ANTHROPOLOGICAL JOURNEYS

Reflections on Fieldwork

ANTHROPOLOGICAL JOURNEYS

Reflections on Fieldwork

Edited by

Meenakshi Thapan

Sangam Books

SANGAM BOOKS LIMITED
57 London Fruit Exchange
Brushfield Street, London E1 6EP, U.K.

By arrangement with
Orient Longman Limited
3-6-272 Himayatnagar, Hyderabad 500 029 (A.P.), India

ISBN 0 86311 752 X

Typeset by
Scribe Consultants, New Delhi 110 029

Printed in India at
Baba Barkha Nath Printers
New Delhi 110 015

For my parents

Aruna Thapan (nee Ahluwalia)
and
Lieutenant General Mohan Lal Thapan

Contents

Acknowledgements

The idea for this book emerged one evening at Professor Baviskar's home on the campus of Delhi University in 1987. I was then teaching at the Department of Sociology at the Delhi School of Economics (where Prof. B.S. Baviskar was the Chairperson). I made a suggestion to Dr. Vinod Jairath, my colleague, that we organise a workshop on the theme of subjectivity in fieldwork. With Professor Baviskar's continuous support and encouragement, Dr. Jairath and I worked hard at organising this workshop later in the year with a follow-up workshop in the following year. It took longer however to bring out the papers in a collection. I left the Delhi School of Economics to take up a position at the Faculty of Education in the same university and Dr. Jairath decided to leave academia altogether. Only five of the original participants (Veena Das, Amrit Srinivasan, Denzil Saldanha, Savyasaachi and Madhu Kishwar) in the workshop have revised and presented their papers in this collection. The other papers included in this volume, with the exception of Kirin Narayan and Loes Schenk-Sandbergen, have been specially written for this book.

I am very grateful to Professor Baviskar for having given me the opportunity to organise the Workshop so many years ago and to Dr. Vinod Jairath for having worked so hard in organising it as well as sharing many thoughts about the possibilities of bringing out a collected volume. In different forms, this book has seen a few publishers' offices and I must admit that it was in complete despair that I wrote to Professor M.N. Srinivas in late 1995 seeking his advice on the volume. His very encouraging response, as well as Professor A.M. Shah's explicit pointer, sent me to Orient Longman where I discovered Vidya Rao. Vidya has restored my faith in publishers by showing me that publishers value ideas as much as scholars do. From the very beginning, she has seen a depth in this volume in the kinds of questions it seeks to raise and the issues it addresses. Many thanks to Vidya Rao for her very precise and sensitive comments, superb editing, and above all, for the sincerity and patience with which she has handled this book.

My preoccupation with fieldwork was of course influenced by my own experience of fieldwork in 1981 at the Rishi Valley School (RVS) in Andhra Pradesh where I experienced both complete absorption in the other as well as an abandonment of the self as an anthropologist. This did not however prevent me from writing a reasonably good dissertation nor did teachers and students at RVS ever see me as anyone other than a nosey anthropologist. How then is the self defined in the context of fieldwork? What happens to the relationship between the self and, what Veena Das has somewhere called, 'the non-self' in the ethnographic encounter? What factors influence, shape, reveal and obfuscate this relationshp between the self and the non-self? What are the implications of this encounter on the nature of fieldwork? And what is the anthropological quest in the contemporary everyday world? How is it defined and what gives it meaning and character? These are some of the questions the papers in this book seek to answer.

I would like to thank Professor T.N. Madan, Maitrayee Chaudhuri, and Saraswati Haider for agreeing to write for the volume and for handing in their papers so quickly. In particular, I am grateful to Professor Madan for the title of this book, which was in fact the title of an earlier draft of his paper. As always, Patricia Uberoi was unfailing in her support and suggestions. I am also grateful to Professor Andre Beteille for his critical suggestions and to Professor D.N. Dhanagre for his detailed, precise and very useful comments.

I have had the privilege of teaching courses on Research Methods at the Faculty of Education, Delhi University and many of my thoughts and ideas have taken shape in interaction with students in the classroom. Many thanks to all the students with whom I have come into contact over all these years.

Finally, I would like to thank my family who are a source of great strength and joy—George, Jyotsna and Ayushya.

New Delhi   Meenakshi Thapan
March 1997

Section I

Introduction

Rethinking Anthropology Anew

MEENAKSHI THAPAN

On Anthropological Discourse

The postmodernist turn in the anthropological endeavour to redefine its quest took place in the 1980s when anthropologists began to question the intellectual and practical moorings of the discipline. Foremost among them were Clifford and Marcus (1986) whose influential book attempted to rethink many issues that seemed to provide legitimacy to the discipline in terms of its positivist underpinnings. It argued for the partial nature of reality as perceived from different points of view; it emphasised the representation of culture in different forms; it stressed the plurality of voices in both the field as well as in the ethnographic text; it posited reflexivity as a tool in the making of the ethnographic text. Clifford and Marcus were representative of a 'new wave' in anthropology which sought to change the direction of anthropology from an objectivist discipline, grounded in a tradition of observation and thick description, to one which sought to allow more space to the polyphony of voices and partial truths that emerged from a collective and shared understanding of social reality.

The postmodern challenge to conservative epistemology was based on essentially two arguments. First, that 'knowledge is not acquired through the abstraction of an autonomous subject from a separate object, but, rather, that knowledge, along with subjects and objects, is constituted collectively through forms of discourse' (Hekman 1990:63). The second argument defines knowledge as 'plural and heterogeneous' as well as questions the existence of a single, true method of acquiring such knowledge. The concepts of subjectivity and objectivity therefore become problematic and the goal of acquiring 'objective' knowledge is no longer a desirable one.

The post modernist 'reimagining of anthropology' (Escobar 1995:16) has been critiqued across disciplines and political affiliations. It is not necessary to go into the different kinds and dimensions of the critique here and I will only focus on what is central to the issues addressed by this volume. The most important aspect of the critique has dwelt on the notion of 'culture' that has been elaborated by the postmodernists.[1] The other major criticism has been that the postmodernist definition of anthropology has tended to ignore the social and material world in its entirety. The task of anthropology should really be the attempt 'to understand the external world as clearly as we can' (Knauft 1994:122). It has been argued that anthropology needs to '"reenter" the real world' (Escobar 1995:16), as it were, and that its 'romantic rebellion' results in the complete 'relativisation of the world including ourselves' so that 'all statements about "the other" are expressions of our own culture' (Friedman 1987:163). It has been suggested that a comprehensive anthropology needs to be 'global' as what 'lies at the foundation of the ethnographic enterprise is the hierarchical relation to the other, ... not just the fact of "otherness" ... but specifically of the hierarchical relation characteristic of the world system implying the necessary silence of the other for whom we speak'. Anthropology also needs to be 'transformational' to the extent that it is not only aware of the differences but more significantly of 'the way in which they are generated' (Ibid:164).

Feminists in particular critique the postmodern move in anthropology for its lack of political will (for example, Mascia-Lees et. al., 1989). The feminist researcher is seen by some as one who is engaged in applied research primarily because she focusses on what is absolutely essential, that is, on what women themselves want and need. The postmodernist, on the other hand, is seen as one with a 'yearning to know "the other"', a 'romantic component [that] has been linked to the heroic quests, by the single anthropologist for 'his soul' through confrontation with the exotic "other"' (Ibid:25). The lack of the political element in postmodernist thought has resulted in a view that sees postmodernism as promoting the 'romantic tradition' in anthropology.

Clearly, while the study of different cultures and the

valorisation of cultural diversity is a significant enterprise, it is equally important, if not more so, to point out and examine the unequal nature of social relations in any culture. This is a kind of 'critical humanism' (Knauft 1994:120) that should inform anthropological discourse today.

The question we then need to address is not so much of how to radically alter or modify the discourse of anthropology but one of 're-thinking' it in the context of emergent political challenges. What is it about the discourse of anthropology that needs to be considered anew? There are new agendas and new expressions of the modern episteme in contemporary discourse on anthropology. Undoubtedly the postmodernist assertion for the presence of a plurivocality and multiplicity in our understanding of the world is a significant contribution. But how do we move beyond this to evolve a more meaningful anthropology? What is it that is crucial to its transformation is perhaps the moot question. Feminism, among other things, has provided a politicisation of the discipline in its concern for the invisible and the unequal in society. More than anything else, anthropology needs to reorient itself to the social and political reality of the everyday world. It perhaps needs to 'move away from the organisation of knowledge in which it exists—abstract, disembodied and disembedded from popular social contexts ... and start to participate more explicitly in local questions and activities' (Escobar 1992:419). As anthropologists, we need to selfconsciously and emphatically assert that we are not in 'the spectacle business' (Friedman 1987:169) of only providing pictures of strange events, exotica, and other trivia but more into a meaningful, transformational anthropology that sets out to understand the world in all its thorny, complex aspects.

The Nature of Anthropological Fieldwork

The construction of reality as intersubjective requires that the self must be seen as simultaneously the self and the non-self or the other.

VEENA DAS 1989:324

This volume is a celebration of the intersubjective element in anthropological research and argues for a humanism that is cross-cultural and cuts across academic boundaries. It presents the view of the anthropological 'other' (in this volume, the subject) as central not only to the research but also in transforming the life and consciousness of the researcher. The self and the subject are therefore viewed in an intersubjective relationship with very fine demarcating lines. In this sense the self is not external to, or different from the subject, whose life and being is often internalised or reproduced by the researcher. As Hastrup points out, 'self and other, subject and object are categories of thought, not discrete entities' (1992:117). It is when the boundaries between self and the non-self collapse that we can speak of fieldwork being in effect 'a social drama confronting the performers with their unbounded selves' (Ibid). We are then 'ourselves' in the field, trying to decipher and understand social reality which is never fixed but always in a state of flux and movement.

Perceiving the self simultaneously as the non-self or the subject is a somewhat complex issue. Anthropological writings abound with stories of anthropologists having 'gone native' in the field. Anthropologists therefore always fear losing their objectivity and strive for the mandatory distance between self and subject. Fieldwork is also often perceived as an arduous task as papers in this volume will testify. More importantly, fieldwork does not take place in a vacuum: it is located centrally in the professional life or career of the anthropologist and contributes significantly to anthropological discourse. To this extent, fieldwork is dominated very much by the external world, the 'outside'. Undoubtedly, the anthropologist works from a position in the field of power. The 'intellectual field', as Bourdieu puts it, is therefore central in locating the ethnographer's political affiliations, his or her educational background, cultural and social capital, all of which influence, in one way or another, the anthropologist's relationship to, and understanding of, fieldwork and the field.[2] Fieldwork is thus always bound by the rules of the discipline and by its own intention, as it were, that is, to make a contribution to anthropological knowledge. We must acknowledge that the anthropologist lives in many spheres at the same time and experiences reality depending on his or her cultural, political and personal identities. These are, to a large extent, influenced by professional and intellectual considerations.

This collection of papers does not seek to dismantle anthropology or to break down its inherent objectivism. There is also no attempt to romanticise subjectivity in the ethnographic process. There is however a call to focus attention on the vital position of fieldwork through examining some key issues that are of concern in the anthropological endeavour to comprehend the world. That the subjective is as important as what is considered the objective element in fieldwork, and in our writing about it, is the central problematic of this book. This volume focuses on specific methodological issues arising out of the fieldwork situation. These include the old, but still very prevalent, dilemma of objectivity and subjectivity in fieldwork and in the social sciences; the crucial problematic of what constitutes the self and the other in fieldwork and in anthropological discourse; and the place of partial visions and situated knowledges in relation to gendered selves in fieldwork. The issue of political engagement remains central to the major themes of this book.

Much has been written about fieldwork especially by anthropologists, who almost narcissistically, and often obsessively, seek to define, explain and analyse the ethnographic process through which they try to 'understand' the distant, sometimes strange and often exotic 'other'. The other becomes the 'other' because the researcher distinguishes the subject of research from the self, both consciously and unwittingly, so that the distancing effect is realised and the anthropologist is able to 'objectively' study what becomes the object of research. In other words, the subject *becomes* the other and thereby the object of research.

It is true that the people or community studied become the other in fieldwork primarily because anthropologists often do research in situations or contexts far removed from their own academic, social and cultural worlds. The writing of the ethnographic text itself creates barriers, creating a distancing effect, 'which leads us to speak of individuals as "others", as actors who perform cultural roles' (Byron 1992:170). Clearly, these others are created, by anthropology and anthropologists, *as* others. It has been suggested that the 'assumption of difference, or rather *distance*' between the knower and the known is supported by the view that the basis of scientific knowledge is achieved by interposing 'a system of concepts (a method or a logic) between reality and the mind' (Fabian 1990:754). It is important to understand that the concept of 'othering' is based on the premise that the 'Other is never simply given, never just found or encountered, but *made*' (Ibid:755). Representing the other is therefore something anthropologists actually do and to that extent, Fabian suggests, we need to realise that 'our ways of making of the other are ways of making ourselves' (Ibid:756). The process of othering however indicates a movement from a there to a here, from a then to a now, and this movement implies a *presence*. It is this presence that needs to be restored to the discourse of anthropology so that we are no longer engaged in representing the other through interpretation or by giving voice but rather in allowing the other to be present.

We need to see the other very much as part of our own world:

> The realisation that the other is not simply beast, heathen, savage, evolutionary fossil, or another experiment in culture, is the understanding that the other is in a significant way a product and a part of the same system as ourselves (Friedman 1987:165).

As long as the other remains the object of research, an intersubjective relationship between the anthropologist and his or her subjects is unlikely to be established. An 'object' is something that can be constructed and deconstructed, manipulated and shaped into a ready-made anthropological mould. This is the 'other' of anthropological research. The 'subject' is a person with whom the anthropologist seeks to have an intersubjective relationship in the ethnographic process. It is only when the distinction between the self and the other is not so sharply defined, *and* one is acutely aware of the social and political conditions of the subjects in the ethnographic encounter, that we can attempt a truly human (*critically* human, as Knauft would have it) understanding of society. The manner in which the other is defined, and the implications this has for objectivity and subjectivity, is one of the main concerns of this book.

This volume focusses on the question of intersubjectivity, not merely as a methodological device, but as having deeper implications for the way anthropologists relate as human beings to the people they study. In one way or another, all the papers in this volume reflect a consciousness of the need to see the other as the subject rather than as the object of study. In this sense, the papers in this volume are all concerned with the problem of the other's agency, the voice/s of the other, and how anthropological writing may reflect rather than obfuscate these.

The question of an intersubjective relationship between the anthropologist and the people/communities studied has perhaps been present in anthropological and sociological writings for many years.[3] Undoubtedly, it was Max Weber who revolutionised sociology by defining social action, a fundamental category in sociology, as being constituted by the bestowal of subjective meaning by the social actor. He argued for the 'interpretive understanding of social action' in order 'to arrive at a causal explanation of its course and effects'. Such action is social because of the 'subjective meaning' attached to it by individuals and 'takes account of the behaviour of others and is thereby oriented in its course' (1947:88). In this sense, the nature of human interaction is very much intersubjective. Max Weber certainly attempted to break away from the positivist underpinnings of the discipline by asserting that for sociology 'the object of cognition is the subjective meaning-complex of action' (Ibid:101). It has been suggested that Weber engaged in a long and complicated dispute, with the positivists and subjectivists of his time, to establish a 'different kind of objectivity in the social sciences, ... that rests on the study of subjective meanings and the subjective choices of social scientific investigators' (Hekman 1990:98). It is also clear however that Weber did not completely abandon his own positivist intellectual ancestry in his search for establishing sociology as 'scientific knowledge'.[4]

The crux of the problem of establishing the social sciences as providing 'scientific knowledge' lies in the process through which subjective meanings *become* objective facticities. How is social reality constructed?[5] What is the process through which social reality is both constructed and transformed? What is the role of individual subjects as well as social forces in this construction and transformation? The question of how the individual constructs meaning as well as the role of the dominant social forces that shape, define and legitimate reality are both of equal concern to the anthropologist.

In the study of social reality, the anthropologist has tended to focus on cultures other than her/his own. This raises the question of 'location' in research. What is an 'other' culture and for whom? The anthropologist in India studying, for example, war-torn Beirut is seen as studying an other culture. The Indian anthropologist in North America, born and raised there but with distinct Indian ties, sets out to study her own community in India. Is she studying an other culture or returning to study her own?[6] A Kashmiri Pandit studying other Kashmiri Pandits in a village in Kashmir: did T.N. Madan study an alien culture or one with which he could completely identify?[7]

In India, in recent times, it was M.N. Srinivas who first articulated the importance of the study of one's own society as against that of other cultures (1966:147–63). He argued that the discipline of sociology in fact emerged with the study of one's own society by scholars such as Marx, Weber and Mannheim and suggested that the process of rapid change which was affecting, and still affects, all areas and levels of Indian society needed to be examined in some depth. The study of these 'ongoing social processes' in one's own country was for Srinivas the most important task for the anthropologist and the area in which he or she could make the most significant contribution.

More recently, Srinivas (1996) has suggested that Indian anthropologists have acquired sufficient experience in the study of their own society and now need to 'move/ from the study of the "self-in-the-other" to the "the self" itself' (Ibid:657). Srinivas's argument is that every life reflects the society in which it exists as well as the changes taking place in that society and an anthropologist can therefore consider his or her own life an ethnographic field and study it. It is perhaps the case that underlying Srinivas's somewhat simplistic assertion is a deeper insight, viz. there is a need to understand oneself and, in that process, dismantle the self-other dichotomy prevalent in anthropological discourse. It is self-understanding alone that can lead to the complete elimination of seeing the other as other or as self-in-the-other. The implications of this view for anthropological research in India are enormous: it is bringing to

Indian anthropology a perspective from within, of self-understanding and reflexivity in the ethnographic process. Such a view also suggests that the question of location is then immaterial to the extent that it is the anthropologist who becomes the subject of study regardless of where he or she may be located.

The question, or the politics, of location is nonetheless central to contemporary discourse on the subject in fieldwork and in ethnographic writing. It has been suggested that there is a direct link between the politics of location and the production of knowledge.[8] The 'place and mode of enunciation (who speaks and how) and that of its reception (how it is interpreted and why)' (Mani 1990:25) is a question of critical significance. There is no general mode of knowing reflecting a common understanding of a universal truth. In fact, caste, class, gender, race, historical and personal experience mark and shape the social world as we experience it and as we understand and interpret it. Feminism has perhaps made a crucial contribution to highlighting the importance of the identity and position of the subject in its interventions on the relationship between experience and knowledge.[9]

It is clear that the relation between experience and knowledge is not simple but one 'fraught with history, contingency and struggle' (Mani 1990:26). The social and material world is undoubtedly one of conflict and contestation, of inequality and struggle. People, both women *and* men, construct this world, define it and give it meaning. It is human agency (the Weberian subjective meaning-complex of action) that creates social reality which in turn constrains, influences, and defines human behaviour. It is therefore a dialectical process: individuals create society and society acts on the individual.[10] Both the agential aspect of social reality in terms of the complexity of individual behaviour as well as that of social processes are of equal importance to the anthropologist engaged in research that seeks not only to 'add on' to the corpus of anthropological knowledge but is also committed and transformational in intent and purpose.

Fieldwork has been considered the best method by anthropologists for understanding the complexity that characterises social life across national and cultural boundaries.

The importance of fieldwork in the careers and lives of anthropologists is exemplified by Beteille's comments in a recent paper (1993). He refers to the importance of fieldwork, 'the encounter with life as it is actually lived', and claims that its importance is highlighted for him as he 'has never been a successful fieldworker' (Ibid:296). Beteille's preoccupation with the fact that he considers himself a poor fieldworker is reflected elsewhere where he states, 'Bose and Srinivas were both superb fieldworkers but I failed to become one' (1991:5). This recognition of the importance of fieldwork is reflected in the considerable debate and writing on the subject.[11]

Earlier writing on fieldwork in India, notably Beteille and Madan (1975) and Srinivas et. al., (1979) have provided us with essentially experiential accounts of fieldwork. *Encounter and Experience*, edited by Beteille and Madan (1975), focusses mainly on accounts of fieldwork in rural India (with two pieces on fieldwork in other cultures) and seeks to place the problem of the subjective element in fieldwork centre-stage by underscoring its significance, albeit with reference to 'the personality of the researcher, his cultural background, and the nature of his academic training' (1975:4). All these factors would arguably affect the nature of fieldwork, the kind of data collected as well as its analysis. The papers in the volume are avowedly personal accounts of fieldwork experience in different cultural and social contexts. These essays highlight the problems encountered by the ethnographers in their field situations, how these problems were resolved, and provide us with rich descriptions of encounter and experience in the field. We can see the interplay between the ethnographer, his or her academic background and training, the problems of studying one's own society as against other cultures, of gaining access to and finally being accepted by a community—in short, of much that goes on in the field to understand which is essential to formulating an adequate methodology for understanding society. In a sense, the ethnographer as person is an important constituent of this volume and to this extent, the editors' emphasis on subjectivity is accounted for. The volume however does not quite draw out the many strands of significance of the ethnographer's relationship with the subject in the varying contexts and situations of fieldwork.

The Fieldworker and the Field (Srinivas et. al. 1979) attempts to cover more ground by including rural and urban India, 'complex organisations' within the country, and it also takes into account fieldwork outside India. The book focusses on intensive fieldwork, as a methodological tool, identifies issues related to the study of other societies by Indian anthropologists and sociologists, and examines the process of studying one's own society taking into account India's linguistic, social and cultural diversity. As such, this volume is really a presentation of the view that sociology and social anthropology are both 'field-oriented' disciplines in India and that fieldwork is about the study of one's own culture and society in its different forms, contexts and situations. With this purpose, the volume contains personal accounts of fieldwork in different settings in rural and urban India.

Objectivity and Subjectivity

Sociological methods of analysing experience and of writing society produce an objectified version that subsumes people's actual speech and what they have to tell about themselves; its statements eliminate the presence of subjects as agents in sociological texts; it converts people from subjects to objects of investigation.

DOROTHY E. SMITH 1990:31

'Objectivity', as the term is commonly understood is an outcome of the positivist tradition in the social sciences and is seen as the testing ground of any 'good', 'valuable', or 'meaningful' research in sociology or social anthropology. No doubt, objectivity has been examined, argued for and persuasively presented in the annals of research. It has also often been contrasted with 'subjectivity' which is considered to be over-representing the view of the subject, the other, or even, the researcher. The positivist tradition often presents objectivity and subjectivity as polar opposites, and suggests that true objectivity in social science research needs to first eliminate the subjective element in order to be 'valid' and therefore acceptable to the academic community. To achieve objectivity, it has often been suggested that distance is first required between the ethnographer and the subject, between the observer and the observed, between the knower and the known. Identification with the subject or presenting the subjects' voices as authentic representations of reality are seen as privileging a particular gender, group or community and therefore indicative of a subjective trend in social science research. As Diane Bell puts it:

> ... it is the association of objectivity, the hallmark of science, with an absence of connection to one's subject matter, that have drawn the ethnographic lines in the sand. If one passes beyond the line, speaks of self as feeling, interacting, or as an element in a relational field, one becomes 'subjective', and one's work is no longer 'good science' (1993a:29).

Clearly, the postmodernist emphasis on subjective, situated, partial, and several versions of reality remains unacceptable to those who believe that 'genuine science' continues to be judged in terms of validity, replicability and other such criteria. It is argued that the influence of postmodernism has resulted in the decline of objectivity in the social sciences and has affected the nature and quality of fieldwork. Subjectivity in research is after all a suspect quality in the social sciences which are modelled in the tradition of positivism, and postmodernism is seen as having contributed to the valorisation of this subjective element.

Why have the dichotomies of subject/object and subjectivity/objectivity remained central to the social sciences? This is a problem that needs serious consideration. The epistemology of the social sciences is clearly located in the 'the desire for an objective knowledge of the social world rooted in the knowing, rational subject' (Hekman 1990:96). Yet as early as the first and second decades of the twentieth century, Weber and other critics of the positivist trend in the social sciences did try to challenge the notion of objectivity in the social sciences. Their critique was based on the manner in which the social sciences had begun to take on the positivist agenda including the myth of objectivity. They were however unable to reject the goal of objectivity itself perhaps because of the lack of a formidable alternative or of an adequate language in which to frame the alternative. More importantly, there clearly was a hesitancy to totally abandon the emphasis on objectivity. The attempt was therefore not a critique of objectivity per se but of redefining objectivity in the context of the social sciences.

In this volume, Veena Das critiques the 'overdetermined' view of the human being in anthropological knowledge where the 'native' is always the object and 'civilised man' alone the subject. She however recognises the complexity of the subject/object dichotomy and seeks to examine the nature of self-knowledge: 'the anthropological journey to distant lands may be seen also as a journey to the unreachable parts of the self'.

Das argues that anthropology eliminates the subject in its search for objectified truth and questions the necessity for '*empirical* truth'. She suggests that one possible reason for the emphasis on objectivity is the anthropologists's fear of the objective truth of the subject's reality in contradiction to his or her own lived reality. Complex cultures are therefore simplified and made intelligible through a rational language that has universal appeal. She also argues that Weber's theory of social action lacks a true place for the subjective in his definition of rational action as the normative ideal type. In this context, she points to the violence common to several cultures across the globe and poses the question of the 'rational' in such situations.

Reason is clearly suspect as is the possibility of reflecting in its mirror-image. Is it possible then, asks Das, to experience that which is not apparent, not visible? Indeed the ethnographer has to develop a 'sensory alterity' in order to 'engage in the anti-real'. Instead of then fearing the unreal, and therefore avoiding it, or perceiving it as an incomprehensible or even as a savage other, it becomes necessary to comprehend the unreal in everyday life as part of the experience of a lived reality.

Rather than the obvious 'grasping at any objectified thought', Das seeks to offer 'the image of holding back' in anthropological writing, to the extent that everything in the realm of the human is not knowable in advance. This is based on the understanding that our own reality is often founded on the unknown and unacknowledged aspects of one's existence. She then turns to the anthropologist's 'autobiographical voice' in ethnographic writing and, based on anthropologists' autobiographical experience, poses some questions: does the anthropologist's description of reality begin, in some senses, to constitute reality? Is the anthropologist in fact offering us false testimony? Or does the turning within by the anthropologist and reaching into the self to find the other indicate a remarkable moment in anthropological discourse? There is no doubt that the autobiographical voice in ethnographic writing indicates a return to the self and provides the possibility of a transformation in the nature of ethnographic writing the implications of which remain fully unknown and unnamed as yet.

To return to the preoccupation with objectivity in the social sciences. The concern with objectivity as being an indicator of good research is undoubtedly rooted in the West. A noted feminist social scientist, Sandra Harding, has declared that

> we think of objectivity as an 'indigenous resource' of the modern West and we 'modernise' it so that it is capable of functioning effectively in the science based society that the West has generated and that today is arguably its major cultural and material export (1993:26).[12]

This statement is apparently made in defence of objectivity which is seen as being a 'central Western value', related to Western notions of fairness, principled decision-making, and therefore embedded in 'Western personal, communal and institutional ideals' (Ibid). Thus any agenda for research must obviously be an 'objective' enterprise. Any deviation from the norm, or attempt to abandon it (if this were at all possible), is seen as a 'bohemian strategy' which clearly has certain negative connotations.

There is no doubt that there are certain political implications of a viewpoint that considers objectivity and research problems grounded in objectivity to be based on Western ideals of modernisation and rationality, and further that considers these paradigms and their ideals as 'superior'. Such a viewpoint suggests that 'other cultures' are necessarily 'backward', 'irrational' and 'traditional'. However such a view represents only one stream of thought in Western academia. This concern for 'objective' research has been questioned not only in terms of what constitutes 'objectivity' in the social sciences, but also in terms of whether or not we ought to consider other indicators for understanding society.[13]

Amrit Srinivasan argues in her paper that the dilemma of subjectivity versus objectivity is rooted in Western science. She suggests that it was the

rational growth of 'interest' in the moral and material nature of mankind as a whole which led to the epistemological emergence of the Subject as a thinking Western person, sharply segregated from all others who were pre-logical and confused, mixing fact with fantasy, reason with emotion and observation with imagination.

She points to 'Malinowski's insistence on the study of the concrete Other' as being 'symptomatic of a peculiar dualist brand of scientific Humanism to which the liberal British state was committed' and argues that the glorification of science, in value terms, in the West, 'preceded and legitimated ethnography and gave it tremendous prestige in the colonies'. She is however critical of the mode of fieldwork as a method of scientific experimentation arguing that 'it was a cultural understanding of what ought to constitute science which gave imperial fieldwork the guise of science'. An Indian programme of fieldwork therefore needs to first question or evaluate the underlying theory of knowledge before accepting it as a model.

Srinivasan makes the point that Indian sociologists and social anthropologists need to break away from their dependence on Western theory and models and generate indigenous theory and method in the social sciences? Although this has perhaps been the preoccupation of sociologists in India, her reiteration of this point here is important. Change has to occur not only in the field of practice or in the goals of fieldwork but in the theory of fieldwork itself. She turns to Gandhi for this. Gandhi did not provide us with a formally worked out 'method', as he was essentially an activist and not an academic or theoretician. Yet, his life offers us an alternative vision. Srinivasan suggests Gandhi's theory of the experiment as one of the available alternative possibilities in the field of activism that could be considered by social scientists in India. She notes however that the search for, and triumph of, modernity in Indian intellectual and national life has led to the rejection of Gandhi's method. In this, cautions Srinivasan, we are denying ourselves and the world an independent and unique opportunity.

It is the hegemonic nature of fieldwork itself that troubles Savyasaachi who questions its 'dualist character' that makes it an instrument of power. Fieldwork is not only a method but generates knowledge that has become linked to power and domination. Based on the premise that 'scientific knowledge' is 'capital intensive' and 'self-justifying', Savyasaachi suggests that such fieldwork has to be unlearnt so that it is really a method of inquiry which 'derives its form and content from the nature of questions' asked by the ethnographer in the course of everyday life. Essentially, argues Savyasaachi, unlearning is about the 'conduct' of the fieldworker which must be appropriate to the task of inquiry. Socially conditioned 'habits of thinking' and practices have to be unlearnt to allow the phenomena of everyday life to unfold without the intrusive presence of the ethnographer. He compares the practice of unlearning to the flight of the Arctic Tern across the globe which is a 'mode of homecoming'. It is through unlearning that dialogue and discourse can be opened up which help us to understand the complexity of the human world.

Savyasaachi traces the origins of fieldwork in India and views this period as one that used fieldwork as an instrument of domination. He critiques colonial notions which considered the language of the Koitors, in Bastar, backward, irrational and redundant. This view restricted knowledge of the language of the subject except for an instrumental purpose. Savyasaachi however considers the language of the subject absolutely essential for understanding through the mode of questioning. He set out to learn Marhia, the language of the Koitors, through first dissolving his fear of the forest. Savyasaachi carried with him, in the forest, his 'life-saving kit' which was made up of medicines, food, his bedsheet, and so on, and which were 'symbols' of his 'social and cultural certainties.' The life-saving kit provides the material link between the self and the subject but this link has to be severed in order to learn the Koitors' language and their perceptions of the forest. Savyasaachi highlights the significance of language in breaking barriers and removing distances in the field. This language can be learnt through learning the Koitors' method of work in the forest, through children, by forming a routine with the people and their way of life, and so on. Once the presence of the ethnographer becomes acceptable, then 'the strangeness dissolves' and his vision is freed and the field of inquiry opens up.

For Savyasaachi, fieldwork was an intensely personal experience, questioning his mode of understanding and transforming his relation to, and experience in, the field. It is no doubt apparent that the ethnographer is 'a person with a distinct biography', and that fieldwork is a 'personal adventure and belongs between autobiography and anthropology' (Hastrup 1992:119). The experience of fieldwork is therefore always a very personal, even intimate experience as the ethnographer's self is in a continuous process of intense engagement with the other, a process where, often, the boundary between self and other dissolves.

Moving from a critique of anthropological theory and method to a critique of broad generalisations and anthropological categorisations that often do not reflect 'reality' as perceived by the people themselves, Denzil Saldanha questions 'scientific categories' such as those of 'class' in rural India in the course of fieldwork among the Warlis of Maharashtra. Defining analysis as an 'intersubjective act of interpretation', Saldanha seeks to understand what might be termed 'collectively shared meaning systems on class in particular historical contexts'. He argues that social structural imagery and self-identification forms one component of the total conceptions held by individuals with respect to their class existence. Saldanha distinguishes between what he calls 'objective identities, scientifically perceived', 'primary polarised identities, subjectively perceived' and 'subordinate differentiated identities, subjectively perceived' and tries to understand these through an interpretation of peoples' narrative accounts. He finds, for example, that the primary collective identity of adivasi and *garib* is distinct from the totally different 'eco-cultural' existence of the other: the *shrimant seth*, and is at the 'forefront of consciousness' as different from the perception of subordinate differentiated identities which emerge spontaneously in peoples' accounts. The question that troubles Saldanha is, 'On which point of the objective scale of class differentiation would one place the descriptive categories used by the people?'

He tries to find the answer to this question in the criteria that are popularly used to differentiate between these subordinate categories, the description of their economic conditions and the location of the category of self-identity.

In questioning the dominant methods of perceiving and defining class categories, Saldanha brings the voices of his subjects, as constructing their own class categories, into anthropological discourse. The crux of his paper lies in the following question: in a particular context, how do subjects see themselves in terms of their class existence? Social science must take into account 'popular common sense' in its intersubjective understanding of social movement phenomena and recognise the point that in fact popular conceptions serve to provide the most severe criticism of the categories of science.

The problem of subjectivity in fieldwork is discussed in the papers in this volume in different ways. At the experiential level, some papers attempt to lay bare the manner in which subjectivity was encountered and presented problems and challenges in the ethnographic text. The question of the possibilities of a reconstruction of the observer-observed relationship, which incorporates rather than eliminates subjectivity is also discussed as is the possibility of developing an alternative theory and method in fieldwork.

Subjectivity in fieldwork is also expressed in terms of the ethnographer's political engagement with the other. The ethnographer's political affiliations are in fact responsible, to a large extent, for the emergence of the mainly voiceless and invisible other. In this context, Schrijvers poses the meaningful question, 'How could my research become a meaningful contribution that would benefit the women for whom I really cared?' (1991:165). She found the answer in 'dialectical, reflexive anthropology' that allows for a 'specific, reciprocal manner of exchange and communication during the research interaction' (Ibid:169). Such anthropologists view research as being meaningful or responsible only if they can, in some measure, contribute to bringing about a change or transformation in the lives of the people they study. There is no doubt an element of power in this process, as the 'better life' is seen in terms of the ethnographer's values. Nonetheless, political engagement appears to be necessary for any meaningful research on the complexity of social forces and individual agency that is characteristic of contemporary society. It is obvious that merely writing about the subject within the limits of anthropological discourse is a position that possibly fails to take account of the complex nature of caste, class, gender, race and other inequalities in relation to both the subject and the ethnographer. This is not a position that is however acceptable to all anthropologists. In this context, an anthropologist has clearly asserted,

> an anthropologist's chief concern is academic, not political; his duty is to understand, and not to change; his goals are definite, *where the distinction between the Self and the Other is perpetually kept* (Srivastava 1991:1475; emphases added).

This viewpoint, while not representative of the anthropological community at large, suggests that fieldwork should remain free of political engagement with strict boundary lines between the ethnographer and the subject in order to understand society in academic terms. However, fieldwork always has political consequences to the extent that the outcome of fieldwork is viewed as a political act. There is thus always a gap between the anthropologist's intention, or lack of political engagement, and others' perception of the fieldwork. In other words, fieldwork is always grounded in the political although it perhaps may not be explicitly stated or even acknowledged.

The Self and the Other in the Anthropological Context

In anthropology, ... there is no experience apart from the experiencer, no knowledge without a knower. This makes it pertinent to investigate the position of the actual experiencing anthropological subject, so curiously absent in the literature as a real person in flesh and blood....

KIRSTEN HASTRUP 1994:224

Beginning with the anthropological self, in the process of inquiry, it is important to understand that this self that seeks to understand the subject through complete immersion has its own persona, its own reality that is markedly different from the subject. How does one seek to understand the anthropological self and why is it important to do so? Clearly, an understanding of the anthropological self is as important as our attempt to understand the subject. This ensures that in understanding ourselves, we are careful not to objectify the subject as other in the research process. As earlier suggested, it is self-understanding alone that can eventually break the sharp division between self and the non-self or other.

The core of the self is no doubt biography, for it is in terms of one's biography that one places one's self, and is placed by others, in the complex nexus of relationships and experiences which, for that person, constitutes reality. Anthropologists in India have been somewhat reticent about the making of anthropological selves.[14] Andre Beteille has very recently written about his childhood (Beteille n.d.). He speaks with immense clarity, intensity, with acute attention to detail, and remarkable memory about the conflicting cultures he experienced as a child at home and at school. In his writings, the anthropologist reaches into the innermost recesses of his lived experience and provides, through what Das refers to in her paper, 'the autobiographical voice', an evocative narrative on his childhood in a specific context. However, the anthropological voice is nonetheless also present when Beteille comments on his sensitivity to social exclusion and other social practices vis-a-vis brahmin widows, for example, as being influenced by his own experiences and understanding as a child. Similarly, as a young boy in a boarding school, his identification of certain spaces being 'out of bounds' remained with him throughout his life and possibly enhanced his awareness of such spaces as an anthropologist. Clearly, the use of the autobiographical voice in anthropological writing emphasises the significance of facing and drawing out one's self, and not only investigating the other, in our attempts to understand the world. This move in anthropological writing indicates the development of a new genre in anthropology, the implications of which are perhaps not yet known.

In his paper, T.N. Madan tells us about what he calls his 'anthropological quest' spanning four decades in terms of the problem of objectivity and that of the study of 'other' cultures. Madan discovered, as a student of anthropology at Lucknow University, that the model for anthropological fieldwork (following D.N. Majumdar) was the laboratory experiment: ethnographic data therefore had to be 'reliable' and analysis was 'rigorous and guided by theory'. In his essay, he shows us how his own career trajectory was influenced by his teachers to the extent that they in fact selected and decided for him his field of study and methodological tools. Finally, however, Madan decided to study his own community, the Pandits of the Kashmir valley, thereby transforming the 'familiar into the unfamiliar'. He did encounter with his teachers, however, questions relating to subjective bias in studying one's own community. They cautioned him by suggesting that he keep away from Indological texts, rely on 'formal anthropological tools of analysis' and stay with the study of observed behaviour rather than people's observations of the same. Such advice was essentially an outcome of the times, as a positivist approach, exemplified in the use of 'formal' anthropological tools, guided anthropological research at the time.

Later Madan discovered that the opposition between objectivity and subjectivity ceased to bother him and he was able to combine methods and perspectives in his work which led him through the study of the family and the household, of work (the medical profession) of religion and its interlinkage with politics in the form of the ideologies of secularism, communalism and fundamentalism. In each of these areas, Madan was able to work with a combination of different methods and tools of data collection. However, he did realise that the use of statistical techniques did not give him the 'emotional satisfaction' that he found through participant observation in the field. Finally, he arrived at the understanding that anthropology was not only about the study of other cultures but really about the 'mutual interpretation of cultures'. He calls this a 'form of consciousness which arises from the encounter of cultures in the mind of the anthropologist'. The anthropologist learns about her/his own culture from the cultures she/he studies and also understands the cultures she/he writes about from her/his own cultural experience and anthropological perspective. It is thus always an intersubjective encounter grounded in the complex and multiple nature of the anthropologist's identity as well as of the people he or she studies.

In this context, Kirin Narayan rejects the dichotomy of the outsider/insider or observer/observed and suggests instead that we view the contemporary anthropologist as someone with multiplex identities in the 'field of interpenetrating communities and power relations'. Although she presents herself as a 'native' anthropologist, or indigenous ethnographer, she argues that this in no way means that she can provide an 'authentic insider's perspective'. She sees herself as made up of many cultures which have resulted in developing many different aspects of her identity. Through a personal narrative, Narayan outlines her cultural identity as American, German, Indian and suggests that she is clearly not a native or a non-native but a 'halfie' instead. She traces her childhood in Bombay with regular visits to other places, notably Nasik and Kangra, where she experienced her identity in many different ways including the influence of cultural and gender factors. She concludes therefore that *every* anthropologist exhibits what she calls, following Rosaldo, a 'multiplex subjectivity' which is uncovered in different contexts and situations in very many different ways.

Narayan argues that it is however the Indian side of her ancestry which defines her identity as a 'native anthropologist' in the U.S. and thus she becomes an 'insider' in studying Indian society despite her complex background. This is something she questions as she does the position of the non-native anthropologist who nonetheless establishes certain ties and deep relationships with the community she chooses to study. She argues that the latter are 'insiders' in the same way as 'native' anthropologists are and therefore it is less important to find out who is more or less authentically 'native' than it is to examine the anthropologist's relationship with the people she studies.

Narayan also comments on the emphasis on partial truths and situated knowledges recommended by postmodernists and feminists and cautions against the perspectivist element in such approaches which cannot provide generalisations for global truths. Narayan however strongly asserts her defence of subjectivity and her position that knowledge is 'not transcendental, but situated, negotiated, and part of an ongoing process' which spans the domains of the cultural, personal and professional. She concludes by emphasising the 'hybrid' nature of ethnographic writing which is based on an understanding of the anthropologist as both an ethnographer located in an anthropological tradition and a person with 'multiplex subjectivity'. This 'enactment of hybridity' in anthropological writing will ensure anthropological understanding allowing a place for 'outsiders' as well. Narayan's paper clearly argues for a major shift in anthropological goals and concerns and eventually questions the nature of anthropological theory which unreservedly emphasises 'objectivity'.

Questions of identity, culture and location are also central to Maitrayee Chaudhuri's paper. In conducting fieldwork among Asian Indian immigrants in the U.S., she examines both her definition of herself as 'Indian' as well as her subjects' definitions of themselves as Asian Indian Americans and as Indians. She also closely examines the concept of culture which is central to questions relating to identity for Asian Indian Americans. She suggests that culture is often linked to nation and especially for Asian Indian Americans there appears to be an urgent need for a 'strong cultural identity' as they have travelled away from their land and have broken their roots, as it were. This cultural identity is therefore linked to India and to symbols of Indianness such as food, festivals, music, dance forms, language, clothes, and national heroes like Tagore and Gandhi.

Chaudhuri also examines the location of the Asian Indian American, as well as that of herself, in American society. She suggests that the 'American experience' (that is, of the immigrant) has different meanings depending on one's colour and origin. She also suggests that the Asian Indian American has a very different notion of 'Indian culture' as opposed to herself. Their views seem to be based on their experience of American culture as well as their memory, or that of others, of what Indian culture is. Their ideas appear to be vastly influenced by American notions of 'Indianness' or what Chaudhuri calls 'America's own form of Orientalism'. She suggests in fact that Asian Indian Americans are pursuing an essentially American quest for cultural identity and that the India of their dreams has nothing to do with the real India. It seems to me that Chaudhuri is in a sense pointing to a false or a failed quest, as it were, for surely one cannot pursue something which does not exist although it remains very much a part of one's dreams and aspirations.

Chaudhuri's own identity as an Indian is rooted very much in modern, contemporary India whereas that of her subjects in an India defined by America as well as in that country's 'discourse on race and multiculturalism, affirmative action and cuts in immigration, identity and lifestyle politics'. She sees a vast gulf between her own identity and that of her subjects although they tend to perceive her as belonging to a common, shared culture. She was also for them a true Indian as well as one who had traversed with time, one who was educated and modern. They were however totally unaware of the complexity and change that characterises modern India and Chaudhuri finds it hard to accept this aspect of their Indianness. She also tends to find herself fitting in very easily into the pattern of normalcy expected of her as a 'housewife' in the U.S. although she also finds it very difficult to express her own Indian identity to her subjects.

The notion of location is central to Chaudhuri's paper, not merely in the sense of her own location as opposed to that of her subjects but relatedly and more importantly, for her, the 'Western location and the Third World'. This is an unequal relationship, asserts Chaudhuri, and the question of cultural identity is posed within this relationship. 'Home' can therefore never be 'boundless' but is in fact always well defined and articulated within this relationship as well as to the extent that she was slotted into a pre-defined category at various academic seminars and workshops and expected to perform in a particular way. She thus experienced herself as what she most pertinently calls, following Appiah (1992), an 'otherness machine' in relation to the Western Self. She concludes that the categories of 'native', 'home' and 'cultures' remain clearly demarcated and fairly well defined in relation to both the self and the other in the context of the 'positional superiority' of the West. Clearly, the notion of self and the subject pertains not only to location in terms of the ethnographic encounter but the larger political question of location in terms of the hegemony of the Western world in relation to both the Other in itself as well as external to it, that is, the postcolonial intellectual.

Gendered Selves in Fieldwork

... it is in the everyday life of women, articulating the poisons that enter social relationships, that the act of hearing and recognition gets done, and through which I propose that culture acquires a soul—that it is born.

VEENA DAS 1995:16

Identifying gender as an important element of ethnography and as a significant factor influencing fieldwork has generally remained the prerogative of women anthropologists.[15] Women's voices, *and* their silences, have rarely been heard, their perspective or vision rarely acknowledged or valorised. Feminist theory has sought to place the experience of women centre stage in social science research. In turn, once heard and acknowledged, 'women's standpoint discredits sociology's claim to constitute an objective knowledge independent of the sociologist's situation' (Smith 1990:21). Dorothy Smith, who has extensively argued for a sociology based .on experience rather than *separation* from direct experience, argues that in fact 'the only way of knowing a socially constructed world is by knowing it from within' (Ibid: 22). Sociology then takes everyday life as its problematic with research focussed on actualities rather than on ideology. Such a perspective is grounded in reality and therefore is more meaningful than research which follows certain set patterns and principles which are seen as being 'scientific' precisely because they are far removed from the everyday world.

We need to address ourselves, then, to the question of hearing women's voices speak about their particular, and thus varied, experiences, to recognise these voices and to be able to present an adequate understanding of the complex and varied nature of social relations without being labelled as those espousing 'partial' (in a perspectivist sense) and thereby incoherent and incomplete truths.[16] I would like to emphasise, following Haraway, that 'feminist objectivity means quite simply *situated knowledges*' (1991:192). Such objectivity is about 'particular and specific embodiment' (Ibid: 194) and not about some transcendental truths located in the general and abstract constructions of society. Is it possible, then, to argue for an objectivity that

> privileges contestation, deconstruction, passionate construction, webbed connections, and hope for transformation of systems of knowledge and ways of seeing (Haraway 1991:191–2)

without falling into the trap of providing only partial perspectives and very personal versions of reality? Such subjectivity will however always be suspect for it is seen as something that 'threatens to overwhelm or pollute "pure knowledge"' (Harding 1992:189). It is nonetheless crucial that women speak about their experiences as this will help in understanding and perhaps transforming the complex character of social relations. We need, however, to be absolutely clear that women lead very varied and structurally opposed lives defined by class, caste, race, and other cultural and social factors. If we therefore accept the fact that there is no universal women's perspective we can, then, conclude that although experience does contribute to the 'creation of knowledge', it does not *'ground* knowledge in any conventional sense' (Harding 1992:185). Experience nonetheless remains essential for a mapping of the field, as it were, to begin to understand social relations from the point of view of women, *and* men.

Almost twenty years ago, Leela Dube (1975) wrote a pioneering paper where she took account of the role of gender in fieldwork. In her paper that scans three important periods in her life and work, she relates her womanhood and her femininity to her work, initially, as an apprentice to her anthropologist husband conducting fieldwork among the Gond women as a 'well-protected daughter-in-law;' as a fieldworker, a 'research associate' to her husband, in a Rajput village in U.P. where she had to more or less comply with the rules of the setting in terms of what was expected of her as a young woman and as a brahmin; and finally as an independent fieldworker on the island of Kalpeni near Calicut. She found here that it was not important that she belonged to a different religion or spoke a different language: she was accepted 'as a human being especially as a woman' (1975:172).

What is important about Dube's account is her very honest

identification of her fieldwork experiences in terms of her gendered self whether she is in the field as an appendage to her husband or as an independent ethnographer. She thus concludes: 'In my own case my femininity was a constant, but my other statuses—as young married woman, as daughter-in-law of an important officer, as educated and employed, as middle-aged mother, and as teacher—made a difference' (Ibid: 175). Dube's perception and articulation of her gendered self in the field and the manner in which it shaped situations during fieldwork is what makes her piece a significant contribution to ethnographic writings in India.[17]

There is no doubt however that women's engagement with the subject in the field has moved beyond the identification of oneself and one's persona in gendered terms. Saraswati Haider focusses on the method she uses to elicit what she considers 'more authentic' data. She suggests 'dialogue' as a mode of inquiry and herself uses this method in her inquiry into the lives of lower class slum women in Delhi. This method entails complete 'honesty, openness and forthrightness' on the part of the ethnographer whose life becomes open to inquiry from the subjects and therefore ensures an equal, 'two-way communication' between the anthropologist and her subject. This, argues Haider, is essential for understanding the lives and experiences of women in the context of the pain and suffering of their lower class status. Haider elaborates on the method used by her in this context: honest and open dialogue, and informal and unstructured interviewing without the use of anthropological paraphernalia such as a tape recorder or even a notebook.

Haider recounts her dialogue with Shanno, one of the women she interviewed, which reveals to us the anguish, pain, as well as warmth and affection, involved in such an encounter. Shanno is not only unwelcoming and uncommunicative in the beginning but also questions the educational qualifications and upper class status of the ethnographer. She has her own opinions about upper class people and their ways and modes of interaction with others. This comes through in her incessant questioning of Haider and in her continuous critique of the ways of upper class people. However, differences recede when Haider and Shanno discuss their first experience of menstruation which has many similarities and thus becomes the source of a bond between them. Somehow the experience of being a woman overrides all other experiences and their sharing and bonding lies in this. In examining the nature of the dialogue, Haider concludes that often she became the other for Shanno who questioned her on many aspects of Haider's life and her experiences as a woman and a wife. Haider therefore emphasises the importance of an equal relationship between the anthropologist and his or her subject in the ethnographic encounter. Not only is this a preferred mode in terms of the ethical questions raised but it also allows for the collection of more authentic material.

The dialogue was also a process of self-discovery for Haider who had to be patient and persevere with Shanno, and the other women she was interviewing, to allow them to trust her with their life experiences. She also felt completely helpless in being unable to alleviate their suffering and lower class circumstances for which she 'in a vague way' felt responsible. This led her to the understanding that anthropological research *has* to be linked to action research of some kind either directly or through policy planners who have the power to actually help alleviate the conditions in which lower class people survive in this country.

Political engagement with the subject has clearly become an important component of women's writing on research in the social sciences. Loes Schenk-Sandbergen seeks to speak 'in a different voice', as it were, not only because it is feminine but also because she subjectively participates in the lives of the people under study, sympathising, empathising, and feeling with them and, at the same time, engaging in rigorous fieldwork. Her paper is an example of the political commitment of the feminist ethnographer to fieldwork which in this case consists not only of the collection of data but also of assisting the underprivileged, whether men or women, in the field.

Schenk-Sandbergen makes a distinction, following Margaret Mead, between those whom she considers 'feminine' and 'masculine' oriented women researchers and suggests that women are neither one or the other but 'in different degrees, and depending on the setting, more feminine or masculine oriented.' She argues that this in fact contributes to a 'double consciousness among women, as both scholars and women, which gives them the opportunity to conduct, as she puts it, 'committed action research'. There are however some problems that Western anthropologists encounter in fieldwork in the Indian setting. These include problems of access to both male and female worlds and especially of conformity to gender ascriptions, restrictions on mobility and questions of reciprocity. In Schenk-Sandbergen's discussion of her own experience, as well as illustrations from the experience of other anthropologists in India, it becomes clear that the woman anthropologist is engaged in a continuous strategic process of negotiation and intervention in order to achieve easier access, more mobility or simply more information.

The last paper in the volume, by Madhu Kishwar, significantly interrogates the very process of fieldwork as a methodological tool. She highlights the complexities which underlie processes of investigation in any context or setting. In a village setting in the Punjab, where she was investigating the lives of peasant and landless households, Kishwar felt she relied too much on women's voices alone and therefore perhaps did not arrive at an accurate picture of the overall social reality. It is important to take into account as many different perceptions and voices as possible to understand the different dimensions of any given problem. However, multiple versions, argues Kishwar, do not necessarily reflect reality.

In this context, she argues that in the case of communal conflict, for example, the researcher may receive more or less the same version of the truth from several members of the dominant community. But this need not necessarily reflect the situation. In her investigation of the Meerut riots in 1987, she found the reality of the Muslim experience very different from the Hindu articulation and explanation of it. It is therefore very important, suggests Kishwar, to keep prejudices in check and look for 'hard evidence' in establishing facts. Relying entirely on people's versions of the truth may not suffice.

At the same time, Kishwar argues that there is a felt need to 'take people seriously' when they talk about what men or women may need or want in order to survive. Most researchers and policy makers impose their values, in terms of what they consider 'good' for the community or the society as a whole, on to the people. But, in fact, suggests Kishwar, people's needs have to be recognised and understood before imposing strictures on them and the researcher plays an important role in this process. In such situations, however, the multiplicity and authenticity of subjects' voices can become a problem. Whereas plurivocality can be taken care of by allowing subjects to speak for themselves in the text, the issue of authenticity poses problems and requires greater attention for understanding the processes involved in rendering voices and silences coherent and meaningful.

Kishwar also questions her apparent advantage as a woman to gain access to women's lives. The 'absent presence' of men, as it were, is a constant impediment in conversations with women and acts as an 'effective censor' except in times of crisis when the pain, dishonour or trauma is so deep that it temporarily wipes out the ever-watchful male gaze. Kishwar's account tells us that being a woman researcher is not a particular advantage in gaining access to women's worlds unless one is able to somehow circumvent the situation and concentrate on aspects of women's lives that are revealed during the course of fieldwork.

Concluding Comments

To conclude, what is the contribution made by this volume to the analysis of fieldwork in India? Questions relating to the nature of anthropology today—objectivity/ subjectivity, the self and the other, and gendered selves in fieldwork—can be addressed in different ways depending on the contexts and situations, the politics of the anthropological voice, and the problems, contradictions, and dilemmas of fieldwork itself. The diversity of field situations and theoretical and methodological issues presented in this volume are testimony to this. It would appear that gender relations are central to questions of objectivity and subjectivity, in addressing important issues about political engagement and in being 'ourselves' in the field. In one way or another, gender plays an important role in defining the grammar, as it were, of fieldwork for many a fieldworker although this may remain unknown and unacknowledged.

The papers in this volume also point to the breaking down of barriers between the self and the other in fieldwork and in anthropological writing. The emergence of the autobiographical voice offers new possibilities for a deeper understanding of reality where both the self and non-self are understood from a perspective informed by self-discovery. The anthropological self is no doubt located in the specific context of a career trajectory. This finds expression in a reflexive narrative, in this volume, with its attendant complexities and revelations, of an anthropological life.

This volume offers a critique of anthropology as being inadequate in terms of both theoretical and methodological frameworks as well as being incapable of giving voice to the invisible and often voiceless other or of hearing the plurivocality of voices in the field. The postmodernist turn in anthropology undoubtedly has many limitations but it has offered us the means of 'reconceptualising scientific activity ... by challenging the definition of science itself' (Hekman 1990:135). There is no single, all-pervasive, universal truth to be scientifically understood, analysed and explained. Indeed, there are many truths and complex realities in a social process of constant flux and change. This volume concludes by suggesting that we begin to take account of experience and vision, individual, partial and contextualised as these might be. It is only when these many voices, and silences, are heard, and seriously listened to, that we can speak of an anthropology that is truly humane and across cultures.

Notes

1. Scott (1992) for example critiques what he calls the 'contemporary anthropological inflation of culture' in terms of the relations between power and knowledge between the West and its Others. Another critic, Sangren (1992), questions the legitimacy and logic of postmodernist claims and defends the traditional bases of ethnography's authority. He also suggests how anthropology can be reflexive in ways which remain unexplored by postmodern critics. O'Neill (1995) has also critically examined the postmodernist position in the social sciences.

2. Bourdieu defines the 'intellectual field' by suggesting that it is 'like a magnetic field, made up of a system of power lines. In other words, the constituting agents or system of agents may be described as so many forces which by their existence, opposition or combination, determine its specific structure at a given moment in time' (1969:89). This field exists in relation to other fields in social space, most notably, to that of power (that is, economic and political power). In other words, relations within the intellectual field are constituted by relations within the field of power.

3. I am using the terms 'sociology' and 'anthropology' (that is, social anthropology) interchangeably as there are no sharp demarcating lines between the two disciplines in India. Elsewhere, as early as 1974, Beteille has examined the relationship between them in the Indian context (see Beteille 1974).

4. This criticism has been levelled against Weber by many scholars, for example, Hekman (1990). See also Veena Das's paper in this volume.

5. This question engaged Berger and Luckmann (1979) who, using a phenomenological approach, sought to understand social reality from the actors' point of view.

6. Such complex questions have troubled in particular Asian Indian American women anthropologists in the U.S. See for example Viswesaran (1996) and Kirin Narayan's paper in this volume.

7. See Madan (1975) where he seeks to answer such questions and also Madan (1982).

8. See for example Lata Mani (1990) and Trinh Minh-ha (1988, 1989).

9. Feminist writers such as Rich (1986), Haraway (1991), Smith (1990) are some who have emphasised these linkages.

10. This is no doubt an old formulation going back to the writings of Karl Marx and appropriated by sociologists in different ways but this in no way detracts from the significance of the idea that there is indeed a dialectical relationship between the individual and society.

11. The considerable interest in Malinowski's fieldwork diary (1967) is one indication of the interest in fieldwork and its implications in the lives of anthropologists. More recently, Derek Freeman's critique of Margaret Mead's fieldwork in Samoa (1984) has raised many questions about the nature of fieldwork in other cultures and the reliability and veracity of the analysis. Experiential accounts of fieldwork have been present in anthropological writing for a long time and I would like to point out, following Visweswaran (1996), that women anthropologists in particular have provided us with many insights into fieldwork using first-person accounts as a critique of the positivist approach as well as a 'strategy of communication and self-discovery'. See for example Dube (1975), Shostak (1981), Cesara (1982), and more recently Bell et. al. (1993).

12. Amongst feminist scholars, there is a marked tendency among some, like Sandra Harding, to retain an emphasis on 'objectivity' because perhaps of their firm belief in a 'scientific' paradigm.

13. See, for example, Geertz (1973), Clifford and Marcus (1986), Fabian (1983), Smith (1990), Bell et. al. (1993), Hastrup and Hervik (1994), Visweswaran (1996) and several others for a criticism of an 'objective' method per se as an adequate representation of the 'scientific method' in anthropology and the social sciences in general.

14. A noted exception is Srinivas (1973) who in an immensely interesting and witty article presented an autobiographical account of his career in anthropology. More recently, Beteille (1993) has given us a similar account of his career which in turn tells us something about his anthropological persona, as it were, in the particular context of the relationship between sociology and social anthropology.

15. Taking note of gender in fieldwork is important because ethnographers are engaged in fieldwork not just as persons with a particular educational and social background but also as men and women. See Bell (1993b).

16. In this context, it has been argued that listening to voices alone cannot always help us to understand the complex nature of power and authority. We therefore need to also take account of 'silence as a marker of women's agency' (Visweswaran 1996:51). See also Spivak (1988).

17. Panini's collection of papers (1991) also contains some accounts of fieldwork by women in India.

References

Appiah, K.A. 1992. *In my Father's House: Africa in the Philosophy of Culture*. New York: Oxford University Press.

Bell, D. et. al. 1993 (eds.) *Gendered Fields, Women, Men and Ethnography*. London: Routledge.

Bell, D. 1993a. 'Yes Virginia, There is Feminist Ethnography: Reflections from Three Australian Fields,' in D. Bell et. al. (eds.): 28–43.

_____ 1993b. Introduction 1. The context, in D. Bell et. al. (eds.): 1–18.

Berger, P. and T. Luckmann. 1979. *The Social Construction of Reality*. Harmondsworth: Penguin.

Beteille, A. 1974. 'Sociology and Social Anthropology', in *Six Essays in Comparative Sociology* Delhi: Oxford University Press.

_____ 1991. *Society and Politics in India. Essays in a Comparative Perspective*. London: Athlone Press.

_____ 1993. 'Sociology and Anthropology: Their Relationship in One Person's Career.' *Contributions to Indian Sociology*, 27, 2: 291–304.

_____ n.d. 'My Two Grandmothers' and 'Boarding School.' Unpublished manuscript.

_____ and T.N. Madan (eds.). 1975. Introduction, in *Encounter and Experience: Personal Accounts of Fieldwork*. Delhi: Vikas Publishing House.

Bourdieu, P. 1969. 'Intellectual Field and Creative Project.' In *Social Science Information*, 8, 2: 89–119.

Byron. R.F. 1992, 'Ethnography and Biography: On the Understanding of Culture.' In *Ethnos*, 57, 3–4: 169–82.

Cesara, M. 1981. *Reflections of a Woman Anthropologist. No Hiding Place*. New York: Academic Press.

Clifford, J. and G.E. Marcus. 1986. Introduction, in *Writing Culture. The Poetics and Politics of Ethnography*. Berkeley: University of California Press.

Das, V. 1989. 'Subaltern as Perspective', in R. Guha (ed.) *Subaltern Studies VI. Writings on South Asian History and Society*. Delhi: Oxford University Press.

_____ 1995. 'Voice as Birth of Culture.' In *Ethnos*, Vol. 60: 3–4: 159–79.

Dube, L. 1975. 'Women's Worlds—Three Encounters,' in A. Beteille and T.N. Madan (eds.) *Encounter and Experience*. Delhi: Vikas Publishing House.

Escobar, A. 1992. 'Culture, Practice and Politics. Anthropology and the Study of Social Movements.' In *Critique of Anthropology*. Vol. 12(4): 395–432.

_____ 1995. *Encountering Development. The Making and Unmaking of the Third World*. Princeton: Princeton University Press.

Fabian, J. 1983. *Time and the Other. How Anthropology Makes its Object*. New York: Columbia University Press.

_____ 1990. 'Presence and Representation: The Other and Anthropological Writing.' In *Critical Inquiry*. 16: 753–72.

Freeman, D. 1984. *Margaret Mead and Samoa. The Making and Unmaking of an Anthropological Myth*. Harmondsworth: Penguin.

Friedman, J. 1987. 'Beyond Otherness: The Spectacularisation of Anthropology.' In *Telos*. 71: 161–70.

Geertz, C. 1973. *The Interpretation of Cultures*. New York: Basic Books.

Haraway, D. 1991. *Symians, Cyborgs, and Women. The Reinvention of Women*. London: Free Association Books.

Harding, S. 1992. 'Subjectivity, experience and knowledge: an epistemology from/for Rainbow Coalition Politics.' In *Development and Change*, 23, 3: 175–193.

_____ 1993. 'Feminist Philosophy of Science: The Objectivity Question.' Keynote address at an international conference *Out of the Margin. Feminist Perspectives on Economic Theory*, Amsterdam, The Netherlands.

Hastrup, K. 1992. 'Writing Ethnography. State of the Art.' In J. Okely and H. Callaway (eds.) *Anthropology and Autobiography*. London: Routledge and Kegan Paul.

_____ 1994. 'Anthropological Knowledge Incorporated.' Discussion, in K. Hastrup and P. Hervik (eds.) *Social Experience and Anthropological Knowledge*. London and New York: Routledge.

_____ and P. Hervik (eds.). 1994. *Social Experience and Anthropological Knowledge*. London and New York: Routledge.

Hekman, S.J. 1990. *Gender and Knowledge. Elements of a Postmodern Feminism*. Cambridge: Polity Press.

Knauft, B.M. 1994. 'Pushing Anthropology Past the Posts.' In *Critique of Anthropology*. Vol. 14(2): 117–52.

Madan, T.N. 1975. 'On Living Intimately with Strangers.' In A. Beteille and T.N. Madan (eds.) *Encounter and Experience. Personal Accounts of Fieldwork*. New Delhi: Vikas: 131–56.

_____ 1982. 'Anthropology as the Mutual Interpretation of Cultures.' In H. Fahim (ed.) *Indigenous Anthropology in Non-Western Countries*. Durham: Carolina Academic Press: 4–18.

_____ 1994. 'On Critical Self-awareness.' In *Pathways: Approaches to the Study of Society in India*. Delhi: Oxford University Press.

Malinowski, B. 1967. *A Diary in the Strict Sense of the Term*. New York: Harcourt, Brace and World.

Mani, Lata, 1990. 'Multiple Mediations. Feminist Scholarship in the Age of Multinational Reception.' In *Feminist Review*. No. 35: 24–41.

Mascia-Lees, F.E. et. al. 1989. 'The Post-modernist Turn in Anthropology: Cautions from a Feminist Perspective.' *Signs: Journal of Women in Culture and Society*, 15, 1: 7–33.

O'Neill, J. 1995. *The Poverty of Postmodernism*. London: Routledge.

Panini, M.N. 1991. (ed.) *From the Female Eye. Accounts of Women Fieldworkers Studying their Own Communities*. Delhi: Hindustan Publishing Corporation.

Rich, A. 1986. 'Notes Toward a Politics of Location (1984)', in *Blood, Bread and Poetry*. New York: Norton.

Sangren, P.S. 1992. 'Rhetoric and the Authority of Ethnography. "Postmodernism" and the Social Reproduction of Texts.' In *Current Anthropology.* 33, Supplement: 277–96.

Schrijvers, J. 1991. 'Dialectics of a Dialogical Ideal: Studying Down, Studying Sideways and Studying Up.' In L. Nencel and P. Pels (eds.) *Constructing Knowledge. Authority and Critique in Social Science.* London: Sage.

Scott, D. 1992. 'Criticism and Culture. Theory and Post-Colonial Claims on Anthropological Disciplinarity.' In *Critique of Anthropology.* Vol. 12(4): 371–394.

Shostak, M. 1983. *Nisa. The Life and Words of a !Kung Woman.* New York: Vintage Books.

Smith, D.E. 1990. *The Conceptual Practices of Power. A Feminist Sociology of Knowledge.* Boston: Northeastern University Press.

_____ 1991. 'Writing Women's Experience into Social Science.' In *Feminism and Psychology.* 1, (1): 155–69.

Spivak, G. 1988. 'Can the Subaltern Speak?' In C. Nelson and L. Greenberg (eds.) *Marxism and the Interpretation of Culture.* Urbana: University of Illinois Press.

Srinivas, M.N. 1972. 'Some Thoughts on the Study of One's Own Society.' In *Social Change in Modern India.* Delhi: Orient Longman.

_____ 1973. 'Itineraries of an Indian Social Anthropologist.' In *International Social Science Journal,* XXV, 1–2.

_____ 1996. 'Indian Anthropologists and the Study of Indian Culture.' In *Economic and Political Weekly.* Vol. 3(11): 656–57.

_____ et. al. (eds.). 1979. *The Fieldworker and the Field. Problems and Challenges in Sociological Investigation.* Delhi: Oxford University Press.

Srivastava, V. 1991. 'The Ethnographer and the People. Reflections on Fieldwork.' In *Economic and Political Weekly,* June 15: 1475–81.

Trinh Minh-Ha. 1988. 'Not You/Like You: Post Colonial Women and the Interlocking Questions of Identity and Difference.' In *Inscriptions.* 3, No. 4: 71–78.

_____ 1989. *Woman/Native/Other.* Bloomington: Indian University Press.

Visweswaran, K. 1996. *Fictions of Feminist Ethnography.* Delhi: Oxford University Press.

Weber, M. 1947. *The Theory of Social and Economic Organisation.* New York: The Free Press.

Section II

Anthropological Questions

Anthropological Knowledge, Alterity and the Autobiographical Voice

VEENA DAS

Malinowski's famous account of the Argonauts of the Western Pacific invites one to share in his adventure of other lands by an imaginative incorporation of the reader into the voyage of the anthropologist.

> Imagine yourself suddenly set down surrounded by all your gear, alone on a tropical beach close to a native village while the launch or dinghy which has brought you sails away out of sight... (1922).

Thornton (1985) has compared these very words with those of Conrad as he describes the march of the Roman General as he first set foot in London in the very old times.

> Sand banks, marshes, forests, savages, precious little for a civilised man and nothing but the Thames water to drink.... Land in a swamp, march through the woods, in some inland post feel the savagery close around him—all the mysterious life of the wilderness stirs in the forest, in the jungles, in the heart of wild men.

The classical couple of savaged/civilised on which anthropological knowledge is premised is overdetermined, in that the savage man is constituted as the object of knowledge while the civilised man alone is seen to be the subject. Yet the subject/object dichotomy is by no means, a simple one. For one thing, the study of one's own society within the anthropological enterprise raises certain important questions about the 'other' within the self, and also about the nature of self-knowledge. The heart of darkness sometimes lies *within*, rather than in distant lands. Second, the anthropological journey into distant lands may be seen also as a journey to the unreachable parts of the self. I address these issues in this essay not from a position in which a resolution has already occurred but from within the problem, so to say. My formulations are still tentative and should be read as a voice in a face-to-face interaction. More experimental than conclusive.

The Stake in Rationality

In the construction of anthropological and sociological knowledge, it is conventional to make a distinction between theories of social order that rest upon the foundations of social structure in one form or another, and theories of social action. The first type of theory takes the institutional order as its privileged object and has been rightly accused of sometimes creating the impression that these institutions are impermeable and have a thing-like objectivity in relation to the individual. Theories of social action claim to show greater concern with the subjectivity and creativity of the individual and of society but have been criticised for paying rather less attention to institutional constraints in social life. I feel that despite the significant differences in the perspectives of the two theories, there is an underlying emphasis upon rationality and order that masks the relation anthropology bears in its *practices* to scepticism.

Much of the theoretical arsenal of anthropology consists of concepts that can render other societies 'knowable' in terms of laws, rules, and patterns of authority. This is equally true whether we take cultural phenomena that belong to the public domain such as village festivals, or intensely private knowledge such as incest. In each case anthropologists have traditionally been interested in seeing how order is created out of chaos—how, for instance, does the incest taboo create enduring relations between men, and not how it may be violated to create structures of power within the family that do not belong to the official face of culture. For a long time, the entire field of transgressions, of disorder, and of violence remained outside the privileged domains of anthropological enquiry. There was a certain aesthetic satisfaction for many in having carved out the realm of 'objectified thought' from which the subject could be eliminated. It is to this aspect that Levi-Strauss (1975:11) made a reference when he posited a categorising system in mythology that was unconnected to a thinking subject.

But far from considering this reservation as indicating some deficiency, I see it as the inevitable consequence on the philosophical level of the ethnographic approach I have chosen since my ambition being to discover the conditions in which systems of truth become mutually convertible and therefore simultaneously acceptable to several different subjects, the pattern of those conditions takes on the character of an autonomous object, independent of any subject.... I believe that mythology more than anything else makes it possible to illustrate such objectified thought and to provide empirical proof of its reality.

The objectified character of social reality and the virtual elimination of the subject in whose practices this objectified truth comes to be part of a lived reality, has been the subject of much criticism.[1] I do not think that it has been noticed though, that Levi Strauss's formulation is equally an attempt to secure the *reality* of this 'objectified thought'. Why does reality need *empirical* proof? I suggest that a glimmer of this *fear* of the other's reality, may be found in Evans-Pritchard's descriptions (1937) of how he came to suspect that he was falling into unreason when he was tempted by the notion that the moving light he saw from his tent at night, might after all be a witch as Azande theories (the objectified thought among the Azande?) suggested despite his firm belief that *witches did not exist*. I shall return to the theme of the voice of 'unreason' that hovers in the margins of anthropological texts. My point is that one's own reality cannot be so secure that one can live in a different society, interact with people as an honorary member, share the everyday concerns and yet never be touched by the thought that the witches might indeed be real or that the initiation one has taken with a guru might affect one's salvation. Such threats of scepticism (or perhaps lures?) are successfully ironed out from anthropological texts, as other societies are made intelligible by being rendered in languages of order and rationality that can have a universal appeal. Yet this implicit social contract about the nature of the anthropological text seems to have been pried open. But how? For it does seem to me that new forms of writing have now allowed the knowledge of other cultures to permeate notions of the self in remarkably new ways. But first let me return to the themes of order in the other dominant theory—that of social action.

In its stern formulation in Max Weber, the social was characteristically meaningful action. Sociological explanation, cautioned Weber, must be able to take the subjectivity of the individual actor into account. Yet a close examination of Weber's theory of social action shows that the paradigm of social action is defined by rational action. Affective action, for example, is only considered to the extent that it is capable of deflecting the course of a well defined rational action. All the examples of affective action that Weber takes pertain to negative emotions such as anger, fear, jealousy, desire for revenge. As the Polish sociologist Ossowaska has pointed out, there seems to be no place for any of the softer emotions in Max Weber's understanding of social action. Despite his stated intention of treating action as subjective action, there is an overdetermination of man as rational being; hence the category of affective action becomes a residual category in which all that cannot be explained by the paradigm of rational action is sought to be fitted. The individual in Weber's theory of social action is the actor in the capitalist system who exercises an alert control over himself. The category of meaning is reduced to the category of motive; the rationally controlled individual who exercises a constant alert control over himself becomes the measure. All other forms of being—whether of non-Western man or Western woman are understood in terms of a lack—a deflection from the ideal typical action represented .by the paradigm of rational action. Weber feels the threat of this vision strongly, for instance, in his fears of the idolatry of the real. So are we to read Weber's formulation as a cautionary tale?

Such a reading might indeed be supported if we see how the real itself came to be questioned as the secure foundations on which social theory rested were questioned; and sociologists and anthropologists found that even their small worlds which had been strictly delimited for purposes of fieldwork changed unrecognisably. We have examples of this from new anthropological studies of Sri Lanka, Bosnia, Cyprus, Rwanda, Cambodia—each proper name conjuring pictures of violence that were not imaginable if one read the earlier anthropological accounts of these very societies. The voice of unreason that Evans-Pritchard feared came to be the voice of the interlocutor in recent writings in anthropology.

The last two decades have seen the emergence of a new cultural geography of the world in which some places have come to be marked by spectacular violence. It is not that the experience of violence is new to this century: but whereas the events of the holocaust were seen as marking some kind of an end to traditional ways of thinking about moral philosophy or even about science, anthropologists did not consider it necessary to integrate such an event into their theories of society. For philosophers like Levinas, as for many others, the events of the twentieth century and especially the useless suffering, in magnitude and savagery inflicted on the Jews, meant the end of traditional theories of theodicy. 'This is the century,' wrote Levinas (1993),

that in thirty years has known two world wars, the totalitarianism of the right and left, Hitlerism and Stalinism, Hiroshima, the Gulag, and the genocide of Auschwitz and Cambodia. This is the century which is drawing to a close in the haunting memory of the return of everything signified by these barbaric names: suffering and evil are deliberately imposed, yet no reason sets limits to the exasperation of a reason become political and detached from all ethics.

Realism and Alterity

The suspicion of reason came to be articulated in recent works along with the suspicion of pure vision, of a mode of rendering other societies 'visible' by a direct taking in of a reality as in the analogy of the mirror reflecting the real. For example, in his work on Ireland, Allen Feldman[2] talked of doing fieldwork in a zone of emergency. Feldman asks in some of his recent work, what it is to see and to be seen in a society in which everyday life is imbued with violence, and ordinary people are caught between the violence of terrorism and the violence of the State. He describes, for instance, the dangers of photography in the policed zones of working class Belfast where the photo lens is considered equivalent of the gunfight and the pointed rifle. Feldman tells how narratives of photographs displayed in the briefing rooms of security officers become part of the rumours through which secret rituals of the State's repressive apparatus circulate. Such rumours gain their 'authenticity' and their power within the everyday ecology of fear, mistrust and anxiety. Thus the photograph which is the example of a referential reality—the empirical proof that the person exists or existed, comes to be used in interrogation rooms to terrorise. Feldman is then led to ask, what is the genealogy of realism, or rather the multiple realisms through which legal, penological, and economic disciplines are instituted under the constitution of modernity. Who has stakes in these realisms? He then asks, how such realisms are experienced in the zones of terror where being seen becomes the risk of being hyper-visible to the apparatuses of the State. The capacity to survive in such zones of terror may consist not in optical clarity but in the uncanny capacity to *experience* that which is not visible, to be able to have multiple doubles, even to be able to take animal forms as the survival stories from Feldman's fieldwork reveal. In a word, survival may depend upon hiding, changing forms, dissimulating and defusing one's presence. What is important in the constantly changing topography of a place in which violence is not set apart from everyday life, Feldman feels, is the sensory alterity which requires the ethnographer to engage in the 'anti-real.' It is a sobering thought that the very definition of the senses changes in the kinds of zones of emergency and terror that Feldman is describing. I find it salutary to compare Evans Pritchard's fears for his own sanity because of the threat of the unreal, with Feldman's understanding of the stakes in the unreal for those fleeing the 'truth producing' apparatuses of the State right in the midst of a modern industrial society.

Let us take another example—that of Sri Lanka. Daniel[3] takes us to the fieldwork context, where a daughter who had witnessed her father's murdered body being dragged away, tied to an army jeep in the midst of the applause and cheering of soldiers, asks him at one moment to write about the way her father was made to meet his brutal death and at another moment, never to write about her father, because the way he was made to die was a direct negation of all he had lived by. How is the writing to be commensurate to this kind of responsibility? The overwhelming experience in reading about the plantation Tamils in Sri Lanka, subjected to violence that happens through many instrumentalities, is the way in which the most taken-for-granted categories of common experience are altered. For instance, what could be more taken-for-granted than that memory is oriented to events past? Yet, says Daniel, 'Reported facts of violence—especially when the informant relives the experience during the telling—are momentous in this sense, with the then-and-there being radically transformed into the here-and-now.' He goes on to describe the experience of time in the act of telling: 'When the past facts return in memory and experience only to reactualise themselves, the past does not enter the flow of time in the full sense.' Thus victims of violence as narrators appear as those who have already lost the authorship of their stories. In the end, 'violence undermined the narrative of the master as well as the mastery of the narrative.' What Feldman and Daniel do not do is to render the violence intelligible by *normalising* it.

Like Feldman and Daniel, I have also been engaged in a scene of writing in which the moral urgency of the questions of how to render such violence has far outpaced my conceptual responses.[4] What I want to offer as a fantasy of writing is not of grasping at any objectified thought that would give empirical proof of an unshakable reality, but an image of holding back. This image of holding back also recalls, for me at any rate, Stanley Cavell's sketch of philosophy as that which does not speak *first*, its virtue lying in its responsiveness, tireless, awake, when others have fallen asleep. In its wakefulness, what anthropology offers is not a single narrative, but a rendering of that which happens every day, undramatically, repeatedly—and it is this that shows that the range and the scale of the human is not knowable in advance. Societies try to fix the range within which a man or a woman may be confined but the facts of violence (as of hunger, or martyrdom) show how much experimentation happens at the edges of what is considered human. Thus an anthropological engagement with other societies comes to meet the unknown or unacknowledged aspects of one's own life precisely at the point when one begins to allow that the scepticism about the other worlds we have encountered need not be met only by objectifying and translating their concepts into an agreed rational language. It could also point to the fact that our own reality is often secured in the face of illusion, trance and artificiality. Yet very few anthropologists have attempted to describe how their own reality was affected by the intense engagement with other ways of fixing the range and scale of being human. I turn to some recent examples of the use of the autobiographical voice.

Anthropology and the Autobiographical Voice

Audrey Cantlie has recently written an excellent analysis (along with a psychoanalyst, Jessica Storm), using the autobiographical voice in reexamining her relation to psychoanalysis in the light of her fieldwork experiences in Assam and Calcutta.

Audrey Cantlie writes as the wife of an analyst who fell in love with his patients, and in one case even declared his love. His declaration of love for his patient enacted the death of psychoanalysis for Cantlie. It is not the personal pain of a betrayal, but what it symbolises—viz. the structure of possibility inherent in the analytical context, that makes her see the lie in the analytical relationship. The deployment of psychoanalytic techniques can reframe the analytical space as one in which an intense relationship takes place, but can be packed up again and reconstructed as analysis. The analogy with anthropological experience cannot go unnoticed here for the intensity of living in other cultures is also repacked and reframed as the 'gathering of data.'

Cantlie uses the first person in writing her brief memoir of her relationship with her husband/analyst. She describes the events which form the subject of this brief memoir as the most ordinary and commonplace kind. On the one side, she says, there is the familiar theme of love and betrayal, and on the other, the professional 'fall' of a psychoanalyst and his patient. It is in the ordinary structures of possibility in the analytic situation that the actuality of the events to which she bears witness become an eventuality. The ground for this discussion is provided by her experience, something for which one is immensely grateful. 'This is my truth,' she observes. 'I bear witness to what I know.'

But Cantlie's experience is not only that of a betrayed wife but also that of an anthropologist, and images of her fieldwork pervade her text. For instance in one place she says of her husband Tom and his patient/lover Caroline:

Tom and Caroline had broken through the boundaries which set the analytic relationship apart as a love which is not quite love, an as-if illusory love called 'transference,' to be resolved at the end of analysis. It reminds me of a conversation with Lahiri Baba, a tantric guru on the cremation ground in Tarapith, about an Australian disciple who studied under him for six months. He taught her to meditate on the local goddess, Tara Ma, the forms in which to visualise her and the mantra appropriate to each. One day he said, 'Now, consider that this goddess Tara, whom you have been worshipping for six months, does not exist.' For forty eight hours she sat motionless on the cremation ground, without eating and without sleeping, then she packed her bags and returned to Australia.[5]

Cantlie asks: 'At the end of the analysis the patient reintegrates the powers projected onto the analyst, or so I'm told. But if transference like the goddess, is an illusion, is this not true of love itself?'

Transference, like the goddess, is an illusion, and is that not true of love itself? Evans Pritchard's certainty that witches do not exist, but that witchcraft as a set of practices makes sense within Azande life, meets a transformation here. Lahiri Baba teaches his Australian disciple to meditate on the goddess and then withdraws from her the certainty that the goddess exists. Audrey

Cantlie, the anthropologist of this encounter, takes this back into her life and asks—what if transference, like the goddess, is an illusion?

Cantlie's text is extraordinary in another way in that she speaks from a position in which she can see her life as already lived. Could one say that in the process of writing she comes to inhabit a different region of the story of her life? Often she finds it impossible to describe herself because her self-descriptions have been constantly scratched over, overwritten by Tom's descriptions of her. It is not always possible for Audrey to remember an event independent of Tom's descriptions of it. Thus she says of one of her analyses that it was recounted by Tom to friends and acquaintances so often that she does not have any memory of the analysis any longer—only Tom's descriptions of it.

She therefore constantly warns the reader against her text, against *herself*. Perhaps in allowing Tom's words to overwrite her words even in her own text, she herself becomes a bearer of a false testimony? Yet she says forcefully to the reader that if he (the reader? Tom?) would tell her it didn't happen, 'I shall rise out of the page and strike you.' Is this a movement that she makes to break out of the dutiful words imposed on her by Tom (her unreliability, her lack of inner resources) so that she can inhabit the territory of her past differently?

It is in this context that I find that her anthropological understanding of another culture creates room for speculation, provides elements for reconstructing the past after it has been shattered. 'The embodiment of beauty was for me a kind of holy thirst, a movement towards the divine.... And yet I remember—always, always, I remember—those golden nights in the arms of a poet when we were entered by the gods.' Then there is the episode when she is sitting in front of the image of Kali in the morning mangala arati, confronted with the question of whether she should look at the cockroaches running over the dress of the goddess or whether she should listen to the beautiful cadences of the priest's invocation. This is an extraordinary moment of revelation when she can see the private face of Tom and experience the cockroaches running over herself.

It is from her position as an anthropologist then that Cantlie has been able to think with elements of her life that experiment with autobiography as a form of ethnology. From that other place, we get images of her fieldwork. There is the revelation before the image of Ma Kali when she sees the private face of Tom and experiences the cockroaches. Then there is the guru whose disappointment she records in his remark that all his life he worshipped the goddess but did he grow more hands? This becomes for Cantlie a way of speaking of psychoanalysis—she nursed a life-long addiction to psychoanalysis but like the guru she too was disappointed in this god. Shaped by this experience Cantlie records the strangeness with which things appear to her after her fieldwork when she returns home. The reflexivity in her account comes because of her discovery that the strangest of exotic places are not always found far away but that one's own life in its ordinariness reveals the uncanniness of the ordinary. It is a remarkable insight—one that alters not only the notion of psychoanalysis but also of ethnographic reasoning.

These new experiments in writing suggest to me that the anthropological text is probably the textual body in which the fear of scepticism in the life world of the anthropologist lies buried. I leave this thought as a sign post for a direction I would wish to take in some future time.

While Audrey Cantlie's text is written from the perspective of someone who has already lived her life, Andre Beteille in his recent (and as yet unpublished) autobiographical account takes the voice of the child—a voice that has been remarkable for its absence in anthropological writings.[6] This is what accounts, perhaps, for the fact that culture appears so often as a finished product in these writings. In evoking the voice of the child, Béteille is able to show how the scene of inheritance of one's culture takes place not only in the conflict of generations but also in the divided inheritance between the conflict of the sexes. This conflict is perhaps heightened for him in the conflicts between a Bengali Brahmin mother and a French father who lives in the colonies. There is a sadness in his text at the inability to inherit fully the paternal inheritance, something akin to the Emersonian sadness that the scene of inheritance of culture is also a scene of loss. Culture, then appears in the form of several possibilities only some of which can be realised in the life of a person. Audrey Cantlie wrote from the position of someone whose life is already lived. In taking the voice of the child Beteille shows us the conflicting interpretations of culture right at the scene of instruction. For both, though, the text provides the opportunity to live their lives by inhabiting time differently. In having been 'cooked' by their anthropological experiences, they can return to their own realities and its strangeness in a new mode. I do not yet have the name for this process but it should surely be included in the official trajectory of what constitutes the anthropologist's birth into writing.

Notes

1. See for instance, Pierre Bourdieu, (1990).

2. See Allen Feldman, *Formations of Violence: The Narrative of the Body and Political Terror in Northern Ireland;* and 'On Anamorphic History: The Perceptual Structure of Violence in Northern Ireland.'

3. Valentine Daniel, 'Mood, Moment and Mind: Writing Violence.'

4. See my *Mirrors of Violence; Critical Events;* and several other papers on this theme. Also see *Social Suffering.*

5. Did she leave because she had gained self-realisation or because she could not take the burden of the non-existence of Ma Tara? [My query.]

6. The work of Pamela Reynolds has been exceptional on this account. See her contribution in the special issue of *Ethnos* on 'Culture and Voice', 1996.

References

Beteille, Andre. 1996, 'Discord at Home' (typescript)

Bourdieu, Pierre. 1990, *The Logic of Practice*, Cambridge: Polity Press.

Cantlie, Audrey and Jessica Storm. 1996, *Death of the Analyst.*

Daniel, Valentine (forthcoming), 'Mood, Moment and Mind: Writing Violence.' In Veena Das, Arthur Kleinman et. al. (eds.) *Violence, Political Agency and the Self.*

Das, Veena et. al. (ed.) 1990, *Mirrors of Violence*. Delhi: Oxford University Press.

Das, Veena. 1995, *Critical Events*. Delhi: Oxford University Press.

Evans-Pritchard, E.E. 1937. *Witchcraft, Oracles and Marriage among the Azande.* Oxford: Clarendon.

Feldman, Allen. 1991, *Formations of Violence: The Narrative of the Body and Political Terror in Northern Ireland.* Chicago: University of Chicago Press.

_____. (forthcoming). 'On Anamorphic History: The Perceptual Structure of Violence in Northern Ireland.' In Veena Das, Arthur Kleinman et al (eds.) op. cit.

Kleinman, Arthur et. al. (eds.) (in press). *Social Suffering*, Berkeley: University of California Press.

Levinas, Emmanuel. 1993. 'Useless Suffering.' In Keith Holler (ed.) *Dream and Existence: Michel Foucault and Ludwig Binswanger*. New Jersey: Humanities Press.

Levi Strauss, Claude. 1975. *The Raw and the Cooked: Introduction to a Science of Mythology*. Vol. I. New York, Harper and Row.

Malinowski, Bronislaw, 1922. *Argonauts of the Western Pacific*. New York: E.P. Dulton & Co.

Thornton, Robert J. 1985. 'Malinowski and Imagination.' In *Anthropology Today* Vol. 1, No. 5: 7–15.

The Subject in Fieldwork Malinowski and Gandhi[1]

AMRIT SRINIVASAN

I

Fieldwork, or the description of society 'in the flesh' so to speak, was a method introduced into professional social science by Bronislaw Malinowski. Strictly speaking, Malinowski was not the initiator of this method but was its best exemplar and to that extent provides this paper with its main point of focus. Even before Malinowski, in the late nineteenth century, A.C. Haddon of Cambridge had laid down the ground rules for the comparative study of man based on first-hand observation. Organised as excursionary forays made by ship to 'other cultures', these early field-trips were very brief, touching only the fringes, literally, of native social life. The research vessel would dock at foreign ports till all investigations were completed and then move on. Also the scientists—biologists, anthropologists, linguists —worked as an interdisciplinary team and were more absorbed in their own group than in the life of the people they came in contact with. The experimental success of this field method was in fact perceived to be a function of its non-interventionist stance: its superior ability to keep subject and object, life and laboratory and theory and data quite separate from one another. In comparison, the sociological study of one's own society was deemed politically and historically implicated and hence not open to laboratory techniques.

Although clearly opposed to the 'armchair theorising' of classicists and pedants such as J.G. Frazer, this early brand of field 'activism' or philanthropology as it came to be known, always remained oriented towards scientific not political goals. For Haddon, field activism was meant to benefit mankind not directly through 'grass roots' activity as it has more commonly come to imply today but rather through the building up of more accurate and humane knowledge about Britain's subjects in other lands. By the time of Malinowski of course, the fieldworker quite arrogantly set himself apart from others of his own kind—missionaries, imperial administrators and mercenaries —all men of affairs not science. At the same time, with him a more participatory methodology emerged involving longer stays in foreign lands. The fieldworker was now a single individual who combined in himself or herself the efforts earlier distributed over a whole team. The greater intimacy this method of participant observation engendered led inevitably to the first cracks in fieldwork's scientific self-image. It was Malinowski's experience more than anyone else's which provided the outer limit of that supposed political and affective neutrality for which British anthropology considered itself justly famous.

Malinowski, it could be said was both the pioneer and the last great man of the British fieldwork tradition. After him, particularly after the publication of his diary in 1967 (which revealed the man in the instrument), fieldwork could only develop as 'art'. But in his time, a particular brand of inquisitiveness very successfully transformed human experience into science at the same time that it denied the latter any subjectivity. Clearly the problem of the subject in fieldwork needs to be located in the sociology of knowledge and not, as has usually been done, in the ethnography of experience. To stay at the level of the real, the individual and the existential in the methodological exegesis of fieldwork is to fall prey to its very special 'maya' rather than to explore it. It is to lend flesh and blood to the hieroglyph of the social fact rather than to examine the cultural specificity of its production and reproduction as science. The growing trend to document the vicissitudes, dangers, temptations and prejudices of particular field experiences is, in a sense, still to be 'writing' Malinowski's diary rather than questioning the theory of knowledge which insisted on its simultaneous but separate and shamefaced production.

Malinowski's diary, let us be quite clear, is as much a part of his ethnography (and therefore the history of anthropology) as prostitution was of Victorian monogamy: the secret and confessional nature of one only heightened by contrast the public, and accepted, legitimate character of the other. Its publication after Malinowski's death appeared at one level shocking, even pornographic, an unnecessary transgression of the sacred boundary separating science from the self. At another level however it was entirely predictable given the growing hermeneutical influences on the discipline which permitted if not reveled in just such kinds of obfuscations. Malinowski's diary far from questioning the validity of fieldwork as an anthropological method, contributed in fact to its valorisation and the valorisation of its real, biological subject—the fieldworker. So much so that today the sex and even the height of this individual is somehow significant for the discipline and must be confessed and accounted for in the research proceedings (Heider 1988, 73–81).

The glorification of subjective variation—an euphemism for scientific 'error'—in the actual conduct of fieldwork, has not surprisingly resulted in the rejection of its claims to anything but a technique for 'thick description' (Geertz 1973). The secret and hidden subject of Malinowski's diary has now moved to the foreground of anthropological discourse but not without cost to its status as science. What remains significant is that it was the epistemological centrality of the subject which marked both the emergence and the decline of fieldwork as a scientific discipline. For to *have* a subjectivity, no one would dispute is a requirement necessarily prior to learning how to suppress it, or alternatively, giving it free expression. Logically, a cult of the Personality in the Durkheimian sense had to emerge before Life and Experience could be fetishised into science (Durkheim 1951). The preoccupation with the object nature of reality was only the inverse mirror-image of the preoccupation with the subject nature of the self.

In the western epistemological tradition it is well to remember, Mind and the World entered the order of the Other in company with one another, even as sense experience became the basis for an objective knowledge of either but never both together. In the positive cosmology there could be no reciprocal partnership between knowledge of the self and that of the world. Not only was personal or 'subjective' understanding of the

Subject now viewed as a course of error but even the scientific understanding of the latter—the physiology of vision, neurology etc.—could not be validly enlarged to encompass an objective science of man. The hermeneutical 'alternative' now being offered to social science far from questioning the desirability of such a separation, merely acknowledges the impossibility within the positivist paradigm of objectivity ever being achieved vis-a-vis the other. The 'exotic' fact—material and cultural—remains integral to anthropology and its praxis, with the only difference that whereas earlier it had provided empirical evidence of the Object-nature of Others, today in more charitable times it provides reflexive evidence of the same. In the context of the field study of other cultures, 'activism' now implies forswearing all claims to superior knowledge in favour of local knowledge systems which remain open to interpretation. In the context of the field study of one's own culture, on the other hand, activism now implies forswearing claims to theoretical knowledge per se in favour of political involvement with the people and their problems. Neither makes an attempt even at designing an alternative experiment.

In India, this altered understanding of anthropology as political not scientific activism was evident as early as Verrier Elwin and N.K. Bose, both of whom were very deeply influenced by Gandhi's national programme. Precisely because of this real life involvement, academic social science of the time preferred to consider them gifted but irredeemably amateur anthropologists who could only remain on the fringes of the profession. Deemed pre-eminently a politician and trouble-maker, the colonial Indian university, it seems reasonable to assume, could not permit Gandhi to corrupt the value-neutrality of its scholars. But if we consider the reasons for which both Bose and Elwin (the former more dramatically) eventually themselves parted company with their hero, we get a different picture altogether. Significantly, it was Gandhi's experimental methodology, not his politics which became the chief bone of contention between leader and disciples. Gandhi's experiments in Brahmacharya, more specifically, appeared to controvert western conceptions of science and the scientist to a degree unacceptable to both, leading finally to a public separation. The reinstatement later of both these fringe figures into the social science of independent India was not therefore entirely fortuitous. The joint opposition to Gandhian *method* has always rendered an alliance possible between academic and activist. By taking up Bose's differences with Gandhi, the paper hopes to focus attention on the scientific, experimental component of Gandhi's 'field' programme, which has been almost totally ignored. If the Indian university is to continue to reject Gandhi, let it at least be for his academic and not merely political controversiality.

II

The all-consuming interest in the Subject in contemporary discussions of fieldwork techniques has been entirely predictable given the peace-time preoccupations of post-colonial anthropology (Clifford and Marcus 1986). In an earlier period of imperialism and war, fieldwork was able to prop up what was seen as an essentially objective comparative social science quite simply because of its privileged political and epistemological location vis-a-vis the Other (Barnes 1978). If in Durkheim's system the scientific fact was one which was '....ready to be treated scientifically' (1960, 346) and objective social science was one which quite literally *had* an object, then fieldwork—the best known and most successful British adaption of European positivism—set about actually providing it. The crucial point being that it was only the British who by the end of the nineteenth century were actually in a military position to do so. If Pax Brittanica had won the war in global terms it had also won it in intellectual terms. The cause of British nationalism was not unlinked to that of liberal empiricism and significantly both these battles were largely fought on foreign shores. Before Malinowski ever set foot on the Trobriand Islands and despite the dangers and discomforts of getting and being there, 'civilisation' had already preceded him and he could safely set about fashioning a revolutionary new scientific method which would provide the specifically British contribution to the cause of man.

Malinowski's eagerness to carry out his first field research in Mailu was not entirely fortuitous. Britain's military possession in New Guinea had given the maximum headstart to professional anthropology. The very term 'fieldwork' was A.C. Haddon's, a natural scientist who began survey work there as part of the Cambridge University expedition to the Torres Straits as early as 1898–99. The anthropologists Seligman and Rivers, both Malinowski's seniors, had been members of the expedition and many of their students had worked there in the pre-war period. Mailu therefore was as important to Malinowski, …as his first military campaign is to any ambitious commander… . The strategic decision furthermore to publish his research in Australia and not in England enabled Malinowski to gain local government support and funds for the later trip to Trobriand Islands in the sensitive period of 1915–18 (Young 1988).

Malinowski's preferred identification with the British during the war was intimately linked to his identification with what was internationally most progressive in terms of western European scholarship. His functionalism was a conscious shift away from the humanist historicist perspectives of his student days in Poland, to what was officially preferred in British anthropology. At a more personal level, it enabled Malinowski to rebuff Germany's historical insult to Poland (Paluch 1981, Strenski 1982, Gellner 1987). It also enabled him to morally justify the separation of cultural from political nationalism when he chose not to fight for Poland and stayed on in the Trobriands during the war.

The inner turmoil this decision caused him is evident from his diary and his correspondence with Stas, his intimate friend S.I. Witkiewicz— Polish artist, playwright, philosopher—who had accompanied him on the trip to the South Seas as field photographer. While still in Australia, news of the outbreak of war had led to a profound disagreement between the two friends resulting in Stas' leaving the expedition. Unlike Malinowski who proceeded as planned to the Trobriands and went on to become an international celebrity, Witkiewicz joined the Czar's armies in Russia, later to return to Poland where he lived and died by his own hand, shortly before the outbreak of the Second World War, almost completely unknown to the world. Even his resurrection as a Polish culture hero was to come sometime later (Kubica 1988, Paluch 1988).

The personal-political confrontation between the two friends reflected the confrontation between science and art or fact and value in twentieth century European consciousness. In the modern West's self-understanding, to devote oneself to science was clearly to sacrifice oneself as a member of a particular national, ethnic or moral community. But for Malinowski, the expatriate Pole, success at science meant really the giving up of a second-class 'enemy alien' status for a more elevated one—'protected' British subject and Anthropologist Laureate of England. Certainly for Witkiewicz, his friend's scienticism was a function of his 'anglicisation' and deplorable on that count alone (Flis 1988: 124–25), a charge borne out perhaps by Malinowski's eventual acceptance of British citizenship in 1931. Functionalism may have been ahistorical and anti-national in theory but its field-praxis was clearly imperial (British) in its operation.

Early fieldwork in Malinowski's hands was a form of imperial kula, symbolising unlike its Trobriand counterpart, the irreversibility of scientific exchange. While the fieldworker could 'discard' an 'ignorant informant' (Malinowski 1948: 265), he need never turn informer himself. The Object of study never became the Subject vis-a-vis the Self. Furthermore, ethnographic facts collected during fieldwork, took on scientific value only when they were communicated back at home amongst one's own kind. An intense and surcharged 'green-room' activity, fieldwork remained merely a preparation for the real drama that was to take place elsewhere. In other words, fieldwork counted as Fieldwork or Science only in retrospect, when it had been written about and exchanged amongst one's colleagues. This disjunction between its symbolic and its instrumental component, made fieldwork a form of intimate knowledge which was ruled not so much by the principle of speech as by that of gaze (Foucault 1973).

The intensification and localisation of the scientific field and its occupation by the one-man 'army'—the fieldworker—was only possible with the extensification and universalisation of the territorial or national field into Empire. The scientific significance of the We/They, Mind/Body dichotomy, it has been argued, became evident only after the geographical boundaries separating (or uniting) them became certain (Leach 1982: 62). In an earlier time, the 'nobility' of the savage in the works of Rousseau and Montaigne had projected an abstract and alternate conception of Freedom and the Self. Now the 'cannibalism' of the savage permitted the colonial projection of an essentially altruistic, White dominion over him.

The case-history of Captain Cook brings out most clearly how the capitalist philosophy of Eat or be Eaten became transformed into a Christian and civilising morality in a prototypical field encounter with Other Cultures. The commercial and Christian soldiery of the British state, it has been argued, killed and 'consumed' (or proselytised) the Hawaiians because they thought that as heathens they were somehow "less than men". The Hawaiians on the other hand, consumed and immortalised Cook because they thought him somehow more than a man, a god—a sentiment not unshared by western geographers of the time who depicted him after his death as a pure, Christ-like victim sacrificed at the altar of European civilisation (Sahlins 1982: 73–102). The reason why Malinowski and not Captain Cook lived on in anthropology text-books as a field ancestor was quite simply because the former survived while the latter did not.

Captain Cook, history bears witness, certainly 'participated' with the natives but he did not 'observe' nor live to tell the tale. An honest, god-fearing Whig, he had not learnt the scientific diplomacy of culture-contact and failed to protect his separateness from the others around him nor was Britain in a position then to help him very much in the matter. It remained for the liberal gentlemen-scholars of a later time to pitch their tents in native society within the English imperial state, in order to proceed with their field investigations on a relatively more secure and permanent basis. Whether or not anthropology served colonialism, the latter certainly '...served and suited anthropology. The period between the wars was the time when the overseas empires were at their most stable and secure.... [It] is a striking fact that not a single anthropologist who ventured among the savages in this period lost his life in the process.... Malinowskian anthropology was ideally suited for making the best possible use of the research potential of empires' (Gellner 1987).

It was the rational growth of 'interest' in the moral and material nature of mankind as a whole which led to the epistemological emergence of the Subject as a thinking western person, sharply segregated from all others who were prelogical and confused, mixing fact with fantasy, reason with emotion and observation with imagination. The physical (geographical) and metaphysical emergence of Man or the abstract Individual of liberal political and economic theory now found its empirical positivist equivalent in the good scientist or fieldworker. Ironically therefore, the largest expansion in history on the cultural, commercial and military plane was accompanied by the greatest contraction on the scientific plane of the real human individual, the 'instrument' of knowledge whose body and sense- experience formed the basis of an objective understanding of the world.

It was certainly a more confident and conservative, imperialist British nationalism, in successful competition with the revolutionary socialism of France and its intellectual productions, which permitted this glorification of the Subject of science. The marriage of Knowledge and Empire had been attempted even earlier in the Utilitarian experiment in the colonies but it was liberal empiricism of the late nineteenth century which gave it a far more sophisticated and secure expression. To actually dirty one's hands in the stuff of Experience without allowing it to corrupt the objective character of scientific description became possible only in an imperial setting, when aliens were automatically segregated from evaluation on the basis of civilisation and its norms. Newly formulated policies of segregation, an increased humanitarianism and the new professional, unofficial status of scientists—all helped prepare the field as a 'laboratory' ready to yield up facts to the fieldworker. Malinowski's insistence on the study of the concrete Other, was symptomatic of a peculiar dualist brand of scientific Humanism to which the liberal British state was committed. Policies of cultural segregation came to be implemented both at home and abroad in equal measure that the doctrine of monogeny or the species unity of man was constitutionally and intellectually adopted. If, as it has been said, it is really love which '...first teaches man to believe in the objective world outside himself...' (Marx 1954: 21), then fieldwork was encouraged not so much by the love and understanding of real men as by the cause of Man.

The emergence of the Other as a racial, political, epistemological and religious category was absolutely intertwined with the emergence of the category of Man. The latter's universal human rights, his biological and natural unity, his deification in bourgeois Christianity or Protestantism encouraged the idea of the Individual as a standardised scientific instrument capable of the impersonal and homogeneous labour of science. Fieldwork, the hazardous exchange of yore, now merely commemorated the alienation of mind from nature, fact from value, science from human life and labour from itself. In it, scientific observation, a predicate and activity of human beings became Science subjectified. The abstract independent Subject of science now stepped forth, not appointed but 'called' to his task, viewing as his own freedom the uncurbed movement of an autonomous even anarchic science. Men who *did* science now became men *of* Science arrogantly setting themselves apart both in the colonies and at home from those who were without science—heathens and believers, Blacks and Whites.

The Scientific Subject now located an ethically neutral object whereby to reflect the image of his own new-found instrumentality. In the field it was only vis-a-vis the Other that the anthropologist was expected to shed all prejudice—a methodology which was strictly speaking not so much immoral as amoral, neutralising the scientists and his activity from state and religious interference *or* privilege. The selectivity considered possible for the field-observer, between values that were strictly mental/intellectual and those merely personal/emotional was part of the 'inhuman' cultural presumptions of the scientific method itself. By introducing in his methodology the etiquette of contact, not ingestion 'pollution' (to borrow a caste metaphor), Malinowski heroically persuaded the anthropologist to go by way of what he was not, without getting lost or destroyed on the way. Thus the fieldworker learnt the local language but communicated with the scientific community in his own. He lived apart from the expatriate official and civilian white population but not so far that he could not avail of their help and protection in case of need. He cooperated and worked with the natives but did not accept (nor did he need) paid employment in whatever form. Like a lotus in the mud of colonial culture, the anthropological fieldworker demonstrated the superiority of mind over matter, idea over reality and personality or 'character' over custom as a function of the scientific hierarchy between himself and the Other.

Historically the extraordinary value for science in the west, preceded and legitimated ethnography and gave it tremendous prestige in the colonies all through even the most beleagured periods of British rule. The search for the substantial and particular Other seemed in some way to give body and soul to the abstraction that Man had been reduced to in the rational organisation of life and knowledge. What is significant for our purpose here is that a cognitive space for the Subject or Self had already been created in the territories of the western mind and thought, before fieldwork or the search for the actual Other ever even began to take place (Gellner: 1987), just as the *idea* of a Natural Philosophy had, in the seventeenth century, already occurred in the mental and conceptual activity of the virtuosi of the Royal Society (The Royal Society of London for Improving Natural Knowledge), before the activity of natural science as we know it today became institutionalised. Is fieldwork then a redundant system of scientific investigation—a form ironically of omniscience—which sets out to 'test' a hypothesis by furnishing only confirmatory evidence based on the human Subject's observation? We are tempted to come to this conclusion when we consider the peculiar absence of any 'failed' fieldwork in our discipline. What this really amounts to saying is that by the time Malinowski actually set out to *do* fieldwork, it had in a sense, already been done for him in the privileged domain of theory.

Fieldwork's almost erotic fascination and draw for anthropologists is a function of its obsolescence. Like the Bound Foot or the Christian Crucifix, it has become excessively suggestive, testifying to what Durkheim considered the 'Thing' character of social mysteries on the basis of a superfluous and essentially carnal knowledge about them. An empiricist application of theory that went before it—French Positivism— fieldwork has fetishised experience and dressed it up to look like an experiment. Before Malinowski ever came on the scene, Durkheim and even Marx had examined the enigmatic character of society and its social productions as an order of reality, which was simultaneously thing and representation, object and spirit, present as an immanent yet transcendent force amongst us. But with the advent of fieldwork, the search for symbolical truths gave way to the requirement for concrete and linear descriptions. The proof of the pudding was now in the eating and fieldwork came to reflect the triumph essentially of modest realism or experience over the grand 'armchair' theorising of Durkheim, Robertson-Smith and others (Malinowski 1954, Peristiany 1960: 317–24, Evans-Pritchard 1956).

The professed "umble-ness' of the anthropologist's task was of course a necessary consequence of its physical, temporal and spatial limitations which permitted the fieldworker scope to collect only that much detailed information on the actual 'working' of a social system. At the same time the play of what come to be recognised as the Personality factor in this exercise encouraged even its artistic, intuitive and magical understanding. The fieldworker was allowed his vain moments when his performance in the field was gauged on the basis of intangible factors relating to his own subjectivity, its agency and power. It was his success now at maintaining a difficult and delicate social balance between intimacy and restraint, 'joking' and 'avoidance' when dealing with the Other, which marked him apart not just as a fieldworker but as an extraordinary person. His scientific praxis consequently was not so much neutral as informed by an ethical and political morality which was different from that of a layman's. The physical and emotional hardship, the involvement with diarrhoea and dirt, loneliness and exile confessed to in diaries or back at home, in the privacy of academe, formed an important component of fieldwork's heroic self-image. The cultural value laid on western science and its superior truth was matched by the superior morality of its subject—the gentleman-scholar—who together with his adamantine other half—the militaryman—ruled the world.

Historically, the peculiar ascetic-erotic flavour of fieldwork, its characterisation as both science and art is explicable in terms of post-Reformation developments within European society which encouraged the rationalisation of adept activity as of human social action in general (Weber 1948: 129–56). Science as a vocation became possible once its subject emerged as a secular professional, an inner-worldly version of the Christian monk. Fieldwork it could be said, presumed both the rigour and specialised discipline of the scientific 'calling', its devotion even 'frenzy' (ibid), without at the same time becoming the venue for their symbolic mediation. Paradoxically therefore, the marriage of data and theory, participation and observation—a recurrent theme in all the pioneering works of social anthropology—was never actually consummated in fieldwork as a true unity in duality. The preoccupation even with other modes of thought remained at the level of cultural description and could never reflect back as science.

Fieldwork continued to be arranged around the mechanical and hierarchical ordering of precept and concept, sensation and reason, intuition and science, which had marked the positivist endeavour right from the very start—and this despite the indivisibility of its moral human subject (Durkheim 1960: 325–40). Even Weber, recognised today as the champion of a hermeneutic social science, as good as legitimated the positivist organisation of field activity when he remarked:

> Every type of purely direct, concrete description bears the mark of *artistic* portrayal (1949: 107 italics original).

For valid scientific judgements, descriptions had to be subjected to a logical and conceptual analysis. 'Life', 'experience' and 'personality' were not to be confused with the elect activity of science, its 'strange intoxication' and 'passion'. Judgements about the True, the Good and the Beautiful were consequently to be kept entirely separate in the scholar's activity (1948: 148).

What for Weber marked the non-dilletantish and professional character of science, confirmed for Marx exactly its alienation from life. Whether as commodity or science, it was de-personalised and standardised human labour which under capitalism assumed the alien shape of the Other (1954). Fieldwork as we know it today, would for Marx have provided a heightened expression of the separation of man from his own humanity.

In the formal organisation of fieldwork, the wholeness of its human instrument—the fieldworker—has constantly to be denied. Elaborate etiquettes exist to maintain the neutrality of fieldwork's image, precisely because it is so close to life and experience. Two anthropologists for instance, rarely research the same field consecutively. A convention which certainly prevents the 'embarrassment' of disparate results but which simultaneously highlights the redundancy of the field exercise. No scholar furthermore, sticks his neck out to check on the technical prowess or back-stage activity of a colleague. The storm raised by Derek Freeman's expose on Mead's field activities in Samoa (1983) reflected the breach of this unwritten code. The authenticity, sufficiency and proficiency of a scholar's fieldwork remains of course at the heart of much conjecture and gossip within the discipline and for that very reason, its public examination is subject to strict taboos. The delicacy with which the profession deals, or does not deal, with the moral lapses and eccentricities of its members, particularly when they relate to the period of their fieldwork, is on that account alone very great.

In the hard sciences, public legitimacy of the scientist is paradoxically enhanced by playing up his wholeness and fallibility so that an entire mythology exists of the sins and sufferings, talents and habits of the professional community and its members. In the soft sciences, this aspect is on the other hand repressed and kept private. Thus Einstein can be publicly permitted to revere Gandhi and Feynman to booze but it will not do for Malinowski or Evans-Pritchard to 'go native' in their sexual or religious preferences. It is what the discipline has worked to keep *out* of its professional record which has allowed it a facade of objectivity. Fieldwork is clearly not a simple technical act, a mere means to the scientific truth; but in the selectivity of its data, acts on a culturally pre-determined understanding of what is or ought to constitute science both as a form of knowledge and action.

III

In their conception of their own scientific subjectivity, Malinowski, Radcliffe-Brown and Evans-Pritchard amongst others, consciously and aggressively separated themselves from their illustrious but essentially sedentary precursors. It was the revolutionary new 'field' component of their anthropological praxis which constituted for them an advantage over those virgin men of science who lacked first-hand experience of the Other—the object of study. But there is no reason for us in India to fall in with this line of thinking. Fieldwork, Malinowski's example has shown us, was imperial in its experiment, in its very possibility as science and not in the national or racial essence of its Subject. The substantive alteration of the latter consequently in post-colonial times, does not rectify its methodological inadequacy. By extension, the question of objectivity in the field study of one's own society and the very possibility of its achievement, is a redundant issue, however much it may exercise nationalist social science (Srinivas 1966: 147–63; Srinivas, Shah and Ramaswamy 1979). This is particularly true when we consider that it was existential contingency and not methodological necessity which forced more and more Indian scholars historically to focus solely on India.

After the departure of the British, the functionalist school of fieldwork was retained in Indian social science as a nationalist clone of the original. Colonial techniques of fieldwork, quite in contradiction to their logical-positivist and ahistorical spirit, were popularised amongst scholars and students alike as a scientific means to achieving national development and democracy. In the absence of resources and opportunity which had enabled the British to make intellectual capital out of geographic and racial distance, it was now social, cultural and economic distance—India's abundant empirical diversity—that was offered to local scholars as a substitute laboratory:

Fieldwork in an alien society constitutes an excellent preparation for the observation of one's own society, but it is very expensive and developing countries will not be able to afford it. Under the circumstances it is best if the young sociologist begins fieldwork in a section of the society different from that to which he belongs....(In India) a sharp stratification system, considerable regional diversity... compensate to some extent for the non-availability of resources...(Srinivas 1966: 15–16).

India is a vast, an heterogeneous country and offers almost unlimited possibilities to the fieldworker...While it is important to try and combine, or at least to bring together, the perspectives of the 'insider' and the 'outsider', it will be well to remember that the difference between the two is at best one of degree (Beteille and Madan 1975: 7).

The dualisms of insider and outsider, self and other, appropriately watered down to accommodate the 'little' traditions of Indian society, were mimetically adopted by Indian field science from its colonial precursor. The dependence on imperial method while rejecting imperial politics had of course its paradoxical consequences. Indian scholars became busy making scientific virtue of subaltern necessity by feverishly endo-specialising. Displaying India's stigmata of poverty and tradition, its 'backward', 'underdeveloped', 'exotic' and custom-ridden conditions to the world, through independent Indian field-studies, now achieved new heights and provided in fact a powerful vested interest for attracting official and foreign funding and patronage (Majumdar 1956, Saran 1958).

Given the powerful state ideology of development and social reconstruction, the micro-level study of whatever is empirically available in India today—caste, village, factory, school or whatever—has come to define the limits of a specifically Indian and nationalist tradition of fieldwork. In Gandhi's language, this purely local application of an already applied western science amounts to the intellectual practice of swadeshi-enquiry into the particular self without the accompanying swaraj-enquiry into universal truth. But significantly for him, the opposite is equally reprehensible. The search for swaraj in the Indian university, Gandhi is quite categorical, cannot be at the expense of swadeshi (Prabhu and Kelekar 1961: 18–41). And yet one brand of nationalist social science is pursuing just this strategy in the name of swaraj (Uberoi: 1978).

Following what can only be termed the Left-Hand tradition of the British school, some scholars, young and old, have in recent years swum against the current to do their ethnography in Europe, without (and this is important to them) changing sides and 'becoming' Europeans or even NRI's. In a historic and substantive reversal of traditional Indian field preoccupations, it is now mainstream institutions of the First World—European science, religion and politics and not its racial, criminal or 'folk' slipstreams (which have anyway been studied by westerners themselves), that are being subjected to Third World scrutiny. In one such approach dedicated to a critique of modern European science and its dualist cosmos, the disastrous separation of swadeshi from swaraj within the Indian mind itself, is more than apparent. Europe remains here the text and India the context, sounding-board and convenient sparring partner:

India as a culture area will be nowhere, I think, in the world of knowledge, the sciences and the arts, if it does not first defy the European monopoly of the scientific method, established in modern times. It is no solution to propose to wait until we should ourselves become Europeans. We must recognise also other 'non-standard' methods of the organisation of knowledge in the sciences and the arts, within and without the university, and other principles of the relation of knowledge to life, whether European or non-European. This in turn will require independent studies of the development of modern European culture, not only in its relation to India and Asia during the modern colonial period, but also in relation to itself during its period of creation (1500–1650), opening with the Renaissance and the Reformation, its phase of institutionalisation (1650–1800) and finally the phase of its diffusion as a pattern of culture throughout the world (1800–1950) (Uberoi 1984: 9).

By seeking to merely alter the essence of the historic Subject *or* Object of Indian ethnography respectively, both field-strategies outlined above remain forms of neo-nationalism—whether of an incestuous or alternately a more belligerent, pugilistic variety. The question to be considered however is not so much the political as the scientific inadequacy of these two positions. The classical western dualist model of fieldwork, I would like to argue, is not merely unethical and impracticable but impossible for Indian social science to adopt. This is so because the very theory of the relation between knowledge and reality, which must of necessity underly any scientific enquiry into Self and the Other and their relations with one another in nature or in art, is fundamentally different in both. Monogeny or the humanist cosmology on which the activity of fieldwork was predicated, cannot without perversion or extrinsic justification, be applied to conditions of life and thought in India. Indeed this inadequacy is only part of fieldwork's more general theoretical inadequacy.

As a method of scientific experimentation, fieldwork is in principle redundant because, geo-politically speaking, the very possibility of its practice presumed its success. In the absence of a genuine test of its theoretical truth, it was a cultural understanding of what ought to constitute science which gave imperial fieldwork the guise of science. Any serious 'Indian' programme of fieldwork therefore must simultaneously, and from an independent view point, resist or re-consider its underlying theory of knowledge. But this has not happened.

The nationalisation of the Indian field-industry without any concern for theory has compounded its alienation from society and the Self. The field-worker, quite in contrast to his white predecessor, is now expected to go to the field purged of all indigenous cultural *and* intellectual 'bias'. In its more empiricist justification this appalling situation is meant to hold even for the study of one's own society: The social fact of living, sophisticated oral and textual traditions in India is treated here as a peculiarly national malady, a failing which makes the immaculate task of science that much more difficult for Indians:

> Observing one's own society is far more difficult than observing an alien society. In the case of Indians there is an additional difficulty that ideas which are carried over from literary material and from the caste and region to which one belongs by birth, vitiate the observances of field behaviour (Srinivas 1962: 130).

This uncompromising stand by a veteran social scientist of India has of course been sought to be modified since it was first articulated, by the cultural and structural approach to Indian civilisation. Paradoxically however, the latter has only ended up sustaining (albeit indirectly) its empiricist presumptions. The argument for the incorporation of indigenous concepts and categories—oral or textual—into the practice of field research (Dumont 1957) remains a variety of description. So also the monographic approach which focuses more exclusively on a single or a set of texts as the 'field' of study (Das 1977). In all these varieties of Indian social science, it is indigenous institutions and/or the categories of cognition and knowledge relating exclusively to Hindu practice (more specifically ritual and customary practice), which are taken to hold the key to an understanding of the whole of Indian civilisation—its life and thought: and which continue to be understood in terms of the assumptions of modern western thought—its epistemology either being applied directly to Indian empirical reality or indirectly to its texts. The question whether such an application of modern scientific methods to traditional praxis is possible at all in the Indian context, is not considered by any. This failure or laziness on the theoretical front has led one observer to remark that '...Indian social thought is largely Indian sociology' (Saran 1958: 1923). The move within Indian social science to promote in the first instance the marriage of indigenous sociology with social anthropology and in the second instance with indology is symptomatic of its alienation from theory. Both these trends although superficially, vociferously opposed to one another, are injunctions really to look at the Self as the Other's Other, in space and in time.

In the West, anthropology and indology—historically the study of the Other—were separated from sociology, the study of the Self. The positivist dichotomy (between fact and value, science and culture, the object from the subject of study) lay behind the higher scientific status granted to the former two disciplines. Modern empiricist indology, we must not forget, in contrast to its Orientalist precursor was close to the 'field' disciplines of the late nineteenth century—philology, anthropology, archaeology, ethnology—and thus counted as a harder social science than sociology which remained a branch of the philosophy of history.

The neutralisation of cultural bias it was considered was easier when entering an alien (natural or moral) field. Contrariwise, and for that very reason, fieldwork as a method was largely discarded by colonial science vis-a-vis the western Self. When field techniques did come to be adopted for studying the latter, it was initiated by American scholars, (who had never known the colonial discipline of social anthropology in the Thirties); and conspicuously, in the realms of ethnic and community studies which remained closer to folkloristics rather than classical history or sociology. In England, Radcliffe-Brown and Evans-Pritchard, particularly the latter, argued for what amounted to the same thing when they urged the coming together of social anthropology and sociology, under post-colonial conditions. More recently the western emphasis on the use of interpretative techniques closer to history in the field-study of Other Cultures, merely confirms the latter's defeated status now as Art, even 'fiction', in the positivist epistemic hierarchy (Clifford 1988: 92–113). The ethical justification provided for this hermeneutic position is really only proof of its scientific unavailability.

The reconciliation between sociology and social anthropology/ indology in the west was of course a pragmatic one but it involved no cost to theory. The dualist underpinnings of the separation between Self and the Other, art and science remained very much alive. Not so in India where it was the empirical peculiarities of Indian society itself which were used to justify the coming together of sociology and social anthropology as 'field' disciplines. India it was post-hoc argued had tribes and castes but it also had urban classes; it had villages but it also had factories—all of which needed to be studied (Beteille 1974: 17). This territorial celebration of the need for methodological unity had however nothing to say universally. Neither did the coming together of Indian field and textual study (Indology). And how could it? Following the lead given by western science meant really underscoring either the complete absence of indigenous theory or its fossilisation as a historical curiosity—a form of traditional knowledge brought to life by the gaze of the Other.

When fieldwork was colonial, it was understandable that we, as servants of the Raj, acted as modest assistants to the British, sometimes even taking their scholarly place, but only in the data-collecting, 'art' half of the positivist praxis, leaving science to our betters. But today, when fieldwork is post-colonial, it is surprising that things are not so very different. In fact, if anything this surrogate science has been preached with the zealousness of the new convert only after India gained freedom from British rule. Before independence, western science and modern values aroused more scepticism and unease because they were reminders of our political subjection. But with this anxiety over, Indian social scientists have thrown their heart and soul into the intensive study of the actual state of affairs in the nation's villages and cities as both adequate and necessary for understanding or alternately transforming a traditional society in transition. Theory it is felt can wait till the accumulation of data through field techniques yields sufficient generalisations. That Indian thinkers continue to be dependent on the west for their theory is of course also due to the fact that those who had served or studied under the British, became in turn their teachers and superiors in the institutions of social science in free India.

The first Indian Department of Sociology was established in Bombay by the British in 1919, under the charge of Professor Sir Patrick Geddes. As early as 1924, G.S. Ghurye took over headship from the latter. Sent to England as a student on Geddes's recommendation, Ghurye had come under the influence of the Le Play School of Sociology at the London School of Economics. Later at Cambridge he worked with W.H.R. Rivers, the leading British anthropologist of the time. In Calcutta, another presidency town of British-India, it was Dr. L.K. Ananthakrishna Iyer who was put in charge of the Department of Anthropology at the local University, which was started some years after the Bombay Department of Sociology. Dr Iyer had not only been influenced by A.C. Haddon and A.H. Keane but had also been associated with the 'Tribes and Castes' ethnographic project of the British Government. Dr Sarat Chandra Roy also of Calcutta University and a colleague of Iyer's, was encouraged in his anthropology studies by both Haddon and Rivers. At the Lucknow University it was Dr D.N. Majumdar, trained in anthropology at Calcutta and Cambridge, who took charge of the local Department in the forties while in Delhi, a Department of Sociology was begun in 1959, under Professor M.N. Srinivas a student of A.R. Radcliffe-Brown at Oxford. In Madras, the Government Museum since early in its history, had officials interested in anthropology. Fawcett and E. Thurston were both connected with the Museum. Dr A. Aiyappan, who worked in London under the guidance of Professor Raymond Firth became Superintendent of the Museum after Independence.

The west's trusteeship of Indian intellectual life and thought was clearly not over even with the passing of the British Raj. Any discussion of the inadequacy of fieldwork must consequently be located not in the political iniquities of British colonialism but in the methodological principles of western science. To think that one can reject the former and yet retain the latter without injury, is to delude oneself. Fieldwork as a research technique was spawned by the positivist universe of discourse so that ideally the cross examination of one should lead to the cross examination of the other. What this really means is that its problematic is not exhausted by an examination of the works of those itinerant scholars who actually do fieldwork but can equally fruitfully be explored in the writings of a Newton, a Durkheim or a Wittgenstein. Many locally produced critiques of modern scientific method do of course exist but most, if not all, stop short of saying what needs to be done about it vis-a-vis the Self. This is fundamentally illogical since the segregation of the technical from the ethical in human life-praxis is already prey to the methodological presumptions of modern western science. Viewed in this light, the inadequacy of the 'Indian' critique of western European scientific cosmology, both in its internal systemic aspect (Uberoi 1984) and in its external 'application' to Hindu data (Marriott 1989), becomes all too apparent. Certainly, the inadequacy of these scholarly exercises—the one by an Indian national and the other by a westerner—is not equivalent. The West (or the Other more generally) cannot do for us what we have not done for ourselves. By extension, it is not the actual 'doing' of fieldwork in India by Indians or Europeans; or alternately in Europe by Indians or whatever but an indigenous theory and practice of the experiment, which constitutes a genuine, independent Indian contribution, if any, to universalistic social science.

IV

Gandhi's indigenous critique of the 'civilisational imperatives of modern life and knowledge is significant in this regard and quite well known to Indian social science (Gandhi 1908). But what is relatively less known to the latter is his theory of the experiment or *prayog* which as a form of human action, was categorically distinguished both from the realm of duty or *dharma* and that of the transcendental or omniscient (Gandhi 1927, 1928: 212–36; Pyarelal 1956: 567–605; Bose 1974: 147–78). 'Participant-observation' for Gandhi was coterminous with any human method of experiment or enquiry into the nature of the Self or the World and could not be restricted to a particular system or branch of knowledge. The 'field' experiment unlike its more specialised western counterpart necessitated the rigorous discipline and preparation of *both* the Self and the Other and was never bereft of the wider ethical context of action—personal or political. His sustained investigations into the ashrama mode of social organisation and into the satyagraha and brahmacharya modes of collective/individual social action, showed that for him the distinction was truly meaningless. Thus, while the exemplary experiment certainly existed and was available to others as such, it could never be imitated and had to be re-designed and re-discovered afresh by each truth-seeker. Standardisation in human scientific enquiry consequently was not only impossible but undesirable, since the possibility of innovation or failure was itself under test.

At the same time, new and 'shocking' experiences of the Self could only become transformed into truth or knowledge in the context of responsible and disciplined social action, which presumed love of the Other. In this heroic inversion of imperial field methodology, the distinction between Self and the Other or the concept of 'untouchability' in Hindu life, was consistently eroded by Gandhi. All his experiments, whether in the realm of caste, communal, race or gender relations sought to de-classify the Untouchable—harijan, muslim, white or woman—through a non-violent exchange of places and meanings with them. That his field methods were ignored as anything other than a form of political, spiritual 'activism' by the social science of free India and continue to be so even today (Caplan 1987, Parekh 1989), is surely significant. A discussion of the anthropologist N.K. Bose's resistance in particular, to putting Gandhi's experiments to the test in a serious scientific manner, highlights for us the separation of the modern Indian university from society and the Self.

N.K. Bose, associated with Calcutta university since the twenties, was a committed Gandhian who participated in the freedom movement and was imprisoned several times. During the grim pre-partition period of 1946–47, Bose even accompanied Gandhi to the riot-hit areas of Noakhali, serving as secretary and interpreter. Most importantly, it was Bose who attempted to bring into his academic work, Gandhian notions of 'activism' or social involvement and responsibility and the value of personal example set by the teacher. Fieldwork, as he once declared was a means of '...changing the world'. Without this attitude, scientific work '..tends to fritter down into an aimless endeavour, which merely satisfies some idle curiosity or even a sense of personal vanity' (1953: 247). Gandhi's uncompromising rejection of modern civilisation and its science however finally drove a wedge between them as it did for many others at the time who were forced to choose between the two.

Bose's dramatic break with Gandhi in 1947 when he physically left his entourage in Patna and returned to the University, was really only the outward manifestation of an inner, moral and epistemic break with Gandhian method. Gandhi's open experiments in brahmacharya involving sharing his bed with a young female relative, Manu Gandhi, provided the immediate occasion. The timing of this audacious experiment and the leader's outrageous demand that it be discussed openly and freely both at the daily prayer meetings and in writing had truly dismayed and alarmed every close associate of Gandhi's. Coming as it did in the thick of the communal horrors of pre-partition Bengal and Bihar, this apparent whim of Gandhi's had led to much perplexity, even antagonism and impatience on the part of his followers. But for Gandhi himself there was nothing new either in his undertaking the experiment at that particular time or even in its eliciting the response that it did from the people.

A clue to this enigma is provided in Gandhi's own earlier writings where he argued in defense of his experiments in brahmacharya that the supposed 'sensuality' of his unorthodox practices was first publicly articulated only when he began his '...active campaign against untouchability' (Bose 1953: 170). The interconnection, might it be suggested, between the two 'field' trials of 1947—one conducted on his camp-bed in Patna (the microcosm), the other in the violent, riot-torn streets of Bengal and Bihar (the macrocosm)—lay in the unity of their method and goal. The first tested the real success of Gandhi's life-long experiments in the removal of 'untouchability' between men and women, the second between Hindus and Muslims. That both resulted in failure (one almost immediately and the other ultimately) does not in any way deny their validity as indigenous experiments. A genuine contribution to Indian social science after all requires merely that Gandhi's field methods be at least considered along with Malinowski's, or any other's. Their acceptance or rejection is quite another matter. But that this did not, even more importantly, could not be allowed to happen, reflected the spectacular triumph of modernity both in the Indian university and in national life more generally.

Significantly, it was N.K. Bose's commitment to his duty as a university person which legitimated for him both his disagreement with Gandhi over the experiments conducted with Manu Gandhi and his subsequent departure from the Mahatma's service. In a public letter to associates, giving his deliberate and considered opinions on the matter, Bose displayed the intellectual and metaphysical divorce from Gandhi which foreshadowed his actual physical leave taking:

... from a serious study of Gandhiji's writings I had formed the opinion, which was perhaps not unjustified, that he represented a hard, puritanic form of self-discipline, something which we usually associated with medieval Christian ascetics or Jain recluses.

So, when I first learnt in detail about Gandhi's *prayog* or experiment, I felt genuinely surprised. I was informed that he sometimes asked women to share his bed and even the cover which he used, and then tried to ascertain if even the least trace of sensual feeling had been evoked in himself or his companion. Personally, I would never tempt myself like that; nor would my respect for woman's personality permit me to treat her as an instrument of an experiment undertaken only for my own sake (Bose 1974: 150–51).

Gandhi responded to this letter by pointing out that Bose was in error about his experiments in brahmacharya, on at least three counts; (i) that their unorthodoxy implied 'modernity', (ii) that they assumed woman's inferiority and (iii) that they could be understood on the basis of 'second-hand' evidence (ibid: 152–53).

Bose's reply to this consciously put his service to the university over service to Gandhi and reiterated his faith in western methods of observation and analysis as a function of this preference:

Personally, I have practiced the Freudian technique of dream analysis on myself and have derived immense benefit, as it has helped bring to the surface submerged desires which had been causing trouble, and thus helped me to deal with them satisfactorily.

Thus I based my judgement on personal observation of behaviour. I admit it was not wholly adequate. But then, I was sitting in no public judgement.... All that I want to tell you is that I did not base my judgement on 'second-hand' evidence; but on another type of observation, which is valid to the extent it goes....

When I have to choose between the amount of service I can render to you here in Bihar and for science in the University, I would place the latter first (ibid; 154–156).

N.K. Bose's rupture with Gandhi—the man and the method— and at that particular moment of history, displayed all the marks of India's collective rupture with indigenous traditions of knowledge. The experimental techniques now communicated to students ensured that the self, and sexuality in particular, could never itself become the object of 'field' investigation. Theory (western) in the free Indian university was to be completely segregated from cultural, political practice (nationalist/ Gandhian).

For N.K. Bose, as for Malinowski, scientific obligation represented cosmopolitanism and was preferred over 'narrow' political obligation to the nation—whether reflected in the example of a great leader or a beloved friend. In a strictly methodological sense, their actions were wholly legitimate since morally and cognitively and not merely geo-politically, the experimental field was only meant to begin where real life left off. Malinowski, it is significant to note, rejected the Jagiellonian University's offer of the Chair in Ethnology instituted for him at Cracow in 1922, on the grounds of pressing fieldwork commitments which left him little time for teaching and related duties (Paluch 1981: 283).

The requirement to separate technical from ethical action in modern fieldwork methods, ensured the fieldworker's alienation from the Self. For Malinowski, a Pole operating under imperial conditions of war and work it certainly meant a near-total disaffection with any sense of community, history, identity or function. His notorious confession in the Trobriand diary: 'As for ethnology, I see the life of the natives as utterly devoid of interest or importance, something as remote from me as the life of a dog' (1967: 167), suggested a man who had cut loose from the 'natives' in Poland itself. Not entirely surprisingly, Poland condemned him politically as a representative of British imperialism by ignoring his scholarly contribution almost completely in the inter-war period. But what is more surprising is that Britain, the country of his choice, condemned him intellectually as an applied scientist by deeming him a brilliant fieldworker and empiricist but not, definitely not, a theoretician!

The vigorous attack on this position today by Polish intellectuals, operating under a changed political regime, seeks significantly to uncover Malinowski's 'roots' in the realm both of culture *and* theory (Paluch 1981: 276–83, Ellen et al 1988). Quite clearly, the problem of the relation between nationalism and internationalism, swadeshi and swaraj is in the social sciences, intimately linked to the nature of the relation between truth and value and thence to the growth of the discipline. For us in India, another 'outpost of progress' like Poland, to have chosen Malinowski over Gandhi as a field ancestor was of course an entirely predictable event, given our colonial history. But to continue so categorically and unreflectingly to prefer the imported product over khadi even today, is perhaps to deny ourselves and the world, of an independent theoretical possibility. A possibility which scrupulously scrutinises the 'ethnography' and the 'diary', the 'science' and the 'art', the 'object' and the 'instrument' of field praxis together, without epistemic isolation, secrecy or fear.

Notes

1. An earlier version of this paper was published in *Economic and Political Weekly*. Vol. XXVIII, No. 50, 11 December 1993, pp. 2745–52.

References

Barnes, J.A. 1978. 'Social Science in India: Colonial Import, Indigenous Product or Universal Truth'. Burg Wartenstein Symposium. No. 78: 15–24.

Beteille, A. 1974. 'Sociology and Social Anthropology.' In A. Beteille (ed.), *Six Essays in Comparative Sociology*. Delhi: Oxford University Press. Pp. 1–20.

Beteille, A. and T.N. Madan. (ed.) 1975. *Encounter and Experience: Personal Accounts of Fieldwork*. Delhi: Vikas.

Bose. N.K. 1953. 'Training in the Field Science'. In N.K. Bose (ed.) *Cultural Anthropology and Other Essays*. Calcutta: Indian Associated Publishing Company. Pp. 244–49.

_____ 1974. *My Days with Gandhi*. Calcutta: Orient Longman Ltd.

Caplan, P. 1987. 'Celibacy as a Solution: Mahatma Gandhi and Brahmacarya' In P. Caplan (ed.), *The Cultural Construction of Sexuality*. London: Tavistock. Pp. 271–95.

Clifford, J. 1988. 'On Ethnographic Self-fashioning: Conrad and Malinowski'. In J. Clifford (ed.) *The Predicament of Culture: Twentieth Century Ethnography, Literature, and Art.* Cambridge, Mass: Harvard University Press. Pp. 92–113.

Marcus, G.E. (ed.). 1986. *Writing Culture*: The Poetics and Politics of Ethnography. Berkeley: California University Press.

Das, V. 1977. *Structure and Cognition.* Delhi: Oxford University Press.

Durkheim, E. 1951. 'Preface to *L'Annee Sociologique*'. In K.H. Wolff (ed.), *Emile Durkheim, 1858–1917.* Columbus: Ohio State University Press. Pp. 341–52.

_____ 1960. 'The Dualism of Human Nature and its Social Conditions'. In K.H. Wolff (ed.), *Emile Durkheim, 1858–1917.* Columbus: Ohio State University Press. Pp. 325–40.

_____ 1975. *Suicide.* London: Routledge and Kegan Paul.

Ellen, R., E. Gellner, G. Kubica and J. Mucha. (eds.). 1988. *Malinowski Between Two Worlds.* Cambridge: Cambridge University Press.

Evans-Pritchard, E.E. 1956. *Nuer Religion.* Oxford: Clarendon Press.

Flis, A. 1988. 'Cracow Philosophy and Malinowski's Scientific Ideas'. In R. Ellen, E. Gellner, G. Kubica and J. Mucha (eds.) *Malinowski Between Two Worlds.* Cambridge: Cambridge University Press. Pp. 105–27.

Foucault, M. 1973. *The Birth of the Clinic: An Archaeology of Medical Perception.* A. Sheridan-Smith, tr. London: Tavistock.

Freeman, D. 1983. *Margaret Mead and Samoa: The Making and Unmaking of an Anthropological Myth.* Cambridge: Harvard University Press.

Gandhi, M.K. 1927. *Hind Swaraj or Indian Home Rule.* First Gujarati ed. 1908. Ahmedabad: Navajivan Publishing House.

_____ 1928. *Satyagraha in South Africa.* Ahmedabad: Navajivan Publishing House.

Geertz, C. 1973. 'Thick Description: Towards an Interpretive Theory of Culture'. In C. Geertz, (ed.) *The Interpretation of Cultures.* New York: Basic Books. Pp. 1–30.

Gellner, E. 1987. 'Zeno of Cracow or Revolution at Nemi or The Polish Revenge: A Drama in Three Acts'. In Ernest Gellner (ed.) *Culture, Identity and Politics.* Cambridge: Cambridge University Press. Pp. 47–74.

Ghurye, G.S. 1956. 'The Teaching of Sociology, Social Psychology and Social Anthropology'. In *The Teaching of Social Sciences in India.* Paris: Unesco. Pp. 148–60.

Heider, K. 1988. 'The Rashomon Effect: When Ethnographers Disagree'. In *American Anthropologist.* 90: 73–81.

Kubica, G. 1988. 'Malinowski's Years in Poland'. In R. Ellen, E. Gellner, G. Kubica and J. Mucha (eds.) *Malinowski Between Two Worlds*, Cambridge: Cambridge University Press.

Leach, E.R. 1982. *Social Anthropology.* Oxford: Clarendon Press.

Majumdar, D.N. 1956. 'Special Report on the Teaching of Social Anthropology'.In *The Teaching of Social Sciences in India.* Paris: Unesco. Pp. 161–73.

Malinowski, B. 1948, *Magic, Science and Religion and Other Essays.* New York: The Free Press.

_____ 1967. *A Diary in the Strict Sense of the Term.* London Routledge and Kegan Paul.

Marriott, M. 1989. 'Constructing an Indian Ethnosociology'. In *Contributions to Indian Sociology*. 23, Vol. 1: 1–39.

Marx. K 1954. *Capital: A Critical Analysis of Capitalist Production* . Vol 1. Moscow: Progress Publishers.

Marx, K. and F. Engels. 1975. 'The Holy Family or Critique of Critical Criticism'. In *Collected Works: Marx and Engels 1844–45*. Vol. IV. Moscow: Progress Publishers. Pp. 7–161.

Paluch, A. 1981. 'The Polish Background of Malinowski's Work'. In *Man*. 16: 276–85.

———— 1988. 'Introduction'. In R. Ellen, E. Gellner, G. Kubica and J. Mucha (eds.), *Malinowski Between Two Worlds*. Cambridge: Cambridge University Press. Pp. 1–11.

Parekh, B. 1989. *Colonialism, Tradition and Reform: An Analysis of Gandhi's Political Discourse*. New Delhi: Sage.

Peristiany, J.G. tr. 1960. 'Durkeim's Letter to Radcliffe-Brown'. In K.H. Wolff (ed.). *Emile Durkheim: 1858–1917*. Columbus: Ohio State University Press. Pp. 317–24.

Prabhu, R.K. and R. Kelekar (comp. and ed.) 1961. *Truth Called Them Differently: Tagore-Gandhi Controversy*. Ahmedabad: Navajivan.

Pyarelal, 1956. *Mahatma Gandhi: The Last Phase. Vol. 1*. Ahmedabad: Navajivan Publishing House.

Sahlins, M. 1982. 'The Apotheosis of Captain Cook'. In P. Smith and M. Izard (eds.). *Between Belief and Transgression: Structuralist Essays in Religion, History and Myth*. Chicago: Chicago University Press. Pp. 73–102.

Saran, A.K. 1958. 'India'. In J.S. Roucek (ed.), *Contemporary Sociology*. New York: Philosophical Library. Pp. 1013–34.

Srinivas, M.N. 1962. 'Village Studies and their Significance', M.N. Srinivas (ed.), In *Caste in Modern India and Other Essays*. Bombay: Asia Publishing House. Pp. 120–35.

Srinivas, M.N. 1966. *Social Change in Modern India*. California: University of California Press.

———— 1995. *Social Change in Modern India*. Delhi: Orient Longman.

Srinivas, M.N., A.M. Shah and E.A. Ramaswamy (eds.). 1979. *The Fieldworker and the Field: Problems and Challenges in Sociological Investigation*. Delhi: Oxford.

Strenski, I. 1982. 'Malinowski: Second Positivism, Second Romanticism'. In *Man*, 17, Vol. 4: 766–71.

Uberoi, J.P.S. 1978. *Science and Culture*. Delhi: Oxford University Press.

———— 1984. *The Other Mind of Europe*. Delhi: Oxford University Press.

Weber, M. 1948. 'Science as a Vocation'. In H.H. Gerth and C.W. Mills (trs. and eds.), *From Max Weber: Essays in Sociology*. London: Routledge and Kegan Paul. Pp. 121.56.

———— 1949. *The Methodology of the Social Sciences*. E.A. Shils and H.A. Finch (tr. and ed.) Glencoe, Illinois: The Free Press.

Young, M.W. (ed.), 1979. *The Ethnography of Malinowski: The Trobriand Islands 1915–18*. London: Routledge and Kegan Paul.

———— 1988 *Malinowski among the Magi: The Natives of Mailu*. London: Routledge and Kegan Paul.

Unlearning Fieldwork: The Flight of an Arctic Tern

SAVYASAACHI

What is the meaning and purpose of fieldwork in a social context where there are conflicts over differences which arise from social and cultural plurality and from political and economic inequalities? In this context, fieldwork which is designed to equip individuals and institutions with a method, not only to collect and catalogue information but also to understand and to overcome problems that emerge from these conflicts, generates a link between knowledge, power and domination. Knowledge on account of its link with power becomes a source for suppression and a means for the dissipation of creative energies. Progressively it loses its meaning as a liberating force in history. Today it is clearly demonstrated that conflicts lead to violence, impoverishment, disasters and breakdowns. They submerge the collective social and cultural life of people in bad faith and suffocate their everyday life within a growing sense of insecurity and uncertainty. Those who know this method acquire power to study those who are socially disadvantaged and are considered inferior, and not study those who are in power. This kind of fieldwork acquires a dualist character. Such fieldwork, and these ways of knowing, have to be unlearnt because they do not concern themselves with questions which open up themes and issues that derive meaning from day to day living. They do not expose the processes of marginalisation and prepare the ground for continuing dialogues and discourses across differences.

On account of its dualist character this fieldwork becomes an instrument of power. Its design creates monopoly in the sphere of knowledge; privileges the expert; legitimises power structures that give rise to violence, impoverishment, disaster and breakdowns, and inflicts injuries on day to day living. This monopoly conceals the asymmetrical relation between the researcher and the people, between the subject of inquiry and the object of study, between the one who is engaged in research, that is, the self, and the field of study, and accentuates social and cultural differences. Unlearning this fieldwork is premised on the critique of scientific knowledge which is capital intensive and which is derived from those questions which are not only asked but are also legitimised by the community of experts. According to this critique scientific knowledge is self-justifying. It is a closed system for it does not allow questions asked by people outside the community of scientists to gain ground. This critique has emerged from a cross fertilisation between the social sciences and a variety of social movements. It has awakened a concern for the relation between the questions, the knowledge systems and the way of life of the socially disadvantaged. It has shown that the questions they ask are as important as are the questions asked by the experts and together they open up and close down social spaces for inquiry.

From this perspective fieldwork is a method of inquiry which derives its form and content from the nature of questions asked by the expert and by people in general in the course of their day to day living. Accordingly, a more inclusive understanding of fieldwork is required for investigating and understanding these questions and their relation to the course of daily living. The pursuit of unlearning can show the various components of a more inclusive idea of fieldwork. What constitutes the identity of a fieldworker as the one engaged in inquiry, in his field of inquiry? How do questions define the field of inquiry? How does the act of asking questions acquire legitimacy? What discourses emerge from questioning? What conducts are appropriate for an inquiry and for the discourse of these questions? This entails a study of dispositions that precondition the thinking of a fieldworker and of practices that open up spaces in social life. Through this study a fieldworker learns to distinguish between ways of thinking and habits that one takes for granted and which discourage dialogue and discourse, from those that one does not take for granted and which encourage dialogue and discourse.

To observe these social practices facilitates an inquiry for a conduct that is appropriate for unlearning. Unlearning is thus an integral part of the conduct which is appropriate to the task of fieldwork. The question that concerns us here is, in what way does fieldwork facilitate unlearning and encourage an inquiry for the appropriateness of conduct.

Unlearning habits of thinking and social practices that are taken for granted, helps to facilitate the unfolding of phenomena of everyday life in their own time frame, uninhibited and undisturbed by the presence of the fieldworker. The 'manner of their unfolding' is thus the appropriate subject and the appropriate object of inquiry in fieldwork. The practice and discourse of unlearning, is concerned with the manner in which phenomena become accessible for inquiry. It seeks to minimise distortions introduced on the one hand by conducts that inhibit an openness in discourse and on the other hand by social practice that generate different conflicts. In this way it opens up social spaces closed by the hegemony of method.

The practice and study of unlearning is an integral part of an inquiry. It is comparable to the home-coming flight of the Arctic Terns who fly across the globe from the northern to the southern hemisphere. In the course of their marathon flight of over 14,000 miles, there are several imponderables. These birds do not have a built-in weather forecasting system. They respond to barometric pressures and other meteorological conditions. They often get confused in fogs, and often, they are carried off their path by storms and strong winds. But eventually they reach their destination. To lose the path and then to recover it is part of their mode of home-coming. Their mode of existence, which includes this marathon flight, is defined by their search for nourishment and warmth. Similarly, unlearning is a mode of homecoming. It opens up for study several social and cultural practices in day to day living which generate conflict over differences. These neither nourish nor give warmth—materially, intellectually and emotionally—to human beings. Unlearning is a mode of work which seeks to sustain dialogues and discourses, over different questions that emerge from conflicts in the course of day to day living and which give meaning to the search for a sense of certitude in this violent conflict-ridden world. The fieldworker then practices unlearning, in order to learn ways of being which are appropriate to this search.

Fieldwork as an Instrument of Domination

To understand how and why fieldwork fosters dualism and in order then to begin to 'unlearn' this mode, one could begin with a brief description of its history in India. In India the beginnings of the tradition of fieldwork can be traced back to 1772 when Warren Hastings returned to India with a cultural policy. Hastings' policy encouraged learning about Indian languages and about the culture and social life of people in India. This was part of the mode of governing them (Kopf 1969: 1–21). The intention of this policy was to wash away the stains on the reputation of the British government, which were acquired on account of the practices of Robert Clive and his generation of rulers. It created a class of Indians who would rule their own people on behalf of the British. At the same time, it also opened up the Indian subcontinent to scientific ideas on independence, freedom and equality. This generated an awareness amongst Indians about their identity and that of their country, and this in turn inspired the national struggle for independence. Fieldwork was considered part of a concientisation programme. It sought to awaken the people, and eventually enabled them to be free from British colonial rule.

From these developments emerged at least two traditions of fieldwork—one from Hastings' cultural policy, and the other from the national struggle for independence. In the former tradition, fieldwork acquired a dualist character and in the latter tradition fieldwork was equated with the process of generating nationalist consciousness and a sense of social responsibility amongst people, for each other and for India. The notion of fieldwork which developed on account of the cultural policy was based on the idea of ethical and cultural neutrality. In contrast, the notion of fieldwork that developed in the course of the struggle was concerned with defining it as a cultural practice that combined active participation and learning.

Under Hastings' cultural policy the Asiatic Society of Bengal was created to encourage and promote learning about the social and cultural life of the people of India. The studies undertaken by this Society, some of which are reported in the Journal of the Asiatic Society of Bengal, demonstrate that the material, natural wealth and the vast cultural heritage of India was researched and documented. Some assumptions of this mode of learning are recorded in the proceedings of the Society. It is stated,

> The body of scientific men in this country is not so great, nor the interest of the public in a single subject so absorbing, that local ethnological exhibition could be expected to stand alone... (Proceedings of the Asiatic Society April 1866:6).

From the standpoint of the Asiatic Society, India was a magnificent field for the collection of data. On 2 February 1814 it was resolved:

> The Asiatic Society is determined upon forming a Museum of all articles that may tend to illustrate Oriental manners and history or to elucidate the peculiarities of Art and Nature in the East. (Proceedings of the Asiatic Society, 2 February, 1814).

The Indian Museum was thus established as the storehouse of field-collections. Dr. Wallich a professional scientist, who initiated efforts for the setting up of this museum, said:

> Also any person engaged in the study of the history and language of this country or in the investigation of its natural produces must have frequent cause for regretting, that such a purpose should have been hitherto so very incompletely carried into effort. No public repositories yet exist....
>
> A collection of substances which are the objects of science and of those religions, which illustrate ancient times and manners, has always been one of the first steps taken by societies instituted for the dissemination of specific or universal knowledge... (Proceedings of the Asiatic Society, February 1814).

A particular kind of learning about the social and cultural life of people in India ensued from these assumptions. On the one hand, there developed an Indological view about India that was derived from a study of written languages and of classical texts. On the other hand, through fieldwork, British civil servants acquired a view about people's social and cultural practices. This created a generation of outstanding scholar-civil servants who educated themselves in, and catalogued the language, culture and history of Indian people. But these were company servants and their learning of another language, for reasons other than economic gain was inconceivable (Kopf 1969:15). Learning a language was a means to control commercial transactions. This utilitarian approach produced several detailed ethnographies of the social and cultural lives of people, but it did not deepen an understanding of their ways of life.

The understanding of India that emerged on account of Hastings' cultural policy did not question the view of British liberal political thinkers who emphasised, that neither in thought nor in practice, was there an Indian civilisation or a nation. On the contrary, the Indological and the ethnographic view of India acknowledged the existence of territorial units, highlighted their distinct social and cultural history, and negated the possibility of seeing them as part of a larger whole—the civilisation of India. These units were seen to coexist, at times in cooperation, but more often in conflict and confrontation, but never as part of this larger whole.

Hastings' cultural policy did not transform the British mode of domination. On the contrary, it grounded domination firmly and legitimised it by preparing a suitable cultural ground. An important component of this ground is that the relation of power and domination between the civil servant and the people was reproduced in the relation between the scientist-scholars and the people. Macaulay spelt out this political aspect of the cultural policy when he advocated westernisation as a true form of modernisation. He undertook to create 'a class of people, Indian in blood, in colour, but English in taste, in opinions and in morals and in intellect.' The social space created by this cultural policy privileged the culture of the literate people. In this space neither the issues, themes and ideas which derived from changes introduced in the daily lives of people by British rule nor their plural traditions of work, could be accommodated. Accordingly, under this cultural policy learning about people's way of life led to the marginalisation of their oral traditions of knowledge.

The ideas and assumptions underlying a cultural policy derive from a notion of subjectivity. The substance of this notion comes from the scientific method: subjectivity is constituted by cultural and ideological considerations. These are a set of beliefs and practices that obstruct the development of reason, of the individual and of a scientific understanding of society. This idea of subjectivity developed as a discipline, and as a method in Social and Cultural Anthropology. It required of an individual, if he or she wished to know society scientifically, to learn participant observation. The Royal Anthropological Institute of England in 1951 outlined this practice of fieldwork in *Notes and Queries in Anthropology*. In India it carried forward the dualism in fieldwork which was developed under Hastings' cultural policy. Descriptions and debates on fieldwork in Social and Cultural Anthropology that have followed the publication of this text have continued to follow this notion of subjectivity.

According to *Notes and Queries in Anthropology* the task is 'to get access to the natives' view of their own social and cultural world.' In order to accomplish this task an understanding of subjectivity was emphasised. This is an important component of the method of participant observation. Its main characteristics are as follows. In order to ensure that the fieldworker's presence is not disturbing it is important to observe how

> [it] is usual to regard as 'natural' the habits and customs normal in one's own milieu. The observer is apt to consider some behaviour unworthy to record when similar, and abnormal when marked differently from, the customary in his own culture (Royal Anthropological Society 1951:27).

Accordingly, to ensure an uninhibiting conduct by the fieldworker,

> [the] first role in all investigation is to advance from the concrete and tangible to the abstract. Accounts of how 'natives think' or feel are of little value without information as to how they actually behave in concrete situations (Royal Anthropological Society 1951:37).

Finally, it is pointed out that to ensure a non-interfering participation in fieldwork it should be remembered that,

> [the] knowledge of the native language is only the medium of study. Such knowledge does not guarantee accurate information. The duration of fieldwork does not allow for the

mastery of the native language. Further, it requires exceptional skill to master the language (Royal Anthropological Society 1951:41–43).

From the standpoint of the tradition of fieldwork that developed in the course of the nationalist struggle, this understanding of subjectivity is bereft of a sense of social responsibility. The political rendering of this understanding is ethical and cultural neutrality. This was questioned in the critiques of the post-independence political economy of the Indian nation-state. In this critique it was argued that the political translation of a socially responsible subjectivity is the notion of human rights. This notion calls attention to the damage done to the human dimension: the world we live in causes human beings to be torn and strained by conflicts, by violence and by bad faith. Further, it emphasises the need to protect the human dimension equally for all people, that is with appropriate measures sensitive to the conditions of the socially disadvantaged people, living and dead, in all walks of life.

These ideas influenced thinking in social sciences methodology. It was realised that ethical and cultural neutrality was the other face of 'objectification,' which is the process that alienates the being of entities in the world from the larger whole of which they were a part, and from which they derive meaning. Accordingly to maintain a sense of ethical neutrality is nothing but a way of ignoring the significance of the fieldworker's presence on the people amongst whom fieldwork is undertaken, and on the social setting of the field of inquiry. Subjectivity when constructed as ethically and culturally neutral discourages dialogues and discourses across differences, prevents exchange of ideas and becomes a means to accumulate and monopolise symbolic capital.

In contrast, the construction of subjectivity from the standpoint of human rights equips us to observe the variety of languages that give access to the phenomena of day to day living. These languages are of body gestures and pain, of celebrations and lamentations, of emotions and desires, of sorrows and ecstasies; of clothings and maskings; of ornamentations and dismemberment. These components of language are forms of thinking and they come together in subjectivity. These languages of thinking have codes which give rise to a variety of social formations and institutions.

Ethical neutrality suppresses all these aspects of language and becomes thereby a mere medium, a thing of instrumental value to gather information alone. From this perspective, language is not seen as a mode of thought and practice which has a life of its own, quite independently of its specific uses and abuses. When language becomes a mere medium it renders subjectivity passive and introduces irrationalities into an inquiry. For instance, the attempt to protect an inquiry from irrationalities, that come from emotions and other aspects of subjectivity, often prompts the researchers to rely for help on a bilingual middleman, the 'informant'. The need for an informant is an irrationality in fieldwork. The informant's presence as a bilingual interpreter introduces irrationalities and distortions in an inquiry. It covers up the human dimension of the field situation and of its setting. It is not clear for instance who is the 'one who conducts the inquiry'—is it the anthropologist or is it the bilingual interpreter, the informant?

People's language(s) when reduced to mere instruments to elicit information, become politically disadvantaged and the voices of people who speak these language, are marginalised. Instrumentality reshapes and alters the context of the language. This in turn influences its content and obscures its structure of meanings. Clearly it is the language of this intersubjective discourse, between the researcher and the informant, which defines and interprets the field of inquiry. Descriptions of the field situation thus partake of the informant's own active projections because it is he or she who has direct access to the field and who thus interprets it to the researcher. Often it is not clear when they give misleading information. Language expresses, interprets and becomes a mode of 'representational positing.' That is, it covers up individual and collective aspects of the being of an entity, holding it from emerging into a world which is intelligible in intersubjectivity.

This is a brief description of how, the social contexts of people's languages when altered and reshaped, become mere instruments to collect information. In this altered social context anthropologists face several problems. For instance, people are unwilling to give time for interviews, they demand money in return for information. At times anthropologists have to compete for 'informants' with other social science and government researchers and investigators. This is the consequence of making 'informants' an integral part of fieldwork technology. Other components of this technology include multimedia techniques for investigation, recording and representation. On account of all these developments over the past two decades, fieldwork has in a large number of cases acquired the character of a business proposition. It has in a majority of cases become a project-specific and a time-bound programme of investigation. Inquiry here is constrained by this external imposition of a time limit. It does not allow time and space for questions that the people are concerned with to surface in the course of their day to day living. Accordingly, fieldwork becomes insensitive to the role it plays as an instrument of gathering information, that is, to the way it derives knowledge that legitimises power and domination. This insensitivity results from an asymmetrical intersubjectivity wherein the time frame and the rhythm of fieldwork is indifferent to the time frame within which the field is structured and to the rhythm of its unfolding. This indifference has a political meaning: from the standpoint of the community of people amongst whom fieldwork is undertaken it is not always clear when the informant is not the 'informer' and when the fieldworker is not an exploiter.

Dualism in fieldwork is exploitative in its mode of information gathering, because it is a means of domination, of taking away ideas and values from the lives of people. It contributes to the social processes that impoverish their lives. It becomes a source of misrecognition because it does not question its own premise, namely the social distance between the researcher and the people—between the subject and the object of study, and between the one who is engaged in inquiry and the field of his or her inquiry. In this regard Levi Strauss observes:

> At first indeed it [anthropology] was concerned with so-called savage and primitive societies. But this interest is shared by other disciplines. On the other hand we have the strange phenomena that anthropology develops as those societies (primitive) tend to disappear or at least lose their distinctive features... (Levi-Strauss 1963:347).

This observation shows that the presence of a fieldworker which is shaped by participant-observation is neither uninhibiting nor is it undisturbing.

This then raises several questions: what is the meaning of an undisturbing, uninhibiting, non-interfering presence of a fieldworker? How does it define the conduct of the one engaged in inquiry? The ground for this inquiry, as mentioned earlier, was prepared by the tradition of fieldwork that developed in the course of the national struggle for independence and self rule, when it made a cultural critique of the political economy of British rule. This ground was enriched in the post-independence period by the cultural critique of the scientific method, that is of its view of development and progress, and of its inherent violent character.

The problem raised by dualism in fieldwork is that it conceals the fact that a fieldworker has a presence in the field which is defined by his or her code of conduct. To make the presence uninhibiting and undisturbing requires a method to first understand its various aspects. This method is the most important component of fieldwork. Its central concern is a conscientisation of the fieldworker towards the nature of his/her own presence in the field and towards the state of his/her preparedness for inquiry. Accordingly, the fieldworker needs to examine to what extent can the assumptions and preconceptions which generate a sense of certitude, be taken for granted and to what extent can they be questioned. Further, what happens to the fieldworker's sense of certitude when these assumptions and preconceptions are questioned in the course of field inquiry.

The asking of questions is an intervention. Its nature can be known from the intention of questioning. That is when the social assumptions and premises of the researcher's social being are questioned in intersubjectivity, when he makes his self available for questioning to himself and to others, in order that he may ask questions. On account of dualism in fieldwork, articulation of this dimension of intersubjectivity is inhibited by the social distance between the fieldworker and the people, between the subject and the object of study, and between the one who is engaged in inquiry and the field of inquiry. It follows that 'distancing' conceals the ground where intersubjectivity facilitates discourses and dialogues, where there are differences in ideas, in social institutions and in ways of life. It heightens differences to such an extent that it inhibits a search for a conduct appropriate for questioning the assumptions and premises of a way of life.

Unlearning

To be present as a fieldworker necessitates a code of conduct. What are the parameters of this code of conduct? The identity of a fieldworker is determined by the questions he or she asks; it is these questions that constitute inquiry. The norms of social life draw boundaries within which questions may be asked. These boundaries need to questioned if the social phenomena they enclose are to be understood. But this is a subversive activity. To be able to ask questions the fieldworker has to acquire the legitimacy to do so. The definition of the one who questions is determined by his or her relationship with different people and with different objects that constitute the field of inquiry. As the one who questions or as the one who is engaged in inquiry his identity is more than the sum total of the social roles and obligations he has to fulfill as a member of a community, a social group and a social class.

Such a reworking of the relation of power and domination with knowledge, such a questioning of fieldwork amounts to a process of 'unlearning'. Unlearning begins with asking the questions, 'What is the character of a field inquiry which does not impoverish the lives of people'? In what way can it prepare the ground for symmetry in intersubjectivity, for introducing the notion of reciprocity and participation in the process of questioning? By a process of such questioning, unlearning brings the fieldworker closer to intersubjectivity—that is a mode of face to face interaction which draws out these aspects of a manner of being present in the world in a field situation. The practice of unlearning gains in legitimacy as it uncovers irreconcilable differences which are concealed in the assumptions and preconceptions that underlie norms of social life, and at the same time generates a code of conduct to search for open space for discourses and dialogues. Differences lead to questioning routine activities, in the light of changing circumstances. This initiates a search for a social conduct which is on the one hand attentive to questions that are concerned with the meaning of the passage of time and, on the other hand which define the labour to be undertaken to keep in step with the changes introduced by the passage of time. The development of such a social conduct is facilitated by questioning those aspects of subjectivity that inhibit unlearning.

It is in this sense that unlearning attempts to free an inquiry from those assumptions, presuppositions, stereotypes and preconditionings that underlie routine activities, habits and customs normal in one's own milieu. It is by questioning that these assumptions and differences which are generated by the passage of time and which are embedded in habit, are uncovered. In so far as it uncovers, this questioning contributes to an understanding not only of habits and modes of participation but it also shows social 'clearings' concealed by habit. A social life which allows for unlearning codes of conduct and habits which create and accentuate social distances, also prepares the ground to perceive that differences and questioning are part of everyday life.

When unlearning questions the assumptions and premises of one's own sense of certitude it searches for a sense of meaningfulness in the differences introduced by the passage of time. This search draws its nourishment and warmth from the differences that enrich plurality of a social milieu and generate warmth in social relationships. The plurality of time scales, of modes of allocating time for various tasks, of arranging social and cultural life sequences, and of intersubjective experiences are concealed by the disposition of non-interference that define the tendency of the fieldworker to enter the field as an outsider and to eternally remain an outsider. Thus the mode of non-interference and participation is firmly rooted in social distances that generate misrecognition.

The Social Being of a Fieldworker

I have attempted here an examination of my fieldwork which commenced in 1982. The provocation to undertake this task was a question asked by an elder Koitor (Koitors are forest dwellers in Bastar) in 1987. I was to return to Delhi to begin to write my doctoral dissertation. He had observed me for these five years. He asked me: 'Who are you and what is the intention and purpose of your stay in the forest, far away from home for this long duration of time?' My response—that I wanted to, and had been able to learn from Koitors their language of shifting cultivation, see how they live in the forests of Abujhmarh in Bastar and understand their perception of the universe of the forest in the context of industrial deforestation—did not satisfy him. To him my undertaking to do fieldwork was meaningless, for it did not explain how my manner of being present, that is the way I lived amongst them in Abujhmarh, was linked to a means of earning a livelihood.

From the perspective of their way of life there is not much to learn from activities that are not linked to the pursuit of a mode of earning a livelihood. In order to exist, Koitors continue to practice shifting cultivation and supplement their incomes by selling their labour. When law renders the forest inaccessible in part or as a whole, then their reliance on the labour market increases. Where there is no forest, the reliance on the market is absolute. This leads to displacement from their homes and work places. Their work places are endangered by mining operations, nuclear plants, experimental rocket ranges and other such enterprises. Their means of living and their culture are reduced to mere objects—for example, what was formerly a totem pole is now used as a support for the ceiling of a country home, or it adorns the gardens of a museum—a thing of melancholy beauty.

Another elder once said,

You are yet another person, apparently concerned with our lives. You, like others of your tribe, are educated. For the past three generations people like you have visited us, enjoyed our hospitality—I wonder what you come to see. Progressively our living conditions are deteriorating. What is it that you wish to seek and know: I wonder what is your mode of coming-in?

One possible interpretation of the question asked by the elder is, what constitutes the identity of a social scientist as a fieldworker and how does it give legitimacy to his inquiry. I was asked, on several occasions what good would happen to Koitors after information about their lives is written and circulated. Several instances were given of people who came to gather information. They were given information but the people's conditions of living had not improved.

It was not possible to conduct fieldwork in the style of Verrier Elwin. Elders from village Bingli in Bastar recollect the organisation of an 'information gathering camp' by Elwin. They said 'He called villagers together in one place, fed them, and at leisure recorded details of their social and cultural life.' Today the sceptical disposition is ubiquitous. At times it is expressed in the form of a demand for a price for information and sometimes it is visible in the reluctance to share information.

The fact that information about them does not result in any improvement in Koitors' living conditions prepares them to withhold information. It is no solution to seduce them to give information. On account of their scepticism—the ethnographic text is at best a projection of ideas onto a people's ways of life—this information may not appropriately describe their social life. This raises questions about the authenticity of the one who asks, of the one who is supposed to answer these questions and of the response elicited. In short, the genuineness of inquiry itself is in question. Was the concern really with learning the Koitors' language and with understanding the meaning they give to their presence alongside the modern scientific world?

What defines authenticity and genuineness? These are perhaps defined by the manner in which questions are selected and the way their problematic is defined in the field of day to day living. The method of observation in fieldwork is concerned with the authenticity and genuineness of inquiry. It seeks to identify sources of misrecognition that are internal to the inquiry. Unlearning is concerned with removing these sources of misrecognition. This process (of unlearning) begins when the inquiry confronts obstacles in getting access to the experience and to the way of life of marginalised people. The process of overcoming these obstacles is unlearning. These obstacles protect those rules of social structure, which cannot be questioned. For this reason, they conceal an inquiry of the phenomena on which these rules are based or from where they are derived. The process of overcoming these obstacles is what one would call unlearning.

Fieldwork undertaken without any process of unlearning results in misrecognition. When fieldwork becomes merely a method of collecting information, it becomes an instrument of power and domination. It generates misrecogonitions. From these are generated collective lies. These collective lives come to be misrecognised as social facts. In so far as it is true that language conceals more than it reveals, it follows that language itself is an important source of misrecognition, misrepresentation and thus, collective lies.

Does the fact that there is an increase in participation in government development programmes indicate their success? To what extent are these programmes successful? Is this success story a collective lie that covers up marginalised people's perception of these programmes? For instance does not deforestation imply that the modern industrial production systems have no sense of preservation and conservation?

Social facts and the rules of social structure which are constraining, external and general in their relation to individual perceptions, condition the senses and the imagination to perceive the world in a particular way. Experience calls to attention the way we think, see and observe, directly. It can open up social spaces and show how rules of social structure can induce misrecognition. It explores how direct observation can accomplish a 'clear' seeing, that is, develop a vision freed of predetermination and preconception—a habit of thinking or a thinking habit. This process of freeing is a continuous one. This is unlearning. Unlearning attempts to show how social structures of scientific knowledge formed by the community of experts inhibit direct knowing and thereby prevent the creation of open spaces in social life.

The obstacles to 'clear' seeing are located in the subjective aspects of observation. Subjectivity therefore inhibits a selection, an identification and a dissolution of obstacles but it also enables this process.

This process of unlearning and then learning to see clearly involves first a process of dissolution of the obstacles to clear seeing. In the course of dissolution there are several moments of confusion and of distraction; these enhance the fear of losing one's path of inquiry. During these moments the fieldworker becomes a stranger to himself. He begins to reflect on his or her self. In the process he or she becomes the other to his or her own self. He/she confronts a sense of self-estrangement and becomes aware of social conditions and thinking patterns that precondition and predispose perception. In this manner the fieldworker becomes aware that any position of inquiry is relative, and therefore comparable to other positions. At this point the problematic of field inquiry comes into being and the fieldworker sees himself as 'the one engaged in inquiry.' He is concerned and engaged with his own social being and with the social being of others. This is a continuous engagement and it is a prerequisite for unlearning, for it is the interaction of social beings that makes it is possible to identify open social spaces where people come face to face and are able to see each other clearly.

Every position, every way of seeing can be as true or as untrue as any other, in so far as they are derived from different ways of life. But when they come together in the frame of day to day living they generate questions and they initiate discourses and dialogues over differences and inequality. The social spectrum across which these positions are arranged has at one end people marginalised in different sectors of work; at the other end are people enclosed in the routine of the official dominant modes of work. From the standpoint of the latter to be with forest dwellers, to go and live with them, to know and to learn from their experiences and social life is a backward movement in time. This idea misdirects the inquiry.

Non-forest dwellers do not perceive a forest landscape as home, a place of work and a condition of work. For them it is, at best, a resource that can be used to generate revenue, or a retreat from the bustle of the city. The forest cannot be a living space. Accordingly, the forest is merely a mysterious, romantic space where time ceases to exist, a space outside of the ordinary, the everyday, and the real. The forest is therefore not seen as a social and cultural space. It is a place of lurking presences, and distant whisperings of shadows. It is a negative benchmark to define a habitable space. It is the 'other' social space. City dwellers enter this 'other' space briefly only to return to the 'real' space of the city where they resume 'real' work either as traders or as of government officials, as money lenders, or, indeed as field-researchers. The time they spend in the forest is thus empty of any social content.

To the forest dwellers all these people are outsiders who may have directly or indirectly contributed to their marginalisation and to whom the experience and social lives of forest dwellers are inaccessible.

This raises several questions. In what way is the presence of the one engaged in scientific inquiry distinguished from others who are not engaged in scientific inquiry? What is that manner of being present in the field, which does not appear to contribute to the processes of marginalisation? What code of conduct and disposition facilitates the shaping of this manner of being present? Is the process of identifying superimposed categories one way of freeing vision for a clear seeing? Is this simultaneously an attempt to uncover and thereby recover the experience of marginalisation? Does this enable an inquiry of the meaningfulness of the modes of work of forest dwellers and of the fields where they work and live?

I turn to my own experiences in the field to understand these problems. In order to live among the Koitors I travelled from Delhi to Narayanpur. Narayanpur is a point of entry into Abujhmarh, and is a small tehsil town. It is from Narayanpur that development programmes are initiated and implemented for the benefit of the Koitors. People living in Narayanpur—described as *koska* by the Koitors—believe their lives are cursed: they describe their posting to Narayanpur and Abujhmarh as *kala pani*. The only people they meet are traders. The only enjoyments are the traders' booty of exotic artifacts, women and liquor.

The people I met advised me to take care of myself—that is, to take care of my social, mental and physical being. My belongings were examined and some items selected to make a life-saving kit. This kit I was assured, would keep me comfortable and safe and facilitate a quick recovery in case of an emergency.

My destination was Konge. To reach this village, seventy-five kilometres away from Narayanpur, I hired a bicycle, loaded my belongings onto it and set off. A kind-hearted school teacher accompanied me. Halfway through our journey I was tired. In order to lighten my burden I wanted to free myself of some of my belongings. This was not possible. There was nothing I could give up. I could not discard my clothes since my body was not accustomed to the open and raw forest environment. I could not discard my rations for I did not know where I would get food. I could not discard my bedsheet for without it I could not sleep on the ground. I could not discard my medicines because I was afraid of falling ill. I became aware that all my belongings were in fact a life-saving kit, that is, they were symbols of my social and cultural habits, certitudes, through which it was possible for me to maintain a certain sense of familiarity with my self. They were, moreover, reminders of the vulnerability of my self in the forest. I was aware that to live in the forest my self needed to be freed from these certitudes. This was a necessary preparation to be able to learn from the Koitors—learn their language and understand from them their perceptions of the forest.

As one engaged in inquiry, the Koitors' social and cultural habits, and their sense of certitude appeared radically different from my own. For instance, they wore a loin cloth. While travelling they carried an axe and a blanket on their shoulders, and a knife and a tobacco pouch round their waist. They were thus able to carry their belongings very easily. In contrast, my own belongings weighed more than I could carry. There was not only this excess weight from which my inquiry needed to be freed, but also the weight of predispositions, of presuppositions and of stereotypes. This made me aware of the burden of a different kind of awareness of my self, of my body and of its sense of social and cultural certitude.

This was clear to me during a hunting expedition. On a midsummer afternoon, soon after I reached Konge, I was asked to accompany the villagers on a hunt. We walked for several hours across hilly terrain, until we came to a patch of flat land covered with a thick growth of dry elephant grass, ready to be cut and used. We walked on into a different forest, where a blanket of dry leaves covered the ground. We were in the country of wild bisons. I was now bare bodied and I carried only a *gamcha* to clean my eyes and wipe the sweat.

Even so, when we reached the hunting ground, I breathed heavily. But in the forest there was no time to rest and we continued to walk in search of quarry. Abruptly, I was signalled to keep silent and walk without making the slightest sound. My friend had spotted an animal. I tried to walk slowly without making any sound. Not knowing how to read the forest, I lost all sense of direction. I was immediately overcome with fear. For every sound I heard, I missed a heart beat. I was restless and confused. I did not know which way to go. I stood still. I was engulfed by multifarious sounds from the forest, from the wind, from the birds, from the falling of dry leaves, from the movement of the grass. An equally large number of sounds were produced by my body, my moving arms, my footsteps, the movement of my legs, and my breathing. For me, this was the first recognition of my body in the forest.

These two instances opened up for my observation not only the working conditions and lives of the Koitors but also the mind of an outsider, fearful of the wilderness and of the forest. Undoubtedly, fear is an expression of losing one's own sense of certitude and of one's sense of self. It points to the idea that society draws upon to create boundaries between wilderness and civilisation. These are internalised by its members. I recognised that the idea of living suggested by the life-saving kit offers a first interpretation of this field of study. My kit was made up of a set of material things considered essential and necessary to come in and go out of a strange, unfamiliar social, cultural, and physical environment—that is, it enabled me to go, live inside this environment and return home safely. In this aspect the life-saving kit is an aspect of subjectivity which surreptitiously introduces a distance between the researcher and the people, between the subject and the object and between the one who is engaged in inquiry and the field of inquiry. This distance discourages meaningful discourse. However, when a fieldworker questions this distance then his or her own self is opened up for inquiry. The fieldworker now becomes the 'one in inquiry' who examines the sources of his or her own perceptions. The life-saving kit is now seen as a set of symbols that maintain distance in the relation between the 'one in inquiry' and his 'field of inquiry' by ensuring the continuity of disposition and a sense of certitude of social life as it lived 'at home', by ensuring too, that this continuity of disposition and sense of certitude are left undisturbed. The process of unlearning attempts to dissolve them and free an inquiry from such determinations as are contained in the life-saving kit.

To make the unfamiliar familiar it is most appropriate to begin to learn the language of the people. With this understanding that this distance between the researcher on the one hand and the forest, the people and their language on the other hand makes them unfamiliar to each other, I initiated myself into fieldwork. To enable myself to learn Marhia (the language of the Koitors), a school teacher introduced me to the people of Konge village. He told them that I was a student from Delhi who wanted to learn to speak their language and understand its discourse. He then left me in their care, to cultivate as best as I could, an independent relationship with them. At first the social space accessible to me was confined to my hut. Over a period of time my social space extended to the neighbourhood and then to the village and gradually it extended to the totality of the forest universe. In this manner it became accessible as a living space. This process of becoming familiar with the forest induced long periods of silence and of solitary confinement. Intersubjectivity between me and different people in the village was filled with an absence of words. As strangers to one another and as stranger to my own self we observed one another.

I was now prepared to be an apprentice. Learning commenced in the company of children. They laid out a daily 'routine' for me. In the morning and at night we were together. We did all our daily chores together. After eating their first meal children joined their parents in work until evening. During this period I was left to myself. Towards evening as the sun set elders would come and sit in silence until it was time for their second meal. After this meal children would again keep me company. From them I learnt about words in their language and their relation to Koitors' way of life.

The routine made accessible to me a first set of simple terms describing their perception of time and space: *nakame*—morning; *nulpe*—night; *porde*—sun; *leni*—moon; *gato*—food; *tein*—eat; *aghe*—water; *gera*—forest; *uda*—sit, *teda*—get up; *dei*—come; *han*—go, etc. Simultaneously, I learnt that the time cycle of the routine marked boundaries of social space. In the absence of a routine the forest space induces a loss of the 'sense of the passage of time.' By allocating a time and a place for different tasks, the forest became a home, a place and condition of work. Over a period of one year the Koitors took me as a member of their household work team. With this development, the routine of daily life changed, and I was no longer confined to a hut. I was given a place in the house and I was assigned a duty. It was expected of me to live within the means available to the household. Over a period of time I found myself participating in work routines different from the one I was socialised in. Gradually, the social frame of reference into which I was socialised dissolved. An identity of my self, which was represented by my belonging or by my life-saving kit also dissolved. A new social world placed in a continuum of time and space different from the one I was socialised in, became accessible.

It was clear to me that images of a forest captured in photographs and derived from occasional bus rides through it, are in sharp contrast to the image of the forest landscape when it encloses and touches the body of forest-dwellers. The essential character of this touch is that it 'encloses.' This is intelligible to the 'one who is in inquiry' in the following way: as it touches the body, a three-dimensional view of the forest emerges; the forest becomes a living space; not only is it itself alive, it also animates social life and defines the existence of living beings, both human and non-human. This emerging view of the forest dissolves the fear of it and the various dimensions of its universe are rendered intelligible. In turn, this makes the process of learning the people's language easier. It showed its relation to their method of work and it initiated for me the process of understanding the universe of the forest.

Koitors are aware that they would be de-forested, that their practice of shifting cultivation would be disallowed by the *koska*—'the distant ones'—who are government officials in particular, and people who live outside the forest in general. Koitors are also aware that the *koska* do not share their (the Koitors') view of their historical past. In this situation, a field inquiry of the forest-dwellers' way of life faces an obstacle viz., the indifference of *koska* and Koitors towards each other.

On account of the way modern life has impinged on the Koitors' way of life, there is a progressive loss of social contact, a slow degeneration of social interaction and a growing unconcern for the forest dwellers' mode of questioning, which generates their knowledge of the forest and which permeates its relation with their way of life. This is why, to Koitors the fruits of modern civilisation are meaningless and wasteful. But in the eyes of the *koska* to live in the forest as the Koitors live is in total opposition to their view that the forest cannot be a human habitat. Koitors know about this view from the way forests are put to commercial use, and from the way people living in the forest are displaced by those living outside it.

Indifference prevents 'direct knowing'. It accentuates differences between spoken language and between social and cultural habits; it exaggerates the absence of the known and the familiar; it magnifies the image of homelessness associated with the forest universe. In the forest landscape, the quality of air and water, the lack of modern facilities for dealing with illness and wounds, the physical and mental discomforts associated with living in the forest make it a fearful place. Accordingly languages from outside the world view of Koitors are made available to show them that they are oppressed, defeated and depressed. These languages of official government development programmes do not recognise Marhia, the Koitors' spoken language, as the language for dialogue and discourse. Nor is it recognised that the Koitors have a view of the 'outside' which finds expression in Marhia. For this reason the languages used by the *koska* become instruments to communicate to the Koitors their condition as it is understood from the outside. For instance, children going to school are discouraged to speak Marhia, and their parents are advised to learn Hindi and Halbi. The Koitor's language of discourse is thus transformed into a mere form, a passive medium, devoid of intellectual content.

As with language, so with their sense of time and the way they understand their 'past'. The historic moment which defines and questions the meaning of their perceptions and views has at least three parameters: it comes as a chronology of events; everyone in it is affected by historic events; and any act can lead to a historic event which can change the course of history. But Koitors do not perceive the passage of time in this way. They do not know of their past either as a 'chronology' or as a 'record', or as a 'fact'. The moment of questioning therefore could prove insensitive to the Koitors', notion of time, and their notion of their 'history'.

Efforts to preserve their culture and at the same time, facilitate their material development has in fact concealed open social spaces that encourage dialogues and discourses. This has led to a double marginalisation because of which they lose on two fronts: they lose their culture, and they become materially impoverished. There is no open space for their way of life to develop.

Under these circumstances, is it possible to know the language(s) available to the Koitors in particular, and to the marginalised people in general, to enable them to talk about their way of life? To what extent will learning their language equip us to understand their way of life? Will it enable them to talk to us about their way of life, when the entire weight of thinking of the outsiders classifies them as a negative other, i.e., a people whose way of life cannot be allowed to exist alongside the way of life in a modern city? In what manner is it possible to know of their social and cultural life?

How, moreover, are we to make sense of development from the Koitors' standpoint?

It is meaningless to ask whether forest dwellers should or should not be incorporated into the 'mainstream' of national development. The forest dwellers cannot think of themselves in this manner. They cannot ask this question for they have no choice. They become a part of the modern world even before they become aware of it. In their everyday life they are continuously ill-treated and exploited because they are unfamiliar with the historic world of the outsider. This is the way they are socialised into modernity.

To understand the meaningfulness of the Koitors' 'presence' in the modern world it is important to create conditions that will allow their sense of the theoretical and practical to grow and mature with the change of times. It is important too to realise that it is neither the past nor the future which holds the destiny of either but it is in the present that the problematique of the meaningfulness of the Koitors' presence has to be negotiated. For this purpose a field-inquiry needs to be freed from all conditionings of the past.

From this perspective, it is necessary, to learn the Koitors' spoken language and observe its relation to their method of work in the forest. Such learning is also a mode of participation. Through it, it is possible to get acquainted with the forest as the home, the place and the condition of work of the Koitors. In other words, through participation, the strangeness of the forest, the estrangement from the self and the alienation from the lives of forest dwellers can be overcome. An inquiry into this participation enables us to explore the way in which unlearning, and then a fresh learning can prevent misrecognition. In other words learning to unlearn is an essential component of participation.

Concluding Comments

In this emergent position the researcher becomes the 'one in inquiry.' Not only is he the 'one who enquiries', he is also the one about whom enquiries are made. In the course of fieldwork the 'one in inquiry' becomes 'a stranger', to his own social world and to the one he approaches, for unlearning and learning question not only the self of the 'one in inquiry', but also the 'field of inquiry' which would otherwise be demarcated and totalised by the certitudes of the self. This questioning initiates a dissolution, an unlearning of social and cultural conditionings, of ideas taken for granted and of ideas acquired in the course of one's own socialisation. When these are questioned and opened up for examination, a ground for intersubjectivity is simultaneously prepared.

The 'one in inquiry' becomes a stranger to himself (on account of the unlearning). He is a stranger to forest dwellers (about whom he has to learn). At this point, it is required of him to reconsider the boundaries between wilderness and civilisation. This is a basis of rethinking the question of how meaning is generated for culturally diverse people who are situated in relations of political and economic inequality. In these circumstances the very nature of the usual method of fieldwork is questioned as a mode of inquiry. Through this questioning, fieldwork acquires meaning for the 'one in inquiry' as well as for the forest dwellers, and it gains legitimacy. When questioned, fieldwork is examined for the way it establishes a relation between the one who is engaged in inquiry, the subject and the field of inquiry and between the people with whom and in whose presence the inquiry is conducted. The focus of the inquiry is now on obstacles that do not allow the surfacing of those questions, which would seek to understand the preoccupation of a way of life.

The one who unlearns acquires the identity of being the one who is engaged in an inquiry of the official standards. As discussed these standards disallow a questioning of themselves, and therefore inhibit unlearning. These standards do not sanction the unlearning of themselves because such unlearning creates open social spaces for parallel discourse which in turn strikes at the very root of all our carefully nurtured certitudes.

Parallel discourses in open spaces outside the field covered by official standard routine activity, generate a different social being. They generate social and cultural processes which go to make up a social person differently disposed from the one who follows routines and the standard of official discourses. Further, they demonstrate that there are plural views of the world, each corresponding to a way of life. For this reason, each view is as true or false as the social being who shapes and is shaped by these views. Moreover, we see how the truth, or falseness of being is an aspect of the truth or falseness of the held view of the world. The different standards embedded in different ways of life measure the social position of a 'being' in terms of the degree of their authenticity or genuineness.

When social beings come together in a social and cultural discourse, they are able to recognise errors of judgment, measure the authenticity and genuineness of this recognition and they discontinue the use of the categories derived from one way of life to see and understand another way of life. This regulates the hegemony of the method. Unregulated, the hegemonic methodology makes open social spaces inaccessible. But by questioning and regulating this hegemony, fieldwork now attempts to create an open space where an unlearning of the categories of one way of life allows for learning other categories that correspond to different ways of life.

Unlearning is not however the same as 'deconstructing'. Deconstruction does not necessarily question habits and their certitudes in a given social structure. It confines its task to exposing the internal structure of representations. In the case of unlearning, habits need to be destablised. This dissolves certitudes and questions the very being of entities. In the attempt to recover the questions that preoccupy people in their marginalised work sector, unlearning opens the field of inquiry by questioning the legitimacy of the standards of routine work. In the process, it itself gets questioned with regard to the basis of its own legitimacy. To earn legitimacy for himself and for the fieldwork, the one engaged in inquiry must acquire a manner of being present which allows for an openness of a discourse on both his work and his being. The manner in which existence and inquiry affect each other exposes the purpose and intent of inquiry. In order to know this relationship fieldwork initiates a process of unlearning, to identify and dissolve obstacles that cover up or camouflage open spaces in society.

Fieldwork is, at times, contrasted to, and at times opposed to laboratory work, in the same way as a view by the naked eye is contrasted to and opposed to a view through the microscope. The difference of course is that in the field, phenomena are observed in their natural environment in the course of their unfolding and development. In the laboratory, however, phenomena are observed in artificial or simulated conditions.

Fieldwork is an expression of a desire to ask questions and seek answers. These are aspects of human activity shaped by speculative and empirical thinking. The relation between fieldwork and laboratory work, according to the above view, is that a hypothesis formulated in one case can be verified in the other. But this relation does not explain the phenomenon of human activity either in the laboratory or in the field. The meaning of simulation is not clearly understood. Is it a particular way of isolation and of singling out an object for study? What allows for this isolation? Does such isolation not obtain in an open field outside the laboratory? It is clear that principles of observing phenomena in the laboratory need not be applicable when observing phenomena in the field? For instance, the identification and verification in a laboratory of an active principle of a medicinal plant known to forest dwellers, does not explain how without the technical vocabulary of the exact physical sciences and without a laboratory, forest dwellers know of its medicinal properties.

In order to understand human activity inspired by a desire to know, it is important to know how this desire shapes human social behavior. In this instance, fieldwork is a mode of social behaviour in the laboratory and in the open field. The fact that every act, and the process of which it is a part, becomes meaningful in relation to a problematique, implies that they are amenable to questioning at any moment. The occasion to question emerges when human activity faces obstacles. The process of overcoming obstacles draws out its problematique and generates knowledge in relation to a way of life. It is possible, therefore, to derive from a study of the social and cultural representation of obstacles, a mode of questioning and the set of questions that together make up a problematique. This is a way of understanding discourse.

What makes it possible to question the legitimacy of the way a social discourse opens a field for inquiry? It is not indifference, but care, concern and involvement that sustains a continuous discourse with people and prepares the ground for the legitimacy of an inquiry. An inquiry has its own mode of acquiring legitimacy for itself: it defines its subject, opens the field, and shapes the manner in which the 'one engaged in inquiry' is present in the open field. Obstacles encountered in the work raise questions about the legitimacy of the inquiry and thus make available an opportunity to examine oneself, one's ideas and one's work.

An inquiry, as a mode of sustaining and continuing social discourse, also defines a mode of coming into the field. This mode shapes the manner in which the one engaged in inquiry is present. This mode also shapes the very field in which the one in inquiry is present. Further, the manner of being present determines the way obstacles are overcome. The process of overcoming obstacles prepares the ground for the legitimacy of the inquiry, and this in turn determines the extent to which the field will open up. Accordingly, the processes through which an inquiry gains legitimacy are the same as the process which makes the inquiry intelligible to those with whom and in whose presence it is conducted. Thus the legitimacy of an inquiry is linked with its intelligibility.

Initially, the one who inquires, and the people in whose presence the inquiry is conducted, are strangers to each other. The process of asking questions makes a spectacle of the one who inquires. This is so because to ask questions disturbs the people's daily routine and takes them away from the work which they do for a livelihood. An inquiry begins to gain legitimate ground when the inquirer's manner of being present as the one who inquires becomes socially acceptable. With this the spectacle of strangeness and the strangeness of the spectacle dissolve.

One's subjectivity is significant in so far as it encourages or inhibits this dissolution. When it encourages dissolution it opens the field for inquiry and gives it depth. Obstacles define social boundaries which circumscribe a field of inquiry. A transgression of the boundary is necessary to continuously free the inquiry of such circumscriptions. If this subverts an existing order, it can also prepare the ground for a different ordering of social life.

Dissolution of social boundaries is a result of successfully questioning one's socially acquired beliefs, modes of thinking, habits and attitudes. This also includes the questioning of assumptions that inform the construction of the self of the one who inquires. It broadens the vision and opens up the field of inquiry. This process is internal to an inquiry and shows that the task of fieldwork is not confined either to confirming or to negating a hypothesis. Instead, it offers a different view of the field, and of one's self. It makes possible a recognition of dissolution, of learning and unlearning, of the fading in and the fading out of social forms.

References

Asiatic Society of Bengal. *Proceedings of the Asiatic Society of Bengal* 1814–1866.

Bourdieu, P. 1977. *Outline of a Theory of Practice*. Trans. Richard Nice. Cambridge: Cambridge University Press.

———— 1978. 'Three Forms of Theoretical Knowledge'. In *Social Science Information* (12) Pt. 1 Jan-June.

Brown, Dee. 1971. *Bury my Heart at Wounded Knee*. New York: Bantam.

Colby, B.N. 1966. 'Ethnographic Semantics: A Preliminary Survey'. In *Current Anthropology* (7), 1.

Duerr, H.P. 1985. *Dream-time: Concerning Boundaries between Wilderness and Civilisation*. Trans. Felicitas Goodman. Oxford: Basil Blackwell.

Evans-Pritchard, E.E. 1976. *The Nuer*. Oxford: University Press.

Ghurye, G.S. 1963. *Scheduled Tribes*. Bombay: Popular Prakashan.

Grigson, G.V. 1938. *Maria Gonds of Bastar*. Bombay: Oxford University Press.

Guha, R. *Elementary Aspects of Peasant Insurgency in Colonial India*. Delhi: Oxford University Press.

Horton R. Finnegan. 1973. *Modes of Thought: Essays on Thinking in Western and Non-western Societies*. London: Faber and Faber.

Kopf, David. 1969. *British Orientalism and the Bengal Renaissance. The Dynamics of Modernisation 1773–1835*. Los Angeles: University of California Press.

Kultigen, R. 1975. 'Phenomenology and Structuralism'. In *Annual Review of Anthropology*.

Levi-Strauss, C. 1963. *Structural Anthropology*. Harmondsworth: Penguin Books.

_____ 1954. *Anthropology and Myth*. Trans, Roy Wills. Oxford: Basil Blackwell.

_____ 1986. *A View from Afar*. Oxford: Basil Blackwell.

Roy, S.C. 1937. *The Kharias*. Man in India Office: Ranchi.

Royal Anthropological Society, England. 1964. *Notes Queries in Anthropology*.

Schutz 'A'. 1964. *Collected Papers II. Studies in Social Theory*. The Hague: Martinus Nishoff.

Uberoi, J.P.S. 1984. *The Other Mind of Europe: Goethe as a Scientist*. Delhi: Oxford University Press.

Uberoi, P. and J.P.S. Uberoi. 1976. 'Towards a New Sociolinguistics. A Memoir of P.B. Pandit. *Economic and Political Weekly*. 11(7): 637–743.

Vanucci, M. (n.d.). 'Sacred Groves or Holy Forest', Unpublished manuscript.

Winch, P. 1964. 'Understanding a Primitive Society' In *American Philosophical Quarterly*, 1 (4) October.

Subjectivity in Contexts of Objectification: Identity and Structural Imagery Among the Warlis

DENZIL SALDANHA

Introduction

The nature and significance of subjectivity was brought home to me in the sharpest manner during my fieldwork in 1979–81 among the Warlis of Talasari and Dahanu talukas of Thane District, Maharashtra.[1] The study was a historical analysis of the process of class formation under the influence of Kisan Sabha ideology, organisation and state policy. While being sensitive to the subjective dimension (the aspect of agency) within social structure and relations of production in historical process, the study also attempted to comprehend the cognitive aspects of class consciousness in the contemporary context of one village in Talasari taluka which was chosen as a critical case, representative of active participation in the Kisan Sabha movement.[2]

What follows is a presentation of a part-analysis of a specific cognitive area—social-structural imagery and self identification —which forms one component of the total conceptions held by individuals with respect to their class existence. The analysis needs to be seen in the context of its total discourse within the original study. However partial, it serves to draw out certain conclusions that are relevant to the understanding of the nature of individual and collective subjectivity within structured social processes. The objective of this article is to present one analytical approximation to this complex area and to uncover its theoretical implications.

The subjectivity of social science forms the third dimension of the above-mentioned processes. One sees the scientific study of popular consciousness of class as the dialectical meeting point of the categories and conceptual framework of the scientist and the cognitive areas and conceptions of the people—the object of study. The scientific act of analysis is an inter-subjective act of interpretation. It is moreover a conscious interaction that creatively gives rise to concepts that hopefully will be adequate to deal with the subjects studied. The following pages will serve to present the nature of this conscious interaction in the interview and especially in the post-interview analytic situation, which creatively gives rise to adequate concepts. I hope to illustrate the elaboration of my own categories as I cover the ground in degrees of abstraction/comprehensiveness, in the very act of understanding the internal coherence of the consciousness of subjects, its external relation to social context and its dynamism in the historical process. From an initial analytical categorisation of the adivasis' responses to particular questions revealing their own isolated cognitive 'categories', to a synthetical explanation of the interrelation between these 'categories', thus uncovering their underlying meaning and arriving at what might be considered to be the total conceptions held by individuals located in the classes studied. One might then infer from the patterned distribution of these individual 'conceptions' the collectively shared meaning systems on class held by groups of persons in particular historical contexts.

Social-Structural Imagery and Self Identity[3]

An analysis of the socio-historical dynamics of the Kisan Sabha (KS) movement in Thane district (Saldanha 1984:350 ff), had earlier resulted in the identification of the following main classes in agriculture in the region: landlords of various categories, rich peasants (RP), poor peasants (PP) and agricultural labourers (AL). The classification was further concretised with respect to the village (ibid: 506 ff). The category of rich peasant was found non-existent in the selected village, given that a section which produced predominantly for the market and employed mainly non-household labour did not exist. I preferred therefore to categorise that section of the middle peasants who were self-subsistent on their land, slightly better off and tending towards an RP existence—as a result of an operational holding that permitted some degree of sale of grass and toddy, for the market and some degree of exploitation of outside labour—as rich-middle peasants (RMP); thus distinguishing them from the rest of the middle peasants (MMP).

An important aspect of the study was to discover how this supposedly scientifically derived objective social structure and relations of rural society in the tribal areas of Thane districts were perceived by the villagers. Related to this was the question of how the human constituents of particular classes, placed themselves with respect to their subjective conceptions of the ordering of society. The essential question was of scientifically comprehending the subjective perceptions of the various crystallisations of class identities, their structuring, their relation, the self identity and the location given to it within this larger conception.

A critical interpretation of the interview material concerning consciousness reveals certain major trends in the social-structural imagery and self identity held by the various classes of the 15 per cent random, stratified, household sample. It is noteworthy that the first response of the vast majority of the people to the broad invitation—"Tell me something about the people living in the rural areas. Are they the same?"—generally is, as in the words of Lakhma a poor peasant:

All are poor (*garib*). We are all adivasis. There are no rich (*shrimant*) here among the people. The seth-savkar are also there. But where do we look to them and they to us? They are rich (*shrimant*). They live there in their big houses.

The question is of a sufficiently broad character so as to possibly embrace socio-cultural identities. Most of the individuals in the sample understand the question of socio-economic terms, suggesting the relative salience of economic conditions to the people within the particular context of the question. Only an insignificant few spontaneously proceed with a differentiation of the adivasis into Warlis, Dublas, Dhodis, Thakurs, etc., after making the basic distinction of *shrimant seth* and *garib* adivasi. This does not mean that the ethnic identity of the 'adivasi' is less salient or that it is not perceived, but rather that the ethnic sub-differentiation of the adivasis into the various tribal groups is less significant to them in the particular context of the general question, subjectively perceived as socio-economic in nature. For individuals who share in various identities, the salience of a particular identity is contextual in character, the manner in which a particular question is posed in the interview situation forming the context of response.

In fact, from the initial remarks in most cases or from the total context of the interview material of an individual, I came to the conclusion that the terms 'adivasi' and 'garib' are used synonymously and interchangeably in this particular context. This is reinforced by the fact that the objective reality of economic poverty overlaps with the cultural confines of the adivasi way of life. The adivasis are seen to be poor and the poor are termed adivasis. The small minority of lower caste non-adivasis in the village consider themselves as adivasi and follow the Warli practices such as celebrating festivals of the village deity (*Gav Dev*) Vagaya. The Warlis who form the vast majority of the village population accept them as adivasi though not as Warli, for the latter term implies a more ritualistic significance related to food habits, birth, marriage and death. An entire history of oppression by the outsider, non-adivasi, seth-savkar, the broad features of which are still alive in the popular mind, has led to the interpenetration of the cognitive dimensions of the poor as different from the rich and of the adivasi as different from the seth. The *garib* and the adivasi are seen as terms descriptive of each other, leading to the primary collective identity of the *garib* adivasi as distinct from the perception of the totally different eco-cultural existence of the others: the *shrimant seth*. This conjuncture of cognitions—held by all in the samples—forms one of the basic aspects of the collective conceptions of the people. One would suggest that the identity of *garib* adivasi, in this context, stands in the forefront of consciousness as different from the 'ground', the perception of subordinate differentiated identities—either ethnic or economic—which are revealed spontaneously or revealed on further probing, as discussed below.

In the given context and at this stage of the unravelling of the interview material, the basic polarised identities do imply a perception of an unity of the differentiated tribal identities, i.e., Warli, Dhodi, Dubla, etc., as well as an unity of differentiated economic identities, i.e., *changle, sadharan, garib, agdi garib.* (The meanings of these terms will be explained.) This implicit perception of the unity of subordinate identities is revealed by the fact that further probing results in responses that are sensitive to differentiation among the people. The terms *'amhi'* (we) and *'lok'* (people) are used by the large majority of the respondents and in various contexts to mean 'garib adivasi'. For example, 'The savkars had taken the lands from the *lok'*, and 'Here among the *lok* one will not find any *shrimant.* We (*amhi*) are all *garib.* '*Amhi*' meant, we, the collective adivasi, who shared a common fate of being *garib.* Incidentally, this conception of primary unity basically corresponds with the CPI(M)-KS ideology as practiced in the region, of the alliance of classes and of cultural groups in the organised unity of the 'people' as opposed to the landlords and capitalist farmers. This is not to suggest that the majority of the villagers are aware of this in ideological terms. Rather, they experience the ideology in practice through their spontaneous experience of shared economic existence, organisation and struggle. The analysis suggests that the subordinate class, understood as conscious agency in historical process assuming particular eco-cultural and political forms, is effectively the *'garib* adivasis'.

Also implicit in this relatively static, structured and ahistorical perception of primary identities, as revealed thus far, is a dynamic, related and historical perception as one notices in subsequent discussions in response to further questions. In the context of introductory questions, the basic distinction between the *seth* and the *garib* advasi rather than the relation between the two is emphasised by most of the villagers. The 'ground' which is latent and implicit in the 'figure' of consciousness within a particular context, itself comes to the forefront in another context revealing another level of consciousness.

Taking up the question of subordinate identities, one comes to the conclusion that all the people are aware of further differentiation among the 'we'. However, this structuring among the people is perceived to varying degrees, whether it be a two-fold differentiation perceived by 29 individuals (50.0 percent), threefold, by 26 individuals (45.0 per cent), or a complete four level hierarchy perceived by only three persons. The last corresponds with the differentiation that I had arrived at through overt economic indicators. Significantly, the three concerned individuals are among the members of the CPI(M) party in the sample who perhaps had greater access to the methods of class analysis.

If one examines the classes that are mentioned by the people one finds that, despite the fact that the classes perceived vary among individuals, a certain pattern emerges. Firstly, very few of the individuals in the sample use the Marathi equivalents of the terminology of RMP, MMP, PP, AL. These few use the terms *'shet mazoor'* and *'madhyam shetkari'* to indicate the AL and the MMP, respectively, and in varying contexts. But significantly, all the individuals use a descriptive terminology to indicate their perceptions of class differentiation. These terms are descriptive of the general economic conditions of the various classes flowing from their ownership of land and their particular economic activity. The question that arises is: On which point of the objective scale of class differentiation would one place these descriptive categories used by the people? That is, what is the meeting point of scientific categories and popular linguistic usage? An answer may be found in the criteria that are popularly used to differentiate between these subordinate categories, the description of their economic conditions and the location of the category of self identity. The villagers tend to see the other classes with respect to their self identity. The conclusion which emerges from the totality of responses of all the individuals is that the terms *'agdi garib'* (very poor), *'garib'* (poor), *'sadharan'* (all right, so-so) and *'changle'* (good), generally indicate the AL, PP, MMP and the RMP, respectively.

Table 1
Social Structural Imagery Held by Individuals from Classes Among the 'People'

Objective identities scientifically perceived	Primary polarised identities, subjectively perceived by all individuals from all classes				Subordinate differentiated identities, subjectively perceived by individuals from various classes		
					RMP&MMP	PP	AI
		'Te' (they)					
LL	*Shrimant*	*Seth-Savkar*			*Seth*	*Seth*	*Seth*
RMP		A			—	*Changle*	*Changle*
MP	G	d	A				
MMP	a	i	L	m	*Sadharan*	—	—
PP	r	v	o	h	—	*Garib*	—
AL	i	a	k	i	*Garib*	*Agdi garib*	*Garib*
	b	s					
		i					
Number	58/58	58/58			8/13	16/21	18/24
Percentage	100	100			62	76	75

Notes: 1. The terms *seth-savkar, changle, sadharan, garib, agdi garib* refer to the Marathi terms used by the people to differentiate identities.

2. The direction of the arrows suggest the process of 'lumping together' of identities which might be either one of 'subsuming' into one below or 'supersuming' into one above.

There are some important qualifications to this linguistic usage in the case of individuals belonging to particular classes. Those who perceive the class of PP, especially the PPs themselves who identify with this sub-category, refer to the PPs as *garib* (poor) and distinguish this category from the ALs whose condition is seen to be even worse and hence *agdi garib* (very poor). They generally differentiate their economic conditions from the adivasi classes above them by the term *changle*, i.e. the RMP, thus apparently collapsing the category of MMP into the former broad grouping. On the other hand the MPs, by identifying their economic conditions as a median—*sadharan*— refer to both ALs and PPs as *garibs*: they do not require the linguistic usage of *agdi garib* to distinguish themselves from the *garib* ALs. One infers that a process of lumping together of categories takes place, as indicated in Table 1. The MMPs and significantly the RMPs themselves 'underestimate' the RMP category. The process of 'underestimation' appears to continue with the category of PP being collapsed into a broad category of *garib* which includes the AL. Most ALs perceive the subordinate differentiation in the extreme terms of the *'changle'*, i.e., the RMP, and the *'garib'* and identify themselves as the *'garib'* labourers at the bottom of the ladder. One might infer that the median categories of MMP and PP are respectively integrated into the former two categories by the ALs. I have tried to represent the broad trends in structural imagery and self identity held by the adivasi villagers in Table 1 above.

The Interpretation of Narrations

Some extracts from the interview material illustrating the criteria used by individuals from the various classes in order to structure their signified social context, and further generalisations and inferences with respect to their social structural imagery will help to make vivid the foregoing discussion.

An Agricultural Labourer

Dharma is a 40 year old illiterate agricultural labourer, who supports a family of nine on a three acre plot of land and on the labour of his family on the fields of the landlord and adivasi middle peasants during the agricultural season. The produce of 1/3 *hara* lasts his family for only three months. Though the land holding is relatively high compared to the average AL holding (0.9 acres), its quality is extremely poor given that it is partly the land given by the landlord to his father according to the practice of binding the services of annual labourers by giving them a plot of land to cultivate and partly land distributed under the ceiling laws. Dharma says that he was 'tired of working with the seth ... tired of being told what to do'. He consequently left work as an annual labourer and now spends six months from December to May working as a diver for sand off Godhbunder in Bombay. Explaining his decision he says:

If I had land in the village why would I go to die in the city. The expenses of travel and staying in the city are very much. Land is not enough, that's why I go. I would have stayed quietly at home and eaten off the land. From the morning the children keep asking for *bhakri* [a bread made of coarse grains], rice. This I want, that I want. From where will we get? The *garib lok* [poor people] like me need at least one meal a day.

His views on the social structure are:

The *lok* are different. We are all *garib* adivasis but there are differences. Some do not have anything to eat in the afternoon and work the whole day. They don't have even *kanneri* [a watery gruel of rice] to eat, they are so *garib*. Some get, some don't get. Some get *toddy-daru*, get food to eat and get even *kumbdi* [chicken]. Their condition is *changle*. Like that, each doesn't get the same. The *changle* are *mothe* [big, i.e. capable]. They do *dhandha* [business] of grass and toddy. They have lands. Some have less lands or no lands. Some get as much as three *haras* of rice from the land. Others work and give to them. The *garib* don't even have food to eat in the afternoon. Don't talk about the *seths*. They are the biggest.... The poor need land. The *mothe* [i.e. big, another term used for the *changle* RMP] say 'I want this land, that land'. The poor get nothing. The big give the government officials chicken, *daru*, toddy. They put something in the pockets of the officers. The poor cannot do this. If they don't have money in their own pockets how can they put money in the pockets of the officers. The *changle* take most of the ceiling lands like this.... Ceiling lands have been taken but not distributed well. Those who already had lands, they got [more].

Dharma's response is typical of most ALs and is similar to that of others among the people. Some points of critical interpretation might be made.

1. The adivasi focuses on the identity that he is familiar with—the larger collective of the *garib* adivasi—almost to the neglect of discussing the *seth*. He proceeds to differentiate the *garib* adivasi, into two sections, the *changle* (RMP) and the *garib* (AL). The presence or relative absence of landholding and its effects on

economic behaviour and standard of living are the criteria used, i.e., labour or commercial activity, the availability and quality of food.

2. Quantitative differentiation within the 'we, *garib* adivasis' predominates over the qualitative distinction between the 'we' and the 'they, *shrimant seths*', in the context of a question which probes structural imagery. Several reasons might be suggested for this.

It appears that the adivasis might have understood the term 'people' in the introductory question, 'Tell me something about the people living in the rural areas? Are they the same?...' as addressed to their primary group of identification—the *garib* adivasi—given that they often referred to themselves as '*lok*'. Given this perception of the question, differentiation is seen to be more relevant than distinction between *garib* adivasi and *shrimant seth*. Dharma himself, in response to further questions, emphasises the character of the relations between adivasis and the seth.

Another possible reason: Most adivasis, who see the economic conditions of the *seth* as altogether different, as the *seth* as totally other, cannot possibly make comparisons between themselves and the *seth*. All the people in the sample perceive a great divide between themselves and the seth, a divide that cannot conceivably be bridged by social mobility. Differential quantitative comparison is not possible between structured entities which are perceived to be qualitatively distinct. Hence, one might suggest that a perception of distinct identities is at the basis and implicit in the very concentration on internal differentiation to the virtual neglect of discussing the *seth* and the distinction from the *seth*.

3. Apart from differences in living standards, Dharma perceives an internal contradiction among the *garib* adivasis in relation to the *changle*, especially on the question of distribution of ceiling lands. This is perceived by the vast majority of the ALs. He also refers to their tendency to seek individual solutions at the cost of others by way of bribing government officers. Some of the RMPs employ other adivasis for a major part of the year, during the agricultural season and later as toddy tappers, leading to a perception of internal contradictions related to

labour and wages. As Bhimra, a 35 year old landless labourer, says:

> I do *mazoori*. I have no lands. Work the whole day and eat only *kanneri*. I climb the trees. The *changle* who have land and toddy trees sit down and give orders. The *mazoors* are those who have to climb and risk their lives. The *changle* have enough land, trees, do grass business. Even the ceiling lands have been taken by some of them.

A Poor Peasant

To take another example, Dival's response is typical of the structural perception of a PP. Aged 40, he is illiterate, but well versed in the art of the bhagat (the medicine man). He supports his family of eight members on one and a half acres of land whose produce of one third of a *hara* is exhausted by his family in seven months. While he himself works as a labourer with other adivasis during the agricultural season, his elder sons go to the outskirts of Bombay to labour in the salt pans. Bhagat rituals, which he has been practicing for the last six years, gives him a meagre supplementary income. I meet him one morning as he has just completed the rituals for the cure of a sick adivasi:

> All are not the same. There are differences. The *shrimant seths* have money, grains, everything. The *garib* adivasi don't have this. But there is *mothe* and *kami* [less, i.e. small] among the *garib*. Rice does not last with us [i.e. with the *garib*, now signifying the PP. Note the self-identification with the PP and the criteria for differentiation—within a hierarchy of the larger identity of *garib* adivasi—from the *changle* RMP and the *agdi garib* AL, which follows]. There is not enough money even for bidis and tobacco. Those who have land, grains, grass, toddy trees and money, they have become *changle*. We don't have enough land, how can we become big. Land is less and people are more. Besides the quality of land is bad. We don't get good *garvi* [of better quality] lands. We depend on the rains. This year the rains were bad. The seeds died. On *garvi* lands they [i.e., the *changle*] get good grains [i.e. in quality HYV, and quantity]. Then they also have toddy trees. You also have those who have no land at all. Their condition is *agdi garib*.

From November to June they have to leave the village and go out for work. Ceiling lands have not been given to them. Those who had lands [i.e. the *changle*] they took away even the ceiling lands. The *garib* have not got it. They [the *changle*] have insisted that I will do this, I will do that; I will cultivate this and that. Now I don't know if the *sarkar* will take these lands away and redistribute them. Lands were properly taken from the *seth* but badly distributed. The *lok* [people, i.e. the *garib* adivasi] do not go forward together. Those who had land, insisted on having more.

Some important conclusions emerge from Dival's response. They are relevant for the PPs, in particular, and have wider significance for the other classes who constitute the people of the village:

1. Dival's basic identification, stated at the outset, is with the *garib* adivasi as distinct from the *shrimant seth*.

2. He quickly moves on to a hierarchical differentiation within the *garib* adivasi. The hierarchical character is conveyed by the terms big (*mothe*) and small (*kami*), i.e. less. This interpretation is further strengthened by the fact that the possibility for mobility within this hierarchy is formally conceived, though the real difficulties which make it improbable are acknowledged—'We don't have enough lands, how can we become big...'. As for the theoretical possibility of social mobility across the chasm that structurally divides the *garib* adivasis from the *shrimant seth*, that is totally inconceivable.

3. In the course of the narration Dival shifts his self-identification to the *garib*, now to mark the PP as different from the changle RMP. Still later the term *garib* is used to express a sympathy with the AL, whose insecurity and total dependence on labour for others as a result of landlessness is recognised. This also implies a differentiation from the ALs who have at least some lands—the term *agdi garib* being now used in indicate the ALs. There is a recognition of occupying a middle position as *garib*, closer to the *agdi garib* and different from the *changle*. The same term, i.e., *garib*, expresses different subjective meanings depending on the focus of attention.

4. The criteria for differentiation that are used are—land, its quantity and quality, and the manifestation of this on general

economic conditions and activity. This was the dominant factor which guided the differentiation of all the respondents among the people. Within this broad perspective, seemingly trivial factors such as who climbs trees and who sits on the ground and orders, as in the case of the previously mentioned AL; whether one has money for bidis or not and how one earns money, whether from the sale of grass and toddy or from the sale of labour, as in this case—acquire varying subjective significance to individuals in their attempts at differentiation.

5. There would appear to be a general concern among the adivasis regarding the symbolical commodity—money—which relates to their preoccupation regarding the produce of the land, grains. How will money be acquired? How long will it last? What commodities will it fetch? Money has perforce acquired a crucial significance within the adivasis' economy, thrust on to them by the advance of the market economy, despite their limitations in handling it. It has introduced a real differentiating feature even among the adivasis. While the ALs live a below subsistence existence from the money acquired from the sale of labour in a situation of scarcity of employment, they have some flexibility in the choice of commodities that they might purchase—grains, toddy, clothes, etc. The RMPs subsistent landholding permits some commercial activity in grass and toddy and the acquisition of money for extra consumption expenses. The MMP, with a barely subsistent landholding, face a real problem as to how to get money for other requirements. Some of the family members have therefore got to sell their labour. The PPs experience a bitter conflict. On the one hand they are tied to a below subsistence land holding, labour on which during the agricultural season being essential to acquire grains which barely last half the year. On the other hand they are forced to acquire money through the sale of labour during the rain-fed agricultural season when employment is most available. The resolution of the conflict generally results in the neglect of the field and its possible alienation or lease to the *seth*, despite the PPs attachment to the land.

6. The internal contradictions of the *garib* and *agdi garib* with the *changle* on the question of fair distribution of ceiling lands, results in a blunting of the perceived contradiction of some of the ALs and PPs with the *seth* and in the present, despite the

perception of a basic contradiction with the *seth* in the past. The extract from Dival's narration concludes with a reaffirmation of the primary identity of the *garib* adivasi, although in pessimistic terms, with the use of the term *lok* (people)—'The *lok* do not go forward together'.

A Middle Peasant

Zania, a MP, is one of the three who see the *garib* adivasis as differentiated into the four sections that I had objectively arrived at. He is about 45 years of age, is a literate party member and has one son who attends college and two others who go to school and are literate. He supports his family of eight on five acres of land whose produce of two *haras* of paddy is able to see them through the year. He uses fertilisers and HYV seeds. Till about four years ago, Zania would go every year for four months to do seasonal manual labour in the railways. Work on the railway track would take him as far as Andheri in Bombay. Today he need not labour for others, though a few family members work on the government Employment Guarantee Schemes.

Zania has experienced some degree of individual social mobility over some of the strata of adivasis, from the days when his father came to the village to reside and work at the wife's parental home according to the adivasi custom of *khandadia*; the subsequent forced unpaid labour which his father and he himself as a child underwent; the one acre of tenanted land which he inherited from his father, the low areas of tenant holding being a matter of choice for his father, according to Zania, given the fear of high rentals. Another four acres were later received from the distribution of ceiling lands and through encroachments on forest lands. Today he is a barely subsistent MP, working on his lands with his family labour and is even able to sell some grass to the *seth*. Given this lived experience of socio-economic betterment over the years, Zania is able to perceive the differentiation among the *garib* adivasis in clear hierarchical terms:

> The adivasis in general are *garib*. They have little land and the land is bad. *Halvi* lands [infertile lands on the heights] produce bad crops even with fertilisers. Differences among the adivasis depend on the quantity and quality of land. The lowest position is that of those who are on the first *payri* [step]. They have no

lands. They have to do *mazoori* [labour]. They have to look for work. Sometimes they don't get work and have to starve. Their's is a *bikat paristhiti* [difficult condition]. They are *agdi garib*. The second step is of those that have at least something to eat from the land. They drink *ambil* [a gruel made of flour left to ferment overnight in water]. They have some land of their own and also go out to work. The third step is of those of us who have lands, have grains. They can even give grains to others in need. The fourth step is that of those who have lands and who do *dhandha* [business] in toddy, grass and even paddy. They eat well. The *seth-savkars* are also there but they are different. They are *shrimant*.

Zania went on spontaneously to explain how the *seth-savkars* became *shrimant* and the adivasis remained *garib*, in a narration which reveals a social relational imagery that is dynamic, relational and social-historical in character:

The *seth* became *shrimant* on the sweat of the adivasis. Before the *seths* used to take *veth* [forced unpaid labour] from all the *kuls* [tenants]. One from each house had to go to work. They would take work from us. Their fields had to be attended to first, then ours. Our lands would remain like that only. Doing this over the years they accumulated grain, money and so on. There used to be four people to eat in their house and a thousand to work from among the *kuls*. They stacked their houses with grains that was enough for three years. All the grass from the *kul* lands would be taken by them, by force and without payment. Then they did business in grass. That brought money. Then they had orchards of chikoo and mangoes. Once again money. Thus there was money from different types of sources. They had plenty of grain. As for *mazoori* (wages), they used to give one kg of grain or one anna in cash. They used to earn from us and became big. Adivasis remained *tasech* [like that only]. Two-three generations have passed and the adivasis have remained like that only. How could the adivasis improve? The debts of the father, perhaps even those of the grandfather, would be written in the books of the *seth*. They would have to pay back the debts in money or by being bound for their labour. Thus the *seths* became *mothe* [big]. We remained behind....

Today we cannot come right up. Before, all were on the bottom-most step. Over the years some have come up a little. Some adivasis have done business, taken labour and improved slightly. The lowest group can improve but they have no *adhar* [support]. There is no *marg* [way]. If they have land, it is little and bad. It becomes difficult for one man to support a whole family, food, clothes, *meeth-mirchi* [literally salt and chillies, though observation has shown that the term intends to convey the idea of general consumption needs beyond the basic food requirements]. Till the children grow up they are a weight on him, and it is so for 20 years.... I am now *sadharan*, on the third step. Till five years ago my wife and I would go to do *mazoori*, I with the plough. Two children have now grown up and they also go for *mazoori*. But if we go for *mazoori*, we neglect our fields. As soon as the little infants grow up they demand food as much as any adult. Our adivasi children eat a lot.

Some comments might be made on this narration:

1. Zania's structural imagery is a very precisely defined conception of structured hierarchy within the *garib* adivasi, subordinate to the basic distinction between the *garib* and the *shrimant seth*. Literacy, geographical mobility, and political education as a result of party membership, reinforced by the lived experience of individual social mobility in the context of the general improvement in the conditions of the adivasis under the leadership of the Kisan Sabha—from the time that they were tenants forced to give high rentals and unpaid labour to the *seth* to the present, where about half of them have at least a minimal landholding to their name—are the main factors that contribute to this clear perception.

2. Zania uses certain terms of popular parlance to differentiate among the *garib* adivasis. *Darza* (grades) clearly indicates a perception of hierarchy, the term *payri* (steps) strengthening this perception with the notion of mobility. The manifestations of differentiation strike individuals in an idiosyncratic manner, as for example, Zania's description of the PPs as those who have at least *ambil* to eat. The term *sadharan* when used by the MP to describe himself conveys more than its literal meaning—the condition is so. It expresses a quiet relief at being self-subsistent,

yet, given the delicate balance on which one is placed and the sympathetic perception of the insecurity and rootlessness of the landless AL, there is the lurking fear that the present conditions might take a turn for the worse. 'The adivasis remained *tasech'*, is the expression used to describe the conditions of the adivasis under the past oppression of the *seth-savkars*. This term, also used by several others to describe the present conditions of the ALs, conveys the idea of stagnation without hope or possibility for change. Viewed presently from a superior MP position, the term could describe a situation of isolation. Zania, like most MPs in the sample, is sensitive to the problems of the ALs. Possibilities for their mobility are perceived in pessimistic terms... 'there is no *marg'*. Given the lack of an organised total alternative, change is seen in terms of the need for *adhar* and *'margadarshan'* (guidance along the way).

3. A social *relational* imagery, which in most cases is implied in the spontaneous responses to the introductory questions (that is, it lies in the background of attention at this particular moment and, I suggest, in the subconscious of awareness most of the time) is spontaneously and clearly stated by Zania in social-historical terms. The relatively static and unrelated structure of the present is perceived and explained by him in terms of the dynamics of the past. Zania's four-fold perception of structure within the *garib* is an exception to that of the MPs and of the people as a whole. The typical MP perception—held by 62 per cent of the sample MPs—is of two sections, *sadharan* MP and *garib* AL, within the identity of the *garib* adivasi.

Some Analytical Conclusions

In the light of the above discussion certain conclusions, relevant to the different sampled classes among the people of the village and at times relevant to the sampled people as a whole, may be made in a summary form:

1. The primary identity perceived by all the people is that of the unity of the people, the 'we', under the economic-ethnic identity of the *garib* adivasi as distinct from the altogether other *shrimant seth savkar*, the 'they'. This identity has a real social and historical basis and corresponds to the lived experience of the

people. Both distinction from the *shrimant seth* and the overlap of the economic and cultural dimensions, strengthen this identity which is further reinforced by organised struggle.

2. The identity of the garib adivasi stands in the 'figure' of awareness of all the individuals in the context of the introductory question and, one would suggest, also for most of the individuals most of the time. It forms a basic aspect of the collective conceptions held by the people.

3. Structural differentiation within the *garib* adivasi, which lies implicit in the perception of the primary identity, comes to the forefront as attention shifts in the light of further questions.

4. The subordinate differentiation perceived by all the people is carried out according to essentially similar criteria: landholding, its quantity/quality or its relative absence, and the effects of this on economic activity and general standard of living. The effects are seen along varying dimensions; and may be identified as follows: Independence and security on land or dependence through wage labour and insecurity of work and food. Food, its quantity and quality or relative starvation. The sale of particular commodities and the acquisition of money through business in toddy and grass based on a subsistent holding or *mazoori* (wage labour) based on landlessness.

While the basic criteria are common to all, their manifestations strike individuals differently, vividly and in an idiosyncratic manner. For example, Bendya described the *garib* PPs as ones who 'don't get into fights', who lack the economic security to assert themselves on the question of land distribution. Some examples have already been given. Here is yet one more, which is most vivid. Lakhur is a 30 year old, literate, party member and MP. His produce of five haras of paddy from his four acre land lasts his small family of five throughout the year. He has to employ a few adivasis at the height of the agricultural season and he himself goes off-season to work in the salt pans. Lakhu has a very interesting narration, but I will concentrate here on the criteria he uses to structure society:

> The agricultural labourers are the poorest. They get money
> from wages only when they go to work. Otherwise they have
> to stay at home and starve. They don't get enough work.
> Theirs is the worst condition. But people like us have some

land, we have some grains. We can stay at home and eat. We can even save some seeds for sowing. If there is a wedding, I can take two days off. I can go and dance at the wedding. I can eat at home [i.e., signifying both place of eating—some ALs receive meals at the place of work as part of wages—as well as eating off one's own land].... Land is what makes the difference. Land gives grain. Those who have excess lands, their lands must be taken away and the landless should be given at least four acres of land. The *seth* has given some lands under the ceiling but the *changle* adivasis have cornered more land. I say, that even if I have excess land, it should be taken and distributed to the poor landless.

Land is the important criterion for Lakhu, which helps him to differentiate between the *garib*, the *sadharan* (himself) and the *changle*. He is sensitive to the internal contradictions that the land question has created among the adivasis. What stands out vividly is his particular perception of the manifestations of landholding which differentiate him from the AL: freedom from the daily quest for and the drudgery of wage labour; being sufficiently carefree so as to participate in the spontaneity of communal cultural expressions—'I can take two days off and I can dance at the wedding'; and the independence that landholding gives—'I can eat at home'.

5. Given the above basic criteria, the various classes/sections within classes are popularly termed by adjectives descriptive of general economic condition along the dimension of rich to very poor.

6. Self-identification within the subordinate differentiation is generally perceived in relation to one's objective classification, by individuals from various classes: 20(83.0 per cent) of the ALs identity themselves as ALs, as the lowest class and as garib; 18(86.0 per cent) of the PPS identity themselves PPs, as next to the lowest class and most of them use the term *garib* to distinguish themselves from the *agdi garib* ALs; while 12(92.0 per cent) of the MPs identity themselves as MPs, most of whom use the term *sadharan*, distinguishing themselves from the lowest group of the *garib* ALs.

7. The social structural imagery is perceived to varying degrees of differentiation, by different individuals, identifying

different classes. Thus 19(50.0 per cent) of the individuals perceive a two-fold differentiation; 26(45.0 per cent) perceive a three-fold differentiation; 3(5.0 per cent) perceive a complete four-fold differentiation which corresponds with my own objectively derived categories. This differentiation of the significant social whole should be seen in the light of the basic distinction of *garib* adivasi and *shrimant seth*.

8. Considering the classes mentioned by the various individuals, a certain pattern emerges in the structural imagery corresponding to class, as earlier depicted in the table.

9. Given that five classes (strictly speaking, three plus two sections of one class) were objectively derived, and that three persons in the sample perceived this complete structure, one might ask what are the processes involved in individuals from particular classes tending not to perceive certain other classes. The data suggest that a process of collapsing and lumping together of other categories takes place, depending on the category of one's identification. There is an element of under-and overestimation of the economic status of other sections depending on one's self-assessment. This process has been described earlier in the text.

10. At a more general level, it might be suggested that the act of categorisation is an essential and inevitable constituent of human and intersubjective existence, corresponding to cognitive, linguistic and social capacities. What remains within a domain of contingent flexibility is the value load given to a particular category. Perhaps social science itself could be defined (categorised) as the art of social categorisation. With reference to the categories of social imagery presently under discussion, one sees that the number, size and quality of particular groupings are related to self definition, social distance and over/underestimations that change over historical processes.

The Dynamics of Consciousness and the Dynamism of History[4]

The social structural imagery and self identification discussed so far refers to a people's perception of the ordering of their society and to their self placement in this structuring. The focus of 'scientific' attention is on the 'popular' understanding of the relatively static aspect of their significant social whole and on the static aspects of a people's total understanding. The resulting structural imagery and identities are found to be relatively unrelated and ahistorical, with an emphasis on the present. The individual subject's attempt is to order his society and the resultant patterns are stylised. The focus of attention is on the process of production and, in particular, on the ownership/control over the means of production. As regards the criteria used for structured differentiation one sees that landholding, produce and their general effect on economic conditions feature predominantly.

On the horizontal dimension, the process of arriving at differentiated identities—it may be inferred—is a process of generalising towards individuals of similar economic conditions and of generalisation beyond the self so as to arrive at a generalised self identity, i.e. a process of summation of individuals, each being perceived to have a similar economic condition and adding up to a strata. This might explain why the resulting structured identities have an additive character. On the vertical dimension, the resulting structure is perceived in a hierarchical manner of quantitatively different strata with a wide qualitative difference separating the *garib* adivasis from the *shrimant seth*. It is significant that the vertically graded structure that is perceived is expressed generally in the symbolism of the steps of the ladder, an object which is useful and familiar to people in a rural economy, rather than in the architectural imagery of floors of a building. Society is seen in terms of vertically graded strata.

But we have seen that even in this relatively static structural imagery which perceives additive identities structured as differentiated strata and in the present, there is a definite implication of dynamic social historical relations. The very perception of differentiation within the basic identity of the *garib* adivasi contains an explicit distinction of the *garib* adivasi from the *shrimant seth*. One has seen that a few individuals proceed spontaneously to diagnose the present structure through a narration which reveals the historical dynamics of social relations. A few individuals, even at this stage of the narration, speak of internal contradictions between the *agdi garib* ALs and the *changle* RMPs on the land and labour questions and some spontaneously speak of the basic contradictions with the *seth* which explain their present condition and the great divide that separates their conditions from that of the landlords.

One might suggest that while a structural imagery figures prominently in the consciousness of most individuals most of the time, an awareness of social relations lies implicit in this perception and is generally held at a subliminal level. Individuals generally go about their lives with a structural frame of reference and with a relational, historical perspective in the background. This would correspond with the character of social existence where structures generally predominate and dynamic relations are a determining instance. A social scientific analysis which limits itself to the social structural imagery of a people, stopping short of an understanding of their social relational imagery, does violence both to popular consciousness and to the nature of social reality. Within the social sciences this limitation might be seen in the analysis of stratification to the exclusion of class relations. Structural imagery is but one dimension of the people's consciousness, the other being relational imagery, at times giving rise to collective, organised identities seen in the context of a historical past and towards a future alternative. An examination of all these cognitive areas would help one to arrive at some understanding of the underlying, internally coherent rationale held by individuals as a total conception of their social location as related to productive activity.

Social relation imagery is seen as the dynamic, relational and socio-historical dimension of social imagery. While structural imagery tells us about an individual's perception of differentiated and relatively static strata in the present, relational imagery throws light on the individual's diagnosis of these structures in the social relations of the present and their roots in the past. Structural imagery emphasises the differential ownership of the means of production with the resulting differences in conditions of existence. The criteria for relational imagery, on the other hand, are to be found in individual needs, collective interests and relations and in the organised actions that arise from these different existential situations in the process of production. It is interests that lead to interactions and to self-assertive relations, these relations, in turn, reinforcing and confirming interest. The ecocultural identities in structural imagery have a character of a unity of individual entities with common eco-cultural existence—an additive identity. Relational imagery, however, relates to a level of understanding where identities are seen to be based on shared interests, collective relations and united actions—a collective identity, i.e. a class.

The process of generalisation of experience involved in arriving at a relational imagery is one of 'abstraction' from the particular, unlike in structural imagery where a process of summation is stressed. It is for this reason that relational imagery requires a greater capacity for conceptualisation and, one might suggest, occupies a subliminal and relatively less articulated level of awareness in the subject. On the part of social science it calls for greater sensitivity in comprehension, more intensive probing and deeper analysis.[5]

In Conclusion

The discussion in the foregoing pages suggests that subject-object phenomena, aspects of agency and structure might be considered as dimensions/poles of a continuum that interpenetrate each other. These dimensions of social reality and existential experience cannot be analytically comprehended in any pure exclusive form by the social sciences. Scientific critical enquiry can only suspend its comprehensive focus at a given point of time so as to approximate either one or the other pole. It is suggested that a more relevant approach to the understanding of social movement phenomena would be an attempt to harmonise the two poles through a process of simultaneous approximation. One such approximation would be to consider the residues of intersubjectivity within individual consciousness, which arise from social processes that attempt to break through structured relations. Such an analysis would have to consider consciousness in both its internal coherence and in its rootedness in external social historical context.

Social scientific reflection on contextualised subjectivity is itself an intersubjective act, at least as regards two aspects: that between science and popular 'common sense',[6] and the fact that the former emerges from and is influenced by the prevailing consonance/dissonance within the social scientific community. While scientific empathy with a people's categories of social comprehension is not seen to be an uncritical intervention that romanticises popular conceptions in a populist manner, it needs to be recognised that the latter have the potential of serving as the most potent critique of the very categories of science. The social scientific community would do well to be receptive to such a popular critique arising from an endogenous context.

This article has had as its object of analysis the subjectivity of individual adivasis at a given point of time; a subjectivity that is constructed through intersubjective relations in structured historical processes. The adivasis' quest for a relevant meaning system (objectivity) is part of the process of breaking the confines of the social relations that objectify them. If this paper has provided an illustration of one approximation to subaltern social phenomena in their totality, it would have served its purpose.

Notes

1. This article is based on fieldwork towards an unpublished doctoral thesis entitled, *A Socio-Psychological Study of the Development of Class Consciousness*, Department of Sociology, University of Bombay, 1984.

2. A brief historical outline of this region which lies about 120 km north of Bombay would be in order. The year 1818 marks the establishment of British rule in the region. Colonial land and forest policies during the first half of the nineteenth century led to settled agriculture for the large part of the hunting and shift-cultivating adivasis. Towards the latter half of that century the adivasis experienced alienation of their lands to incoming traders, money-lenders and liquor vendors. Tenancy, bonded labour and a history of extortion of produce, torture and sexual oppression followed. The entry of the Kisan Sabha in the region in 1944 marked a militant phase of struggle till 1948. The post-independence interplay of party and non-party based peasant organisations—the latter of phenomenon of the 1970s and after—with state intervention by way of land reforms and development measures has resulted in a predominantly subsistence economy for the adivasis who are rendered poor peasants and agricultural labour. Over a period of a little more than 150 years the adivasis have been forced into a subordinate location over several modes of production to suit the hegemonic interests of the larger economy. The contexts of 'objectification' are the structured relations that have reified adivasi existence and resulted in the

alienation of land and labour. The focus of this paper is on the extent and nature of conceptualisation and articulation by the adivasis of this historical process.

3. I had, at that time, drawn heavily from a tradition of empirical studies on industrial working class consciousness. Some of the major works are listed below. These studies were subjected to critical adaptation, interpretation and enlargement of scope as would be appropriate for an analysis of class consciousness in a rural, tribal context.

4. The enlargement and relevancing of the scope of empirical studies of working class consciousness, as mentioned in footnote 3, has been influenced by readings in the Marxian classical tradition and the writings of G. Lukacs, A. Gramsci and L. Goldmann, in particular. While I have drawn on the extensive literature on peasant movements, modes of production and the class analysis of the peasantry in the Indian context, empirical studies of cognitive aspects in peasant movements are marked by their absence. Some major theorisation on the consciousness of the peasantry that had influenced my study at that time are included in the references given below.

5. An elaboration of the methodological implications of this approach may be found in D. Saldanha (1988).

6. The concept of common sense is used in the Gramscian meaning of the term.

References

Alavi, H. 1973. 'Peasant Classes and Primordial Loyalties'. In *The Journal of Peasant Studies*. 1:1.

Bain, G.S. et. al. 1973. *Social Stratification and Trade Unionism: A Critique*. London: Heinemann Educational Books.

Banks, J.A. 1972. *The Sociology of Social Movements*. London; Macmillan.

Berger, J. 1978. 'Towards Understanding Peasant Experience'. In *Race and Class*. 19:4.

Beteille, A. 1974. 'Ideas and Interest'. In *Studies in Agrarian Social Structure*. New Delhi: Oxford University Press.

Beynon, H. and R. Blackburn. 1972. *Perceptions of Work*. London: Cambridge University Press.

Billing, R. 1976. *Social Psychology and Intergroup Relations*. NewYork: Academic Press.

Blackburn, R. 1976. *Union, Character and Social Class*. London: B.T. Batsford Ltd.

Blauner, R. 1960. 'Work Satisfaction and Industrial Trends in Modern Society. *Unionism*. New York: Wiley.

Bulmer, M. (ed.). 1975. *Working Class Images of Society*. London: Routledge and Kegan Paul.

Genelleti, C. 1976. 'The Political Orientation of Agrarian Classes: A Theory'. In *European Journal of Sociology*, 17.

Giddens, A. 1973. The Class Structure of the *Advanced Societies*. London: Hutchinson.

Goldthorpe, J.H. and D. Lockwood. 1963. 'Affluence and British Class Structure'. *The Sociological Review*. 11:2.

Goldthorpe, J.H. et. al. 1969. *The Affluent Worker in the Social Class Structure*. London: Cambridge University Press.

Gross, N. 1953. 'Social Identification in the Urban Community'. *American Sociology Review*. 18.

Holmstrom, M. 1978. *South Indian Factory Workers*. New Delhi: Allied Publishers.

Landsberger, H. 1973. 'The Problems of Peasant Wars'. In *Comparative Studies in Society and History*. 15.

Lahmann, D. 1972. 'Peasant Consciousness and Agrarian Reforms in Chile'. In *European Journal of Sociology*, 2.

Lane, R. 1962. *Political Ideology*. New York: The Free Press.

Legget, J.C. 1968. *Class, Race and Labour: Working Class Consciousness in Detroit*. New York: Oxford University Press.

Lockwood, D. 1958. *The Balckcoated Worker: A Study in Consciousness*. London: Allen and Unwin.

_____ 1966. 'Sources of Variations in Working Class Images of Society'. *Sociological Review*. 14:3.

Mann, M. 1973. *Consciousness and Action in the Western Working Class*. London: Macmillan.

Miliband, R. 1971. 'Barnave: A Case of Bourgeois Class Consciousness'. In I. Meszaros (ed.) *Aspects of History and Class Consciousness*. London: Routledge and Kegan Paul.

Mintz, S. 1974. 'The Rural Proletariat and the Problem of Rural Proletarian. Consciousness'. In *Journal of Peasant Studies*. 1:3.

Moorhouse, H.F. 1976. 'Attitudes to Class and Class Relations in Britian. In *Sociology*, 10(3).

Parkin, F. 1971. *Class Inequality and Political Order*. London: MacGibbon and Kee.

Populitz, H. et. al. 1976. 'The Worker's Images of Society'. In T. Burns (ed.) *Industrial Man*. Harmondsworth: Penguin.

Portes, A. 1991. 'On the Interpretation of Class Consciousness'. In *American Journal of Sociology*. 77:2.

Post, K. 1972. 'Peasantisation and Rural Political Movements in Western Africa'. In *European Journal of Sociology*. 13:2.

Runciman, W.G. 1968. *Relative Deprivation and Social Justice*. London: Routledge and Kegan Paul.

Saberwal, S. 1980. 'For Renewal'. In *Seminar*. October 1980.

Saldanha, D. 1988. 'Antonio Gramsci and the Analysis of Class Consciousness: Some Methodological Considerations'. In *Economic and Political Weekly*. 30 January.

Scott, J.C. 1979. 'Revolution in the Revolution: Peasants and Commissars'. In *Theory and Society*: 1–2.

Singleman, P. 1975. 'The Closing Triangle: Critical Notes on a Model for Peasant Mobilisation in Latin America'. *Comparative Studies in Society and History*. 17:4.

Taussig, M. 1977. 'The Genesis of Capitalism Amongst a South American

Peasantry: Devil's Labour and the Baptism of Money. In *Comparitive Studies in Society and History*. 19.

Useem, B. 1976. 'Peasant Involvement in the Cuban Revolution'. *Journal of Peasant Studies*. 3:3.

Westergaard, J.M. 1965. 'The Withering Away of Class: A Contemporary Myth'. In P. Anderson (ed.) *Towards Socialism*. London:Fontana.

Wolpe, H. 1970. 'Some Problems Concerning Revolutionary Consciousness'. In *The Socialist Register*.

Section III

The Self and the Other in the Anthropological Context

Discovering Anthropology: A Personal Narrative

T.N. MADAN

> We might say then that both the relativist and his partner, the dogmatist, that is the 'true believer of science', lack the insight that their own form of life is always what it is not and that for this reason one does not become conscious of his own form of life until he leaves it....
>
> But in some sense the researcher will always stay a bit 'between the worlds'. It is the price he has to pay for knowledge: to be forever excluded from the world of talking animals and from the world of talking anthropologists as well.
>
> HANS PETER DUERR 1987

The First Encounter

My 'engagement' with anthropology has now lasted forty years, which is long enough for some reflection on what it has come to mean to me. In this essay I will discuss some issues, which have had a significant place in my anthropological quest from the very beginning. These include the problem of 'objectivity' and the notion that anthropology is essentially the study of 'other cultures', defining otherness to refer to, narrowly, non-Western cultures, or broadly, cultures other than the anthropologist's own.

My first encounter with anthropology, as I now recall it, was almost fortuitous: I stumbled upon the word in a university prospectus! My way to a career in anthropology led through history, English literature, and economics. Although history emerged as the preferred subject when I first deliberated upon what to study after finishing high school, I was unable to make this choice. Instead I read natural sciences during the first two years in college and social sciences (economics and political science) during the next two. In the latter period, I chose English literature as my Honours subject, and found immense delight in it.

Yet, flowing with the stream, as it were, I opted for economics as the subject for my M.A. In the early 1950s, soon after independence, while English language and literature seemed to harken to the past, economics via its connection with planning was the subject of the future. I decided do join the Lucknow University, much against the advice of my economics professor at Amar Singh College (in Srinagar, J&K). He warned me that one did not get a good education in economics at Lucknow, but only a miscellany of courses, including sociology; one would thus earn only a 'hybrid degree'. I did not let this opinion deflect me from the journey I had planned to undertake, which was to become more than a journey from one city to another, and which was to lead to the choice of a vocation.

On enrolment in the Department of Economics and Sociology at Lucknow University I found that, during the first of the two-year M.A. course, I would have to study micro- and macro-economic analysis, with institutional economics thrown in, and also introductory sociology including social ecology. Besides, I had to choose a 'paper' from among three optionals that included cultural anthropology. I did not know what anthropology was, and the dictionary I consulted defined it as the comparative study of races and cultures. The details of the course appeared interesting. On enquiry I found that it would be taught by one of the more popular teachers, D.N. Majumdar. The prospectus identified him as a 'reader' with a Ph.D. from Cambridge and the distinction of being a Fellow of the National Institute of Sciences. All this was impressive, and I opted for cultural anthropology, unmindful of my college teacher's warning. In the event, and not at all surprisingly, I learnt very little economics!

As for anthropology, in order to get us started, Majumdar asked us to read Robert Lowie's old classic, *Primitive Society* (1922), which had recently become available again. This book was supplemented by selected chapters from several others including Majumdar's own works. Anthropology interested me, but I cannot really say that the engagement with it began then. The emphasis on the culturally specific datum recaptured for me something of the excitement of reading history. Ethnographic examples might have called to my mind aspects of the novel and the short story, but not only were we not required to read any monographs in the first year, Majumdar's insistence that anthropology was a 'science' also was not conducive to such anticipations.

The way sociology and social ecology were taught to us (by Radhakamal Mukerjee and D.P. Mukerji) was more like anthropology rather than economics, in the interpretative rather than the analytical mode. Robert MacIver's *Society* and Radhakamal Mukerjee's *Social Ecology* were the introductory texts. The third teacher, A.K. Saran (who was a stern critic of positivism began with the theory of symbolic interactionism a la G.H. Mead's *Mind, Self and Society*, which left me rather dazed. MacIver had a philosophical approach and a literary style, and I recall reading his discussion of themes like 'code and custom', 'the sociological significance of the family', and 'contrasts of urban and rural life' with enormous interest. D.P. Mukerji's exegesis of these and other themes was itself immensely absorbing. He introduced us to the Marxian perspective, but not at all in the high-handed manner of the copy-book marxist intellectual. Together, anthropology and sociology seemed to me to be an invitation to consider everyday life worthy of serious study in a manner that economic analysis, with its graphs and curves and general concepts did not—concretely rather than in the abstract. (I will not say anything here about the economics courses and how they were taught.)

At the end of the first year a clear choice was offered to us in respect of the courses to be taken up in the second year: straight economics or a combined set of anthropology-sociology courses. I opted for the latter. Besides the history of social thought and theories of culture and civilisation, we now had to study a broad-based anthropology course. Beginning with some lectures on palaeontology, Majumdar guided us through the monographic and theoretical works of Alfred Kroeber, Robert Lowie, Bronislaw Malinowski, Ruth Benedict, Margaret Mead, and Ralph Linton. He also often referred to his own fieldwork among Indian tribes such as—the Ho, Tharu, and Khasa.

Anthropology, Majumdar taught us, was 'the science of man in totality'. Although the syllabus contained very little on biological anthropology and prehistoric archaeology, he always insisted that any anthropologist worth the name must know all three fields. He did not include anthropological linguistics in this 'core' or 'sacred bundle'. Besides its holistic character, Majumdar expounded at length on anthropology's scientific and applied character. Anthropology is a 'laboratory' science, he used to say, and a 'field' science. He considered the work that he did in his laboratory (serological classification, anthropometric analysis, etc.) continuous with what he did in the field (collecting blood samples, taking body measurements, etc.). And he regarded the collection of data for his ethnographic work as an important aspect of the larger enterprise of fieldwork, guided above all by the ideal of objectivity.

The ways of life of the people being studied—their beliefs and behaviour—were as 'real' as their body weight, skin colour, and blood groups. There was, therefore, no more scope for spinning out tales in ethnography than there was in physical anthropological description. One had to ensure that ethnographic 'data' were reliable and their analysis was rigorous and guided by theory (which for him was functionalism informed by evolution). The ultimate test of 'scientific objectivity', which was his ideal, was that what one claimed to be the facts of the case, should be verifiable by another well-trained investigator. The model was the experiment in the laboratory.

D.P. Mukerji, who taught us the history of social thought, was rather disdainful of the conception of anthropology as narrative ethnography. He advocated an approach to the study of human cultures which was explicitly historical but not historicist—evolutionary but sensitive to cultural specificities. Without an interest in the general and the abstract, the study of the specific and the concrete, he used to say, would surely turn out to be an intellectual bog.

When he lectured on the theories of culture and civilisation, the scholars whose contributions Mukerji discussed included sociologists such as Max Weber and Pitrim Sorokin, and historians like Jacob Burckhardt and Arnold Toynbee. The only contributions by anthropologists that he discussed were Bronislaw Malinowski's thesis on the mutual entailment of 'freedom and civilisation' and Ruth Benedict's notion of the 'stubbornness of the core of a culture'. Although he did not find the ethnographic narrative particularly interesting, he acknowledged its value as a 'shock absorber'. He was a relativist, but not philosophically naive. He considered the position of absolute value-neutrality wrong and also stressed the dangers of uncritical functionalism. Mukerji was committed to the notions of the unfolding of the possibilities inherent in every social formation and the arriving at the next higher stage through the dialectical process. He maintained that anthropologists and sociologists would discover the true promise of their subjects only if they cultivated an interest in history and philosophy. Over the years, I myself have come to embrace this twin emphasis whole-heartedly, limited only by the elementary nature of my knowledge of philosophy.

The third professor, Radhakamal Mukerjee, lectured on 'the social structure of values' and 'the dynamics of morals', using his own books for the purpose. He was very eclectic in his approach. A prolific author, he had written on a wide range of themes in the fields of economics, sociology, psychology, and religious studies. He had a greater interest in ethnography than D.P. Mukerji.

There was thus no single over-all approach to the study of society, and to explicating the character of the social sciences, in the lectures and published work of the four professors who taught us. D.N. Majumdar, I should add, was not alone in his conception of the social sciences as essentially *scientific*: his approach found sympathetic echoes in the lectures and published work of practically all the economists in the Department. None of them showed much concern for the role that personal preferences or ideological commitments play in the so-called sciences.

As for my own predilections, it was the courses on the theories of culture and civilisation, taught by D.P. Mukerji, and on anthropological theories of culture, taught by D.N. Majumdar, that I found most interesting. I particularly enjoyed reading Toynbee's *A Study of History*, of which the first six volumes were then available. Also available was an excellent and helpful abridgement by D.C. Somerville. Reading Toynbee was for me a welcome return to history and comparative literature. The books of Malinowski and Ruth Benedict also interested me greatly: they were rich in ethnography and also very readable.

By the time I finished my M.A. (in 1951), it was obvious that research and teaching were to be my vocation in life. Radhakamal Mukerjee and D.N. Majumdar both offered me scholarships for doctoral studies. Mukerjee suggested I work on the composition of the working class in Kanpur, but this did not attract me at all. Majumdar proposed fieldwork among a tribal community in the Almora (U.P.) area, with the focus on problems of rehabilitation. D.P. Mukerji, mindful of the interest I had evinced in Toynbee, suggested that I consider working on Toynbee's 'method' (or lack of it). After some vascillation I settled for a career in anthropology.

During the early years at Lucknow University, I had the opportunity to hear, besides my teachers, a number of distinguished scholars including A. Aiyappan, N.K. Bose, Louis Dumont, Irawati Karve, S.F. Nadel, and M.N. Srinivas. The subject of Srinivas's talk (winter 1954–5) was fieldwork and he spoke about the qualities of a good fieldworker, emphasising, above all, total commitment. Not only must the fieldworker be a genuine participant observer, he must consider his relationship with the community he chooses to study as more than a strategy for data collection. He must recognise that there is a moral dimension to the relationship. He went so far as to suggest that the best fieldworkers are single individuals without family obligations. It is worth recalling here that Srinivas himself did his fieldwork among the Coorgs and in the village of Rampura in Karnataka before he got married.

Srinivas also stressed in his talk the importance of fidelity to facts. The importance of memory and imagination that are a distinguishing feature of his book, *The Remembered Village* (1976), were not, of course, anticipated in his talk. Actually, the discussion that followed his presentation was marked by a sharply stated difference of opinion between him and A.K. Saran on the issue of positivism in the social sciences. For Srinivas sociology was at its best when it was grounded in observable data in the manner of social anthropology. In fact he considered a distinction between the two domains to be a colonial hangover. Saran's commitment was above all to a metaphysical perspective on social reality.

I would also like to mention the powerful impact N.K. Bose made upon some of us when he spent a day with the students in the winter of 1950. He lectured on caste in modern Bengal, on temple architecture in Orissa, and finally on Gandhi. The range of his interests seemed wide like D.P. Mukerji's, but while the latter was a social theorist, Bose was, first and foremost, a fieldworker and a man interested in practical affairs. There was something earthy about him in the best possible sense of the term.

It was apparent from Bose's first and second talks that, for him, observation was a broad-based and wide-ranging engagement with a social phenomenon (caste, temple architecture), which was not to be bound by a narrowly conceived rule-book. A great deal of what he told us about changes in the caste system was based on his own day-to-day interaction with people than fieldwork in some village or hamlet. In contrast his work in Orissan temples was obviously based upon carefully planned and painstaking research, carried out practically single handed. And when he spoke about Gandhi, he spoke more as a social activist with a deep moral concern for human suffering than as a social scientist interested in the form of social life, a subject on which he had written insightfully in Bengali (*Hindu Samajer Garan, 1949*). In our day with Bose, social anthropology was presented to us as a part of our own lives, not a study of primitive cultures. The objective and the subjective were both accommodated in his method.

The Quest for Objectivity

Anthropology, I had learnt from Majumdar, was the study of 'primitive societies', of cultures other than the literate and the industrial. The so-called tribes of India were what Indian anthropologists had studied. It was inexpensive and convenient to do fieldwork within the country, and there was no dearth of tribal people. He had done so himself, in Chota Nagpur (Bihar), Mirzapur (U.P.), Jaunsar Bawar (U.P.) and elsewhere, studying communities like the Ho, Tharu and Khasa.

Conscious of my inadequacy and even awkwardness in relating to strangers and cultivating social relationships, and also perhaps attracted to D.P. Mukerji's emphasis on the importance of general if not explicitly stated theoretical issues, I asked Majumdar if fieldwork among a tribal people was an essential requirement of a programme of doctoral studies. He said that, strictly speaking, it was not, for the limited purpose of preparing a dissertation, but one could not hope to make a professional career out of anthropology without it. Accordingly, it was agreed that the subject of my dissertation would be the 'rehabilitation' of Indian tribes. The data for it would be drawn from published sources of various kinds, including anthropological monographs and government reports. At that time the critique of development as a destroyer of cultural pluralism had not yet emerged, nor had the idea that the 'other' was in fact constituted by the anthropological method itself. Development from above was then considered a moral obligation rather than arrogance, and the 'other' cultures were considered essentially so.

About a year later, I joined a group of M.A. students who were being taken to Ranchi (Bihar) for a two-week 'field trip' as part of their training in anthropology. It turned out to be a depressing experience for me. Not that the Oraons appeared to be culturally very different from the Hindu villagers of the same area. What upset me was our behaviour.

Everybody in our group, I found, was asking the villagers questions about their family and economic life, religious beliefs, and similar matters of significance, without any regard for their feelings or convenience. My shyness crippled me, but I did manage to take photographs at an old woman's funeral and cremation, without first seeking anybody's permission to do so. As we came away from the village, I had the uncomfortable feeling that there was something indecent about such field trips. This feeling was accentuated by the fact that one of the girl students in our group had cried at the cremation, but no one else had shown any emotion. A year-long stay in the field by an anthropologist working on his own would be, I thought, far from the kind of 'assault' in which we had been engaged. Nevertheless, a strong feeling that anthropological fieldwork was in a certain sense degrading to the unwilling subject of observation, a violation of his personal life by strangers, took firm hold of me. This feeling was, perhaps, partly a cover for my own incapacity for fieldwork among strangers.

Gradually, almost imperceptibly, it occurred to me that a solution to the problem probably lay in studying my own community, the Pandits of the Kashmir valley, though perhaps not my own family circle and kindred, or any other such grouping in the city of Srinagar where I had grown up. Years later I wrote: 'It is clear to me now, though it was not then, that I was transforming the familiar into the unfamiliar by the decision to relate to it as an anthropologist' (1975: 134).

Early in 1955, the well-known anthropologist S.F. Nadel visited Lucknow. I took the opportunity to discuss my fieldwork problem with him. He told me that he could see no objection to an Indian studying aspects of the caste or community of his birth. He stressed the importance of training in formal anthropological research which, he thought, should help one to overcome the limitations of subjective bias. He also emphasised the importance and advantages of a good command over the 'native tongue' to anthropological research, particularly to the study of kinship and religion, and pointed out that being a native speaker would give one a head start in fieldwork. He had written about the importance of language competence in fieldwork in *The Foundations of Social Anthropology* (1952).

Soon afterwards, I discontinued work on my dissertation on the rehabilitation of Indian tribes. Majumdar, who had by then himself initiated a research project in a non-tribal village near Lucknow, agreed that I could write a dissertation on the basis of fieldwork among the Pandits of rural Kashmir. Accordingly I sent a proposal to Nadel at the Australian National University (ANU) for the study of 'kinship values': Radhakamal Mukerjee's lectures and book on the social structure of values may have had a deeper impact on me than I was conscious of at that time. He had laid considerable stress on family relationships and their underlying values of love, sharing and solidarity.

ANU awarded me a scholarship in the summer of 1955. I could never find out what Nadel actually thought of my research proposal, for he died early in 1956 before my arrival in Canberra. I had been apprehensive that he might not approve of the theme I had suggested. There was no evidence of such an interest in his own published work. My confidence had been somewhat shaken by A.K. Saran, who had summarily rejected the idea of a study of values through fieldwork. My clarification that what I intended was to find out, through close observation, was the norms and values that were not merely verbalised by people, but could be shown to have actually influenced choices and behaviour in real life situations, left him totally unconvinced. This was, of course, in tune with his known opposition to positivism and to the idea of a social science.

After my arrival in Canberra, the first person to discuss my proposal with me at considerable length was Edmund Leach, who was on a short visit to ANU. He told me in a typically forthright manner that, given his structural-functional approach, the focus of my proposed research worried him. He said that I would be making a very serious mistake if I got involved in a theme so vague and so difficult to handle as 'values'. He advised a focus on 'objective facts'. What mattered most in peasant kinship systems in South Asia was that 'people had land and they had maternal uncles'. This was obviously his way of saying that the two most significant factors governing kinship relations and family life are the ownership and inheritance of property, notably land, and the disputes that arise over it among agnatically related kin who are the offspring of different mothers in an extended family. He advised me to collect case studies of family disputes and subject them to careful analysis, so that the existence of cultural norms may be demonstrated, and to avoid getting bogged down in 'an ideal, value-governed, mythical state of existence'.

Leach thus raised doubts about the study of kinship values, as had Saran earlier, but for the very opposite reasons. His advice, as I understood it, was to leave alone the people's notions of ideal behaviour, and to adopt a statistical concept of customary or normative behaviour: to study people's behaviour itself—that is, the objective reality—rather than their ideas about it, which are subjective formulations of objective reality, often no more than distortions and rationalisations. One could trace this distrust of what people say or affirm to the many excellent demonstrations of the gap between word and deed that abound in ethnographical literature, beginning with Malinowski's monographs on the Trobriand Islanders.

Although rather disappointed by Leach's rejection of the

proposed focus of my research, I was greatly relieved that he had not objected to my studying the Pandits, my own people. He had not raised a question which I had feared he might, namely how I could ensure that my research among my own people would be marked by scientific objectivity, as required by orthodoxy. I partially revised my research plan on the lines suggested by Leach.

The question of objectivity was not, however, absent in the discussions I had with various faculty members on my proposed fieldwork in Kashmir. One of them, Derek Freeman, cautioned me repeatedly to steer clear of Indological texts, and not get carried away by people's ideas about their culture and society. He called giving too much attention to such texts and ideas 'the besetting fault' of the work of Indian anthropologists on Hindu society. The anthropologist should, they all said or implied, draw his conclusions directly from observed behaviour, guided by well-established fieldwork techniques. (The Department stocked copies of the venerable *Notes and Queries on Anthropology*, and I too equipped myself with one.)

We understand the import of such exhortations much better today than I was capable of doing then. They emphasised that, in today's language, Indians were not to be trusted to produce objective and reliable ethnography about themselves without the benefit of modern social science perspectives. Even when trained in them, they had to be careful about not losing their objectivity by being overwhelmed (beset) by native categories of thought. The few books that I carried with me to the Kashmir village where I went for fieldwork were what were then considered exemplary anthropological studies of kinship, notably the Nuer and Tallensi kinship books by E.E. Evans-Pritchard and Meyer Fortes respectively. Halfway through the fieldwork I felt the need for an authoritative work in Hindu law, and obtained one (by mail), but that was as far as I went. Irawati Karve's *Kinship Organisation in India* (1953) which I had carefully read was not in my kitbag in the field. On the whole, I thought I had the dangers of subjective bias and a book-view of society well under control, notwithstanding the fact that my Pandit villagers had lots of ideas about the character of their family life.

In fact, they had not merely stray ideas but a coherent and well-articulated ideology of the householder. I assembled this ideology from both statements, made directly by informants in reply to my questions, and observations on all sorts of topics which reflected the ideology. But eventually, on my return to Canberra, I did not include a discussion of this ideology in my dissertation. My focus was on observed behaviour, which would have been fine but for the fact that my notion of what constituted 'behaviour' was rather narrow. Thus I failed to collect sufficient materials on Sanskritic rituals, such as initiation, marriage, and the rituals addressed to manes, because I believed that the quest would soon lead me to the forbidden texts. Caution about presuming that what is given in the texts is also to be found, and in the same form, in real life would have been in order. A total avoidance of the texts, however, was a mistake that I made, but nobody told me that I was doing so. I did not then realise that being objective requires paying attention to the subjective point of view—native 'texts', first-order interpretations, or whatever one may call them.

The Middle Position

Early in 1959, when I was nearing the completion of the writing of my dissertation, I read the English translation of Louis Dumont's inaugural lecture, 'For a Sociology of India', which was delivered (in French) in Paris in 1955. The approach advocated by him, attaching equal importance to Indology and social anthropology in the making of the sociology of India, reopened for me the whole issue of the place of the ideas of the people in anthropological fieldwork and the ethnographic narrative.

Dumont's argument seemed clear and convincing to me. It is quite well-known for me to not need to go into it in great detail. It should suffice to recall here that, after affirming that the study of any civilisation is ultimately inspired by 'the endeavour to constitute an adequate idea of mankind' (1957: 9), he observed that 'modern social anthropology had made a significant contribution' to the definition of social facts as things and as collective representations through 'its insistence that the observer sees things from within (as integrated in the society which he studies) and from without'. Following Evans-Pritchard,

Dumont described 'the movement from one point of view to the other as an effort of translation', but cautioned that 'in this task it is not sufficient to translate the indigenous words, for it frequently happens that the ideas which they express are related to each other by more fundamental ideas even though these are unexpressed' (ibid: 11–12).

Dumont's perspective was welcome to me as it pointed to a seemingly satisfactory way out of the alleged conflict between anthropological and native understandings of the social reality: not by privileging the former and devaluing (and even excluding) the latter, but through a confrontation of the two. To the extent to which my dissertation had considerably relied on the Kashmiri Pandits' own conceptions of kinship, marriage, and the family (see Madan 1965), I felt vindicated. At the same time it was obvious that, in the absence of a solid theoretical position (such as I now found in Dumont's statement), I had not proceeded systematically, not far enough. I attempted to do so later in a number of essays (written between 1976 and 1985, see Madan 1987), which included one on the ideology of the Pandit householder. By then the role of ideas and ideologies in social life, and in anthropology, had begun to receive serious attention. Also, behaviouristic conceptions of culture were being replaced by symbolic ones that emphasised meaning and significance. In some of these essays I turned to notable works of fiction in various Indian languages for insights. With the arrival of the novel on my anthropological desk, I had finally put behind me an exclusive *social science* conception of the discipline.

Dumont's approach came under attack from F.G. Bailey soon after the publication of the English version of his 1955 lecture. Bailey restated the orthodox behaviourist position and advocated evasion of the ideas of the people, 'supposing they have any ideas which is not always the case' (1959: 90). He dismissed Dumont's approach as culturological and stuck in the intuitive understanding of the unique. This was gross distortion. There were a few others who joined the debate, including A.K. Saran, who refused to grant Dumont the privilege of the ground he claimed to stand on. He wrote magisterially: 'social reality *qua* social reality has no "outside":... the only outside is interpretation in terms of an alien culture' (1962:68). The conflict between 'scientific objectivity', so-called, and 'subjective understanding' was presented in a particularly uncompromising form in these criticisms.

Having followed the debate with interest, I tried to formulate my own response to it. I made the following two points, among others. While recognising the significance of the dialectic of the views from within and without, I complained that Dumont weakened his argument by asserting that the sociologist shares the external point of view with the natural scientist. I wrote: 'I am not sure that such a point of view exists.... If it did, it should have been possible for us to study social life through observation unaided by communication with the observed people.... [W]hen the sociologist allows "the principles that people themselves give"... to enter his analysis and explanation, he surrenders a truly external position' (1966: 12).

In response, Dumont argued that if the external point of view had not existed, there would have been no social anthropology, but conceded that the approach advocated by him 'might rather be called positive-cum-subjective' and reasserted: 'Duality, or tension is ...the condition *sine qua non* of social anthropology or, if one likes, sociology of a deeper kind' (1966: 22–23).

Although I may not have stated my position very clearly, what I was trying to suggest was that, beyond a point, a stark opposition between scientific objectivity (howsoever defined) and 'subjective understanding' is sterile: it produces the kinds of negative extremism exemplified by Bailey's and Saran's comments cited above. As social anthropologists we were concerned with the 'concrete' and the 'particular'; to adequately describe and interpret the same, and provide causal explanations when doing so seems appropriate and possible, we need 'abstract' and 'general' concepts. It cannot be otherwise in the human sciences, and I am quite comfortable with this middle position.

Mutual Interpretation of Cultures

As my anthropological-sociological studies continued, I ceased to worry about the opposition between objectivity and subjectivity. I combined perspectives and methods in a self-conscious manner. I also dispensed with the notion of anthropology as the study of 'other cultures', and continued with the study of aspects of the society in which I lived.

In a paper written in 1974, I questioned the requirement of the personal study of an alien culture on the part of every anthropologist. Instead, I emphasised the importance of bridging the gap, or conversely creating it, between the observer and the observed. I described fieldwork as the feat of 'living intimately with strangers' (Madan 1975). I might have added: 'or strangely with intimates', which was what I had done during my fieldwork among the Pandits of rural Kashmir. The anthropologist studying his own culture, I wrote, 'is an insider who takes up the posture of an outsider, by virtue of his training as an anthropologist or a sociologist, and looks at his own culture, hoping to be surprised. If he is, only then may he achieve new understandings' (ibid: 149).

Subsequently, I moved a step further, and argued that anthropology was best conceived, not as the study of other cultures, but as 'the mutual interpretation of cultures' (Madan 1982). I mentioned the dual perspective of the views from within and without, and added: 'we must adhere firmly to the notion that anthropology resides in this nexus, that it is a kind of knowledge—a form of consciousness—which arises from the encounter of cultures in the mind of the anthropologist. What an observer learns about an alien society's observable modes of behaviour will not yield anthropological understanding unless he is able to grasp, in the first place, the subjective purposes and meanings that make these modes of behaviour significant to the people concerned. But the knowledge about one's own beliefs and rituals which an informant may impart to the investigator is not anthropological either' (1982: 5). In other words, anthropological knowledge was not to be discovered, but generated by confronting, first, what people say with what they do, and, then, confronting the view from within with the view from without.

'What people believe in and do, and the relationship of belief and action, has first to be understood in the people's own terms—this is the first order interpretation of facts—before one may translate these understandings into the language of anthropology. The anthropologist's task, then, is to establish a synthesis between the introversion of self-understanding and the extraversion of the scientific method' (ibid: 7). It was thus that I arrived at the conclusion that anthropology was, perhaps, best defined as the mutual interpretation of cultures: learning about one's own culture from the other cultures one studies, just as one uses insights derived from one's cultural experience—one's personal anthropology—as well as knowledge of ethnography to make sense of the cultures one writes about.

Writing as a creative rather than merely recording activity, was soon going to attract a great deal of attention. Naive realism and an uncritical mirror theory of knowledge were under attack. There was a great deal of over-kill in some of these writings, but there was a hard core of genuine criticism of the orthodoxy, which fitted well with my views developed over the years.

In a conference paper written in 1985, I briefly discussed the images of India in the work of American anthropologists, from Alfred Kroeber to McKim Marriott. I identified several images or representations and concluded that all the representations seemed to be grounded in empirical reality: what distinguished them from one another was the perspective of each. Echoing James Clifford, I called these representations partial—committed and incomplete, and added: 'this does not mean though that someone has to piece them together and render them complete. Their utility lies in their being what they are and in their mutual contestation. The assessment of the truth value of anthropological images thus turns out to be not merely a question of information about the present situation or historical roots of institutions, or of future possibilities, but also a debate about appropriate perspectives. Such debates are, of course, notoriously inconclusive. One clear guideline though is that the perspective which enables us to understand more of the facts on the ground economically and in an internally consistent manner, and does not claim exhaustiveness, is to be preferred to those that lack coherence and lay claims to monopoly over truth' (1990: 196).

I returned to this theme of the character of anthropological knowledge in the introductory essay to my book *Non-Renunciation: Themes and Interpretations of Hindu Culture* (1987). Writing about first order interpretations which a people provide when questioned about their culture, I suggested that, while the interpretations fabricated by the people themselves may seem adequate and explicit to them they usually are opaque to the outsider, which is what the social anthropologist is, in one sense or another: if not born in another society, his training as an anthropologist teaches him to turn a sceptical eye at everything that seems familiar. 'Interpretation thus involves the social anthropologist in a process of unfolding or unravelling what are at first riddles to him, by working out their implications: ...it is a search for significance and structure' (ibid.: 7–8).

Just as the internal interpreters one encounters in the course of fieldwork are several, I continued, the external interpreters also may be many, each capturing a particular facet of social reality, a particular cultural theme, and providing a comparative or general perspective on it. To say this is not to surrender to solipsism, but to affirm the legitimacy and value of pluralism. The illusions of completeness and permanence that an ethnographic text creates are useful, each in its own way, but the interpretive endeavour knows no finality. As the questions change—and this happens for a variety of reasons ranging from on-going social change to changing theoretical orientations—so do the answers, and the completeness of description is inevitably deferred. I believe the positivists of yesterday knew this as well as do the grammatologists of today. The aims and the nature of the endeavour are, however, clear: namely the effort to make sense of what the people we seek to understand think and do, and, as Max Weber put it, to grasp how they 'confer meaning and significance' on their lives. Our interpretations thus are not merely pictures of empirical reality. They are descriptive but they are not merely description. In our fieldwork and the subsequent writing, we not only *look* and *listen*, we also *think*. In other words, we inevitably, though not always self-consciously, put ourselves into our ethnographic accounts of others.

As I have, over the years, reflected upon the nature of anthropological fieldwork and knowledge, I have leaned more and more towards the humanities, and found social history and literature richer sources of inspiration in my anthropological work than the natural or biological sciences. I have noted the need for immense caution implied by Karl Popper's admonition that 'the triumph of social anthropology' may have only been 'the triumph of a pseudo-observational, pseudo-descriptive, and pseudo-generalising methodology and above all marks the triumph of a pretended objectivity and hence an imitation of the methods of natural science' (quoted by Banton 1964: 99).

I have also become increasingly conscious of the significance of cultivating a philosophical perspective in the specific sense of comparative ethics. Ethnography merely as knowledge of how other people live their lives can be just baggage, a burden, unless it teaches one to live one's own life better—judged as such in terms of certain ultimate values that enjoy cross-cultural legitimacy. Whether this effort is described as 'the mutual interpretation of cultures', or as the cultivation of 'critical self-awareness' (see Madan 1994), the point being made is the same and obvious. It would be trite to try to illustrate such a worldview by citing particular examples: it must inform all that one does and the way one thinks.

Anthropology and History

I began my discovery of anthropology in the light of what my teachers, first at the University of Lucknow and then at the Australian National University, told me the subject was all about. They spoke to me in several voices at Lucknow, but the dominant voice at Canberra was that of positivism. As I have tried to describe in this essay, the need to choose between the different perspectives emerged fairly early in my research career. I had wanted to begin with a fieldwork based study of kinship values, but ended up writing a structural-functional study of the family and the household. To be told by those whose opinions mattered in the profession that it was the first such study for north India and a successful one, mattered a great deal to me. Besides, the question of what to do with the subjective understandings of the people being studied, what value to attach to them, seemed to me to move towards a satisfactory solution in the work of Louis Dumont rather than that of, say, Edmund Leach.

Doing fieldwork among the Pandits of rural Kashmir had meant dealing with a situation in which 'work' was an aspect of domestic life, even when it took place in the fields or the village shops. The idea of looking upon work on its own, which of course meant looking upon it in modern bureaucratised settings, interested me a great deal. Also, I was curious about the criticism voiced by economists, and some sociologists too, that anthropological knowledge was of very limited practical value. Accordingly, I undertook studies of modern occupations and professions on the basis of secondary data, which involved statistical analysis at the state, national, and international levels. I supplemented these studies with personal observation of clinical medical practice and interviews with allopathic practitioners in an Indian city as well as interviews with the faculty of a major medical teaching and research and health care institution (see Madan 1972, 1980). I found this work, its concern with social development and its quantitative data and statistical analysis notwithstanding, intellectually less appealing and emotionally less satisfying than my earlier work. It had none of the interest of participant observation (in the real sense of the term), and I was sure that I never fully succeeded in finding what the doctors' work meant to them. Their world of subjective experience was not easily captured in interviews and quantified information.

While fieldwork thus remained an attraction, I looked elsewhere too for new perspectives. It seemed to me that besides 'kinship' and 'work', the third major area which the anthropologist should study, particularly in India, is religion. There are many excellent fieldwork-based studies of the meaning and significance of religion in the lives of village communities, or particular categories of people, such as pilgrims. But religion has become intertwined with politics in our times, and appears to us in the form of the 'ideologies' of secularism, communalism and fundamentalism. It is these ideologies that have engaged my attention for much of the last decade.

While the anthropological method of comparison, with the focus on the particular, still guides me, the nature of the subject compels me to study it diachronically. I find, not a single ideology, but secularisms and fundamentalisms, each set of ideologies held together by a family resemblance. Thus, by a circuitous path, I find I have come back to history and, indeed, literature also. But when I turn to history today, I do so as an anthropologist. Actually, these labels and designations do not seem to me all that significant any more. What is significant is the social reality that we seek to know and understand, and what matters is whether our studies—our interpretations—illumine this reality more than the earlier explanations did. The critical question is, are we moving forward? The rest, it seems to me, is the vanity of intellectual fashions of which we seem to have a plethora nowadays.

References

Bailey, F.G. 1959. For a Sociology of India? *Contributions to Indian Sociology* III: 88–101.

Banton, Michael. 1964. Anthropological Perspectives in Sociology. *British Journal of Sociology* 15: 95–112.

Duerr, Hans Peter, 1987. *Dreamtime: Concerning the Boundary between Wilderness and Civilisation.* Oxford: Basil Blackwell.

Dumont, Louis. 1957. For a Sociology of India. *Contributions to Indian Sociology* I: 7–22.

_____ 1966. A Fundamental Problem in the Sociology of Caste. *Contributions to Indian Sociology* IX: 17–32.

Madan, T.N. 1965. *Family and Kinship: A Study of the Pandits of Rural Kashmir.* Bombay: Asia.

_____ 1966. For a Sociology of India. *Contributions to Indian Sociology* IX: 9–16.

_____ 1972. Doctors in a North Indian City: Recruitment, Role Perception, and Role Performance. In Satish Saberwal (ed.), *Beyond the Village.* Simla: Indian Institute of Advanced Study.

_____ 1975 . On Living Intimately with Strangers. In Andre Beteille and T.N. Madan (eds.), *Encounter and Experience: Personal Accounts of Fieldwork.* New Delhi: Vikas.

_____ et al. 1980. *Doctors and Society.* New Delhi: Vikas.

_____ 1982. Anthropology as the Mutual Interpretation of Cultures. In Hussein Fahim (ed.), *Indigenous Anthropology in Non-Western Countries.* Durham N.C: Carolina Academic Press.

_____ 1987. *Non-Renunciation: Themes and Interpretations of Hindu Culture.* Delhi: Oxford University Press.

_____ 1990. India in American Anthropology. In Sulochana Glazer and Nathan Glazer (eds.) *Conflicting Images: India and the United States.* Glen Dale, Maryland: Riverdale.

_____ 1994. *Pathways: Approaches to the Study of Society in India.* Delhi: Oxford University Press.

Saran, A.K. 1962. Review of 'Contributions to Indian Sociology', No. IV. *The Eastern Anthropologist* XV, I: 53–68.

How Native is
a 'Native' Anthropologist?[1]

KIRIN NARAYAN

How 'native' is a native anthropologist? How 'foreign' is an anthropologist from abroad? The paradigm polarising 'regular' and 'native' anthropologists is, after all, part of received disciplinary wisdom. Those who are anthropologists in the usual sense of the word are thought to study Others whose alien cultural worlds they must painstakingly come to know. Those who diverge as 'native,' 'indigenous,' or 'insider' anthropologists are believed to write about their own cultures from a position of intimate affinity. Certainly, there have been scattered voices critiquing this dichotomy. Arguing that since a culture is not homogenous, a society is differentiated, and a professional identity that involves problematising lived reality inevitably creates a distance, scholars such as Aguilar (1981) and Messerschmidt (1981a:9) conclude that the extent to which anyone is an authentic insider is questionable. Yet such critiques have not yet been adequately integrated into the way that 'native' anthropologists are popularly viewed in the profession.

In this essay, I argue against the fixity of a distinction between 'native' and 'non-native' anthropologists. Instead of the paradigm emphasising a dichotomy between outsider/insider, observer/ observed, I will argue that at this historical moment we might more profitably view each anthropologist in terms of shifting identifications amid a field of interpenetrating communities and power relations. The loci along which we are aligned with or set apart from those whom we study are multiple and in flux. Factors such as education, gender, sexual orientation, class, race or sheer duration of contacts may at different times outweigh the cultural identity we associated with insider or outsider status. Instead, what we must focus our attention on is the quality of relations with the people we seek to represent in our texts: are they viewed as mere fodder for professionally self-serving statements about a generalised Other, or are they accepted as subjects with voices, views, and dilemmas—people to whom we are bonded through ties of reciprocity and who may even be critical of our professional enterprise?

I write as someone who sometimes bears the label of 'native' anthropologist, and yet squirms uncomfortably under this essentialising tag. To highlight the personal and intellectual dilemmas invoked by the assumption that a 'native' anthropologist can represent an unproblematic and authentic insider's perspective, I incorporate personal narrative into a wider discussion of anthropological scholarship. Tacking between situated narrative and more sweeping analysis, I argue for the *enactment of hybridity* in our texts, that is, writing which shows up authors as minimally bi-cultural in terms of belonging simultaneously to the world of engaged scholarship and the world of everyday life.

The Problem in Historical Perspective

The paradigm that polarises 'native' anthropologists and 'real' anthropologists stems from the colonial setting in which the discipline of anthropology was forged: the days in which, from the perspective of the West, natives were genuine natives (whether they liked it or not) and the observer's objectivity in the scientific study of Other societies posed no problem. To achieve access to *the native's* point of view (note the singular pronoun), an anthropologist used the method of participant observation among a variety of representative natives, often singling out one as 'chief informant' (Casagrande 1960). A chief informant might also be trained in anthropological modes of data collection so that the society could be revealed 'from within.' As Franz Boas argued, materials reported and inscribed by a trained native would have 'the immeasurable advantage of trustworthiness, authentically revealing precisely the elusive thoughts and sentiments of the native....' (Lowie 1935:133 cited in Jones 1970:252). Or better yet, a smart and adequately westernised native might go so far as to receive the education of a bonafide anthropologist and reveal a particular society to the profession with an insider's eye. Though ordinary people commenting on their society, chief informants friendly with a foreign anthropologist, or insiders trained to collect indigeneous texts were all in some sense natives contributing to the enterprise of anthropology. Yet, it was only those who received the full professional initiation into a disciplinary fellowship of discourse who became the bearers of the title 'native' anthropologist.

Even if such a 'native' anthropologist went on to make pathbreaking professional contributions, his or her origins remained a perpetual qualifier. For example, writing the foreword to M.N. Srinivas's classic monograph on the Coorgs, Radcliffe-Brown emphasised that the writer was 'a trained anthropologist, himself an Indian' and went on to add that he had 'therefore an understanding of Indian ways of thought which it is difficult for a European to attain over many years' (Srinivas 1951:v). As Delmos Jones has charged, it is likely that 'natives' who could get 'the inside scoop' were first admitted into the charmed circle of professional discourse because they were potential tools of data collection for white male anthropologists (Jones 1970:252). Admittedly, in an era prior to extensive decolonisation world-wide, and civil rights movements in the United States, that 'natives' were allowed to participate at all in western based professional discourse was remarkable. In this context, calling attention to, rather than smoothing over 'native' identity perhaps helped to revise the engrained power imbalances in who was authorised to represent whom.

Viewed from the vantage point of the 1990s, however, it is not clear that the term 'native anthropologist' serves us well. Amid the contemporary global flows of trade, politics, migrations, ecology, and the mass-media, the accepted nexus of authentic culture—demarcated field—exotic locale has unravelled (Appadurai 1990, 1991; Clifford 1992; Gupta and Ferguson 1992). Though many of the terms of anthropological discourse remain largely set by the West, anthropology is currently practiced by members (or partial members) of previously colonised societies that now constitute the so-called Third World (Altorki and El-Solh 1988; Fahim 1982; Kumar 1992; Nakhleh 1979; Srinivas et. al. 1979). These scholars often have institutional bases in the Third World, but some have also migrated to Europe and the United States. Furthermore, in the First World, minority anthropologists also hold university positions and their contributions to ongoing discourse have helped to realign, if not overthrow, some of the discipline's ethnocentric assumptions (Gwaltney 1981; Jones 1970; Limon 1991). Feminist scholarship questioning the formulation of 'Woman as Other' has underscored the differences between women, and the multiple planes along which identity is constructed, thus destabilising the category of 'Other' as well as 'Self' (Abu-Lughod 1990; Alarcon 1990; Lauretis 1986; Mani 1990; Mohanty and Russo 1991; Strathern 1987). It has also become acceptable to turn the anthropological gaze inwards towards communities in western nations (Ginsburg 1989; Ginsburg and Tsing 1990; Martin 1987; Messerschmidt 1981b, Ortner 1991). The 'field' is increasingly a flexible concept: it can move with the travels of Hindu pilgrims (Gold 1988), span Greek villagers and New Age American healers (Danforth 1989), or even be found in automobile garages of South Philadelphia (Rose 1987). In this changed setting, a rethinking of 'insider' and 'outsider' anthropologists as stable categories seems long overdue.

Multiplex Identity or Identities?

'If Margaret Mead can live in Samoa,' my mother is reputed to have said when she moved to India, 'I can live in a joint family.' The daughter of a German father and American mother, she had just married my Indian father. Yet these terms—'German', 'American', 'Indian'—are broad labels deriving from modern nation states. Should I instead say that my mother, the daughter of a Bavarian father and WASP mother who lived in Taos, New Mexico, became involved with her fellow student at the University of Colorado: my Indian-from-India father? Yet for anyone familiar with India shouldn't I add that my father's father was from the Kutch desert region, his mother from the dense Kathiawari forests, and that while he might loosely be called 'Gujarati', his background was further complicated by growing up in the state of Maharashtra? Should I mention that

Mayflower blood supposedly mingles with that of Irish potato famine immigrants on my maternal grandmother's side (I'm told I could qualify as a 'D.A.R.'), or that as temple builders, members of my paternal grandfather's caste were always vehemently claiming a contested status as brahmin rather than artisan 'sons of Vishvakarma'? Should I add that my father was the only Hindu boy in a Parsi school that would give him a strictly British education, inscribing the caste profession-based title 'Mistri' onto the books as the surname 'Contractor'? Or would I better locate my father to say that he remembers the days when signs outside colonial clubs read 'No Dogs or Indians?' Also, is it useful to point out that my mother—American by birth—has now lived in India for over 40 years (more than two thirds of her life) and is instructed by her bossy children on how to comport herself when she visits the United States?

I invoke these threads of a culturally tangled identity to demonstrate that a person may have many strands of identification available, strands which may be tugged into the open or stuffed out of sight. A mixed background such as mine perhaps marks one as inauthentic for the label 'native' or 'indigenous' anthropologist. Perhaps those who are not clearly 'native' or 'non-native' should be termed 'halfies' instead (cf. Abu-Lughod 1991). Yet, two halves cannot adequately account for the complexity of an identity in which multiple countries, regions, religions, and classes may come together. While my siblings and I have spent much of our lives quipping that we are 'haylf' (pronounced with an American twang) and 'hahlf' (with a British-educated accent), I increasingly wonder whether any person of mixed ancestry can be so neatly split down the middle, excluding all the other vectors that have shaped them. Then too, mixed ancestry is itself a cultural fact: whether patrilineality is stressed, the localised meaning of colour, the particular groups that have mixed, and the prejudices of the time, all contribute to the mark that mixed blood leaves on a person's identity (cf. Spickard 1989).

Growing up in Bombay with a strongly stressed patrilineage, a Hindu Indian identity has weighted more than half in my self-definition, pushing into the background the Pilgrim fathers and Bavarian burghers who are also available in my genealogical repertoire. This would seem to mark me as unproblematically

Indian, and therefore, when I study India, a 'native' anthropologist. After all, researching aspects of India, I often share an unspoken emotional understanding with the people I work with (cf. Ohnuki-Tierney 1984). When I started taping the stories of a sadhu whom I called 'Swamiji' in Nasik, I had the benefit of years of association with not just Swamiji himself, but also the language and wider culture. Since Nasik was the town where my father grew up, a preexisting identity defined by kinship subsumed my presence as ethnographer (cf. Nakhleh 1979). Similarly, researching women's songs and lives in the Himalayan foothills, I bore the advantage of visiting the place practically every year since I was fifteen, and of my mother having settled there. All too well-aware of traditional expectations for proper behaviour by an unmarried daughter, in both places I repressed aspects of my cosmopolitan Bombay persona and my American self to behave with appropriate decorum and deference (cf. Abu-Lughod 1988).

In both Nasik and in Kangra, different aspects of identity became highlighted at different times. In Nasik, when elderly gentlemen wearing white Congress caps arrived and Swamiji pointed me out as 'Ramji Mistri's granddaughter,' my local roots were highlighted, and I felt a diffuse pride for my association with the Nasik landmark of the large Victorian bungalow that my grandfather had built in the 1920s. Visiting Nathu Maharaj, the barber with buck-teeth and stained clothes, to discuss interpretations of Swamiji's stories, I felt uncomfortable, even ashamed, of the ways in which my class had allowed me opportunities that were out of reach for this bright and reflective man. My gender was important in the observance of menstrual taboos not to touch Swamiji or the altar—injunctions that left me so mortified that I would simply leave town for several days. Borrowing the latest Stevie Wonder tapes from one of 'the foreigners'—a disciple from New Jersey—I savoured a rowdy release, becoming again a woman who had lived independently in a California University town. When Swamiji advised that in written texts I keep his identity obscure ('What need do I have for publicity?' yet his doctor took me aside to advise that I disregard such modesty and identify him by name, 'so people abroad will know his greatness') I felt my role as culture broker with the dubious power to extend First World prestige to Third

World realities. Yet, when Swamiji challenged my motives for taking his words on tape 'to do a business' I was set apart from all planes of locally available identification, thrown outside a circle of fellowship forged by spiritual concerns, and lumped instead with fellow academics who made it their business to document and theorise about other people's lives (Narayan 1989:59–62).

When I undertook research on women's oral traditions in the Himalayan foothill region of Kangra, I had no deep local roots. Unmoored from a certain base for identification, the extent to which others can manipulate an anthropologist's identity came into dizzying focus (Dumont 1978, Stoller 1989). Explaining my presence, some of the village women I worked with asserted that I was from such-and-such village (where my mother lives), hence local. At other times I was presented as being 'from Bombay', that is, a city dweller from a distant part of the country although still recognisably Indian. A wrinkled old woman I once fell into step with on an outing between villages asked if I was a member of the pastoral Gaddi tribe (to her, the epitome of a close-by Other). At yet other times, and particularly at weddings where a splash of foreign prestige added to the festivities, I was incontrovertibly stated to be 'from America... she came *all* the way from there for this function, yes, with her camera and her tape recorder!' In the same household at different times, I was forced to answer questions about whether all Americans were savages (*jangli log*) since television revealed that they didn't wear many clothes, and to listen as a member of a spellbound local audience when a dignified Rajput matron from another village came by to tell tales about how she had visited her emigrant son in New Jersey. In the Kangri dialect, she held forth on how, in America, people just ate 'round breads' of three sizes with vegetables and *masalas* smeared on top (pizza); how shops were enormous with everything you could imagine in them, and plastic bags you could rip off like leaves from a tree; how you put food in a 'trolley' and then a woman would press buttons giving you a bill for hundreds and hundreds of rupees! Bonded with other entranced listeners, my own claims to authoritative experience in this faraway land of wonders seemed to have temporarily dropped out of sight.

Now it might be assumed that I had experienced these shifting identifications simply because of my peculiar background, and that someone who was 'fully' Indian by birth and upbringing might have a more stable identity in the field. For a comparison, I could turn to Nita Kumar's lively and insightful *Friends, Brothers, Informants: Fieldwork Memoirs of Banaras* (1992), which makes many of the same points. Instead, I look farther back (to pre-postmodern times) and draw out some of the implications about identity from M.N. Srinivas's compelling ethnography, *The Remembered Village* (1976). Srinivas was educated in Oxford in the 1940s. On Radcliffe-Brown's advice, he planned to do fieldwork in a multi-caste village called Rampura in Mysore (Karnataka State). Srinivas's ancestors had moved several generations before from the neighbouring Tamil Nadu to rural Mysore; his father had left his village for the city so that his children could be educated. In returning from Oxford to live in a village, Srinivas stated his hope that 'my study... would enable me better to understand my personal, cultural and social roots' (1976:5).

But did the presence of these roots mean that he was regarded as a 'native' returning home to blend smoothly with other 'natives'? No, he was an educated urbanite and brahmin male, and the power of this narrative ethnography lies very much in Srinivas's sensitivity to the various ways in which he interacted with members of the community: sometimes aligned with particular groups, sometimes set apart. As he confesses, 'It was only in the village that I realised how far I (and my family) had travelled away from tradition' (1976:18). From his account, one gets the impression that villagers found him a very entertaining oddity. He struggled regularly with villagers' expectations that he behave as a brahman should (1976:33–40). Growing up in the city, he had not internalised rules of purity and pollution to the extent that they bound local brahmins, and he found himself reprimanded by the headman for shaving himself *after* rather than before a ritual bath. On the other hand, a political activist criticised him for his involvement with the headman, rather than all sections and factions of the village (1976:22). When he did move throughout the village he found himself received with affection: 'word must have gone round that I did not consider myself too high to mix with poor villagers' (1976:24). Yet as he was a respected guest and outsider, villagers as a group also colluded in keeping details of unpleasant 'incidents' regarding sex, money, and vendettas from him (1976:40–47). In a lighter vein, many villagers knew him by the exotic object he sported, a camera that fulfilled not just their ends (such as the use of photographs in arranging marriages) but also his anthropological responsibilities of recording for a foreign audience. He became 'the camera man—only they transformed "camera" into "chamara" which in Kannada means the fly-whisk made from the long hair of yak tails' (1976:20). Villagers plied him with questions about the English, and the headman even planned a tour of England in which Srinivas was to be adopted as guide (1976:29). In short, his relationships were complex and shifting: in different settings, his caste, urban background, unintended affiliations with a local faction, class privilege, attempts to bridge all sectors of the community, or alliance with a faraway land could all be highlighted.

Even as insiders or partial insiders in some contexts we are drawn closer, in others we are thrust apart. Multiple planes of identification may be most painfully highlighted among anthropologists who have identities spanning racial or cultural groups (Abu-Lughod 1988, 1991; Kondo 1986, 1990; Lavie 1990). Yet in that we all belong to several communities simultaneously (not least of all, the community we were born into, and the community of professional academics), I would argue that *every* anthropologist exhibits what Rosaldo has termed a 'multiplex subjectivity' with many cross-cutting identifications (1989:168–95). Which facet of our subjectivity we choose or are forced to accept as a defining identity can change, depending on the context. What Stuart Hall has written about cultural identity holds also for personal identity:

> But like everything which is historical, they [identities] undergo constant transformation. Far from being eternally fixed in some essentialised past, they are subject to the continuous 'play' of history, culture, and power. Far from being grounded in a mere 'recovery' of the past, which is waiting to be found, and which, when found, will secure our sense of ourselves into eternity, identities are the names we give to the different ways we are positioned by, and position ourselves within, the narratives of the past [Hall 1989:70].

Rethinking Connections Through Fieldwork

We are instructed as anthropologists to 'grasp the native's point of view, his relation to life, to realise *his* vision of *his* world' (Malinowski 1961:25). Yet who is this generic subject, 'the native'? To use a clump term is to assume that all natives are the same native, mutually substitutable in presenting the same (male) point of view. Yet even received anthropological wisdom tells us that in the simplest societies, gender and age provide factors for social differentiation. To extend conceptual tools forged for the study of heuristically bounded, simple societies to a world in which many societies and subgroups interact amid shifting fields of power, these very tools must be reexamined. We would most certainly be better off looking for the 'natives' points of view... to realise *their* visions of *their* worlds' while at the same time acknowledging that 'we' do not speak from a position outside 'their' worlds, but are implicated in them too (cf. Mani 1990; Mohanty 1989; Said 1989) through fieldwork, political relations, and a variety of global flows.

Arjun Appadurai (1988) has persuasively teased out some of the underlying assumptions in the anthropological use of the term 'native' for groups who belong to parts of the world distant and distinct from the metropolitan West. As he argues, the concept is associated with an ideology of *authenticity*: 'Proper natives are somehow assumed to represent their selves and their history, without distortion or residue' (1988:37). Those in the position to observe 'natives' however, exempt themselves from being authentic and instead represent themselves in terms of complexity, diversity, and ambiguity. Furthermore, the term is linked to *place*. 'Natives' are incarcerated in bounded geographical spaces, immobile and untouched yet paradoxically available to the mobile outsider. Appadurai goes on to show how in anthropological discourse 'natives' tied to particular places are also associated with particular *ideas*: one goes to India to study hierarchy, the circum-Mediterranean region for honour and shame, China for ancestor worship, and so on, forgetting that anthropological preoccupations represents 'the temporary *localisation* of ideas from *many* places' (1988:46, emphasis in original).

The critique that Appadurai levels at the term 'native' can also be extended to 'native' anthropologist. A 'native' anthropologist is assumed to be an insider who will forward an authentic point of view to the anthropological community. The fact that the profession as practised in the United States remains intrigued by the notion of the 'native' anthropologist as carrying a stamp of authenticity is particularly obvious in the ways in which identities are doled out to non-western, minority, or mixed anthropologists so that exotic difference overshadows commonalities or complexities. My German-American mother seems as irrelevant to others' portrayal of me as 'Indian', as the American mothers of the 'Tewa' Alphonso Ortiz, the 'Chicano' Renato Rosaldo, or 'Arab' Lila Abu-Lughod. For those of us who are mixed, the darker and patrilineal element in our ancestry serves to define us with or without our own complicity. The fact that we are often distanced—by factors as varied as education, class, or emigration—from the societies we are supposed to represent tends to be underplayed. Furthermore, it is only appropriate (and this may be the result of our own identity quests) that sooner or later we will study the exotic societies we are associated with. Finally, while it is hoped that we will contribute to the existing anthropological pool of knowledge, we are not really expected to diverge from prevailing forms of discourse to frame what Delmos Jones has called a genuinely 'native' anthropology as 'a set of theories based on non-western precepts and assumptions' (1970:251).

'Native' anthropologists, then, are perceived as insiders regardless of their complex background. The differences between kinds of native anthropologists are also obliviously passed over. Can a person from an impoverished American minority background who despite all prejudices manages to get an education and study her own community be equated with a member of a Third World elite group who, backed by excellent schooling and parental funds, studies anthropology abroad and then returns home for fieldwork among the less privileged? Is it not insensitive to suppress the issue of location, acknowledging that a scholar who chooses an institutional base in the Third World might have a different engagement with western-based theories, books, and political stances'? Is a middle-class white professional researching aspects of her own society also a 'native' anthropologist?

And what about non-'native' anthropologists who have dedicated themselves to long-term fieldwork, returning year after year to sustain ties in a particular community? Should we not grant them some recognition for the different texture this brings to their work? It is generally considered more savvy in terms of professional advancement to do fieldwork in several different cultures rather than returning to deepen understandings in one. Yet to use people one has lived with for articles and monographs, and not maintain ties through time generates a sort of 'hit-and-run' anthropology in which engagement with vibrant individuals are flattened by the demands of a scholarly career. Having a safe footing to return to outside the field situation promotes 'a contemplative stance... [that] pervades anthropology, disguising the confrontation between Self and Other and rendering the discipline powerless to address the vulnerability of the Self' (Dwyer 1982:269). Regular returns to a field site, on the other hand, can nourish the growth of responsible human ties and the subsuming of cultural difference within the fellowship of a 'We-relation' (Schutz 1973:16–17). As George Foster and the other editors of the book *Long-Term Field Research in Social Anthropology* point out in their concluding comments, an ongoing personal involvement with people in the communities studied often makes for an interest in 'action' or 'advocacy' work (1979:344). Looking beyond the human rewards to the professional ones, long-term fieldwork also leads to the stripping away of formal self-presentations and the granting of access to cultural domains generally reserved for insiders, thus making better scholarship. Returns to the field allows for a better understanding of how individuals creatively shape themselves and their societies through time. Finally, repeated returns to the field force an anthropologist to reconsider herself and her work not just from the perspective of the academy but also that of the people she purports to represent. As Paul Stoller has written about his long-term fieldwork among the Songhay in Niger:

> Besides giving me the perspective to assess social change, long term study of Songhay has plunged me into the Songhay worlds of sorcery and possession, worlds the wisdom of which are closed to outsiders—even Songhay outsiders. My insistence on long-term study forced me to confront the

interpretive errors of earlier visits. Restudying Songhay also enabled me to get a bit closer to 'getting it right'. But I have just begun to walk my path. As Adamu Jenitongo once told me, 'Today you are learning about us, but to understand us, you will have to grow old with us' [Stoller 1989:6].

While Stoller was not born Songhay, his ongoing engagement has given him a niche in the society, a place from which he is invited to 'grow old' *with* his teacher. Like all long-term relationships, his encounters in the field have had exhilarating ups and cataclysmic downs, yet persevering on has brought the reward of greater insight. Do not anthropologists who engage sensitively in long-term fieldwork also deserve respect from their professional colleagues as partial insiders who have through time become bi-cultural (cf. Tedlock 1991)? Need a 'native' anthropologist be so very different?

It might be argued that the condescending colonial connotations of a generic identity that cling to the term 'native' might be lessened by using alternative words: 'indigenous' or 'insider' for example. Yet the same conceptual underpinnings apply to these terms too: they all imply that an authentic insider's perspective is possible, and that this can unproblematically represent the associated group. This leads us to underplay the ways in which people born within a society can be simultaneously both insiders and outsiders, just as those born elsewhere can be outsiders and, if they are lucky, insiders too. Also, as Elizabeth Colson has bluntly stated, " 'Indigenous' is a misnomer, for all of us are indigenous somewhere and the majority of anthropologists at some time deal with their own communities" (Fahim et al. 1980:650). We are *all* 'native' or 'indigenous' anthropologists in this scheme. Rather than try to sort out who is authentically a 'native' anthropologist and who is not, surely it is more rewarding to examine the ways in which each one of us is situated in relation to the people we study.

Situated Knowledge

Visiting Nasik as a child, I knew better than to touch Maharaj, the chubby brahmin cook, as he bent over to fill our shining steel *thalis* on the floor; yet if asked, I would never have been able to explain this in terms of 'purity and pollution'. I knew that servants were frequently shouted at, and that they wore ill-fitting, cast-off clothes, but I did not call this 'social inequality'. I observed that my girl cousins were fed after the boys and that though they excelled in school they were not expected to have careers, but I did not call it 'gender hierarchy'. I listened raptly when the Harveys, a British couple who had stayed on after 1947 told us stories about Viceroys and Collectors, but I did not know the words 'colonisation' or 'decolonisation'. When amid the volley of British authors our minds were shaped by in school, we finally came across poems by Rabindranath Tagore, I noticed that these were different but did not call them 'nationalist'. Reflecting on India with the vocabulary of a social analyst, I find that new light is shed on many of the experiences that have shaped me into the person—and professional—I am today.

In sōme ways, the study of one's own society involves an inverse process from the study of an alien one. Instead of learning conceptual categories and then, through fieldwork, finding the contexts in which to apply them, those of us who study societies in which we have a preexisting experience absorb categories that rename and reframe what is already known. The reframing essentially involves locating vivid particulars within larger cultural patterns, sociological relations, and historical shifts. At one further remove, anthropological categories also rephrase these particulars as evidence of theoretical issues that cross cultures and are the special provenance of trained academics.

Yet, given the diversity in culture and across social groups, even the most experienced of 'native' anthropologists cannot know everything about his or her own society (Aguilar 1981). In fact, by opening up access to hidden stores of research materials, the study of anthropology can also lead to the discovery of many strange and unfamiliar aspects of one's own society (cf. Stewart 1989:14). I have learned, for example, a good deal more about village life, regional differences, tribal groups than what my urban upbringing supplied. Institutions and belief-systems that I took for granted as immutable reality—such as 'caste' or 'Hinduism'—have been dismantled as historical and discursive constructions. Even as a purported insider, it is impossible to be omniscient: one knows about a society from particular locations within it (cf. Srinivas 1966:154).

As anthropologists we do fieldwork whether or not we are raised close to the people who we study. Whatever the methodologies used, the process of doing fieldwork involves getting to know a range of people and listening closely to what they say. Even if one should already be acquainted with some of these people before one starts fieldwork, the intense and sustained engagements of fieldwork will inevitably transmute these relationships. Fieldwork is a common plane binding professional anthropologists, but the process and outcome varies so widely that it is difficult to make a clear-cut distinction between the experiences of those with prior exposure and those who arrive as novices. As Nita Kumar writes in her memoir of fieldwork in Banaras (which she had only visited before as the sheltered, anglicised daughter of a highly placed Indian government official): 'Fieldwork consists of experiences shared by all anthropologists; the personal and the peculiar are significant as qualities that *always* but *differently* characterise each individual experience' (1992:6, emphases in original).

To acknowledge particular and personal locations is to acknowledge the limits of one's purview from these positions. It is also to undermine the notion of objectivity, since from a vantage of particular locations all understanding becomes subjectively based and forged through interactions within fields of power relations. Positioned knowledge and partial perspectives are part of the language that has risen to common usage in the 1980s (Clifford 1986, 1988; Haraway 1988; Kondo 1986; Rosaldo 1989). Yet let us not forget the prescient words of Jacques Maquet from an article in which he argued that decolonisation laid bare the 'perspectivist' character of anthropology in Africa, showing up anthropology's claim to objectivity as entwined with power relations in which one group could claim to represent another. Arguing against objectivity in a polemic at least 20 years ahead of its time, he writes:

A perspectivist knowledge is not as such non-objective: it is partial. It reflects an external reality but only an aspect of it, the one visible from the particular spot, social and individual, where the anthropologist was placed. Non-objectivity creeps in when the partial aspect is considered as the global one [Maquet 1964:54].

Enacting Hybridity

'Suppose you and I are walking on road,' said Swamiji. 'You've gone to University. I haven't studied anything. We're walking. Some child has shit on the road. We both step in it. "That's shit!" I say. I scrape my foot; it's gone. But educated people have doubts about everything. You say, "What's this?!" and you rub your foot against the other.' Swamiji shot up from his prone position in the deckchair, and placing his feet on the linoleum, stared at them with intensity. He rubbed the right sole against the left ankle. 'Then you reach down to feel what it could be,' his fingers now explored the ankle. A grin was breaking over his face. ' "Something sticky!" You lift some up and sniff it. Then you say, "Oh! This is *shit*." ' The hand which had vigorously rubbed his nose was flung out in a gesture of disgust.

Swamiji turned back toward me, cheeks lifted under their white stubble in a toothless and delighted grin. Everyone present in the room was laughing uncontrollably. I managed an uncomfortable smile.

'See how many places it touched in the meantime,' Swamiji continued. 'Educated people always doubt everything. They lie awake at night thinking, "What was that? Why did it happen? What is the meaning and the cause of it?" Uneducated people pass judgment and walk on. They get a good night's sleep.'

I looked up at Swamiji from my position on the floor and tried to avoid the eyes of the others who watched me with broad smiles on their faces. 'What was that? Why was it? What is the meaning and the cause of it?' rang in my ears as a parody of my own relentless questioning as an anthropologist interviewing both Swamiji and his listeners. I had to agree that among the academics I represented, analysis could often become obsessive. But I also felt awkward, even a little hurt. This parable seemed to dismiss all the years that education had dominated my life. It ridiculed my very presence in this room.

In his peculiar mixture of sternness and empathy, Swamiji must have read the discomfort on my face. When the settled back into his deckchair, he turned to me again. 'It's not that you shouldn't study,' he said, voice low and kind. 'You should gain wisdom. But you should realise that in the end this means nothing.'

Once again, Swamiji was needling any possible self-importance that might be ballooning inside me as self-appointed documentator and analyst of what to others was everyday life. While others enjoyed his stories and learned from them, I brought the weightiness of perpetual enquiry to the enterprise. Every action was evaluated (at least partially) in terms of my project on folk narrative as a form of religious teaching. Now Swamiji had turned his technique of instruction through stories on me. Through a parable, he dramatised how we both coexisted in shared time and space 'walking the same road', yet each with a different awareness. The power-relations of 'structured inequality' (Dwyer 1982; Rabinow 1977) that allow anthropologists to subsume their subjects in representation had been turned on its head with such a critique.

This uncomfortable scene dramatises how the issue of who is an insider and who is an outsider is secondary to the need for dismantling objective distance to acknowledge our shared presence in the cultural worlds that we describe. Pioneering works on 'native' anthropology emphasised the need for such anthropologists to achieve distance. Yet, distance, as Dorinne Kondo (1986) has observed, is both a stance and a cognitive/emotional orientation that makes for cold, generalised, purportedly objective and yet inevitably prejudiced forms of representation. As Kondo argues, it can be replaced with the acceptance of 'more experiential and affective modes of knowing' (1986:75) in which the ethnographer's identity and location are made explicit and informants are given a greater role in texts. This is what Michael Jackson (1989) has more recently called, 'radical empiricism': a methodology and discursive style that emphasises the subject's experience and involvement with others in the construction of knowledge (cf. Stoller 1992).

To question the discipline's canonical modes of objective distance is not, however, to forfeit subjective distance and pretend that all fieldwork is a celebration of communitas. Given the multiplex nature of identity, there will inevitably be certain facets of self that join us up with the people we study, other facets which emphasise our difference. In even the closest of relationships, disjunctures can swell into distance; ruptures in communication can occur that must be bridged. To acknowledge such shifts in relationships rather than present them as purely distant or purely close is to enrich the textures of our texts so they more closely approximate the complexities of lived interaction. At the same time, frankness about actual interactions means than an anthropologist cannot hide superficial understandings behind sweeping statements and is forced to present the grounds of understanding. Further, as Lila Abu-Lughod has argued in regard to what she calls 'ethnographies of the particular,' by writing in terms of 'particular individuals and their changing relationships, one would necessarily subvert the most problematic connotations of cultures: homogeneity, coherence, and timelessness' (1991:154).

These insights, then hold radical implications for anthropological modes of representation. As I see it, there are currently two poles to anthropological writing: at one end stand accessible ethnographies laden with stories and at the other end stand refereed journal articles, dense with theoretical analyses. In American universities, such narrative ethnographies are routinely assigned in 'Intro to Anthro' classes (even if these are not written by professional anthropologists but their wives (Fernea 1965; Shostak 1981)) because it is through narratives lively with people, places and events that recalcitrant undergraduates are likely to be seduced by the discipline. Reading these ethnographies, we ourselves may forget we are judgmental professionals, so swept along are we in the evocative flow of other people's experiences. Narrative ethnography is one arena in which the literary critic Mary Pratt's blunt diagnosis that ethnographic writing is boring (1986:33) simply does not apply. Journal articles, on the other hand, tend to be exclusively of interest to academics initiated into the fellowship of professional discourse, and subscribing members of a particular, academically formed society. Journal articles are written according to formulae which include a thesis introduced in the beginning and returned to at the end, and the invention that theoretical frameworks and generalised statements should be forefronted, suppressing vivid particulars. We read these articles with our minds more than our hearts, extorting ideas and references from their pages.

Need the two categories, compelling narrative and rigorous analysis, be impermeable? Increasingly, they seep into each other, and here I want to argue for an emerging style in anthropological writing that I call the *enactment of hybridity* (cf. Abu-Lughod 1992; Behar 1993; Jackson 1989; Kondo 1990; Lavie 1990; Rose 1986; Stoller 1989; Rosaldo 1989, Tedlock 1992). In using the word 'enactment', I am drawing on Dorinne Kondo's view that 'the *specificity* of...experience...is not opposed to theory; it *enacts* and *embodies* theory' (1990, emphases in original): any writing then, can be an enactment of some sort of theory. By 'hybridity', I do not mean only a condition of people who are mixed from birth, but also a state that all anthropologists partake of but may not consciously include in our texts. We are all incipiently bi- (or multi-) cultural in that we belong to worlds both personal and professional, whether in the field or at home. While people with Third World allegiances, minorities, or women may experience the tensions of this dual identity the most strongly, it is a condition of everyone, even of that conglomerate category termed 'white men'. Whether we are disempowered or empowered by prevailing power relations, we must all take responsibility for how our personal locations feed into our scholarly texts. When professional personae altogether efface situated and experiencing selves, this makes for misleading scholarship even as it does violence to the range of hybrid personal and professional identities that we negotiate in our daily lives.

Adopting a narrative voice involves an ethical stance that neither effaces ourselves as hybrid nor defaces the vivid humanity of the people with whom we work. Narrative transforms 'informants' whose chief role is to spew cultural data for the anthropologist into subjects with complex lives and a range of opinions (that as Swamiji demonstrated, may even subsume the anthropological enterprise). At a moment in which scholarship has a 'multinational reception' (cf. Mani 1990), it seems more urgent than ever that anthropologists acknowledge that it is *people* and not theoretical puppets who populate our texts, and that we allow these people to speak out in our writings.

Also, narratives are not transparent representations of what actually happened, but are told for particular purposes, from particular points of view: they are thus incipiently analytical, enacting theory. Analysis itself is most effective when it builds directly from a case evoked through narrative, so providing a chance to step away, reflect on, and reframe the rivetting particulars of the story at hand. In including the perspective of the social analyst along with narratives from or about people studied, a stereoscopic 'double vision' can be achieved (Rosaldo 1989:127–143). Some skillfully constructed analyses can even read like good mystery stories, starting from a conundrum, then assembling clues that finally piece together. Narrative and analysis are categories we tend to set up as opposites, yet a closer look reveals that they are contiguous, with an open border.

Calling for a greater integration of narrative into written texts does not mean that analysis is to be abandoned, but rather, that it moves over, giving vivid experience an honoured place beside it. The key to the coexistence of narrative and analysis is *relevance*. While some orders of personal experience are relevant to the situation described, others simply are not, and including them may be a useless exercise in self-indulgence that gives narrative a bad name. Similarly, some kinds of analysis are relevant to the human situations described, and others are an empty display of theoretical virtuosity high above the ground. By translating professional jargon into 'the language of everyday life' (cf. Abu-Lughod 1991:151), analysis can also be made intriguing to audiences who would otherwise be compelled only by narrative. Admittedly, writing strategies cannot singlehandedly change the inequalities in today's world; yet in bearing the potential to change the attitudes of readers, ethical and accessible writing unquestionably takes a step in the right direction. As companions clothed in non-technical language, narrative and analysis join to push open the doors of anthropological understanding and welcome in outsiders.

Conclusions

I have argued for a reorientation in the ways that we perceive anthropologists as 'outside' or 'inside' a society. The traditional view has been to polarise 'real' anthropologists from 'native' anthropologists with the underlying assumption that a 'native' anthropologist would forward an authentic insider's view to the profession. This view sprang from a colonial era in which inegalitarian power relations were relatively well defined: there was little question about the 'civilised' outsider's ability to represent 'primitive' peoples, and so it was worthy of note when a person excluded from the dominant white culture was allowed to describe his or her own society. With changing times, however, the scope of anthropology has shifted to include industrialised societies even as it is also practised in 'Third World' countries and by 'Third World' and minority scholars. Identity, always multiplex, has become even more complex at this historical moment in which global flows in trade, politics, and the media stimulate greater interpenetrations between cultures.

In this changed setting, I have argued that it is more profitable to focus on shifting identities in relationship with the people and issues an anthropologist seeks to represent. Even if one can blend into a particular social group without the quest of fieldwork, the very nature of researching what to others is taken-for-granted reality creates an uneasy distance. On the other hand, even if one starts out as a stranger, sympathies and ties developed through engaged coexistence may subsume difference within relationships of reciprocity. 'Objectivity' must be replaced by an involvement that is unabashedly subjective as it interacts with and invites other subjectivities to take a place in anthropological productions. Knowledge, in this scheme, is not transcendental, but situated, negotiated, and part of an ongoing process. This process spans personal, professional, and cultural domains.

As we rethink 'insiders' and 'outsiders' in anthropology, I have argued that we should also work to melt down other, related divides. One wall stands between ourselves as interested readers of stories and as theory-driven professionals; another wall stands between narrative (associated with subjective knowledge) and analysis (associated with objective truths). By situating ourselves as subjects simultaneously touched by life-experience and swayed by professional concerns, we can acknowledge the hybrid and positioned nature of our identities. Writing texts that mix lively narrative and rigorous analysis involves enacting hybridity, regardless of our origins.

Notes

1. An earlier version of this essay was published in the *American Anthropologist* 95:3, September 1993, pp. 671–86.

Though I knew Swamiji since 1970, I lived in Nasik investigating his storytelling between June and September 1983 and July and October 1985; my thanks to him for hospitality and generous instruction extend across the years. Kangra has been my second home since 1975 but I undertook a year's fieldwork on village women's oral traditions there between September 1991 and August 1992. My special thanks to Didi Contractor, Sarla Korla, Urmila Devi Sood, Jagadamba Pandit and Veena Dogra for their help. I am extremely grateful for a National Science Foundation Graduate Fellowship, a University of California at Berkeley Graduate Humanities Research Grant, a Robert H. Lowie Fellowship, a Charlotte W. Newcombe dissertation Writing Fellowship, support from the University of Wisconsin Graduate School, an American Institute of Indian Studies Senior Fellowship and a National Endowment for the Humanities Fellowship. My deep thanks to Eytan Bercovitch, Ruth Behar, Ann Gold, Smadar Lavie, Maria Lepowsky, Renato Rosaldo, Janis Shough, Paul Stoller, Anna Tsing, and Kamala Visweswaran for conversations about and comments on issues raised in this essay. I am also grateful to Meenakshi Thapan for her interest and encouragement.

References

Abu-Lughod, Lila. 1988. 'Fieldwork of a Dutiful Daughter'. In S. Altorki and C. Fawzi El-Solh (eds.), *Arab Women in the Field*. Syracuse: Syracuse University Press: pp. 139–61.

_____ 1990. 'Can There Be a Feminist Ethnography?' In *Women and Performance: A Journal of Feminist Theory* 5:7–27.

_____ 1991. 'Writing Against Culture'. In Richard Fox ed., *Recapturing Anthropology*. Santa Fe: School of American Research Press: pp. 137–62.

_____ 1992. *Writing Women's Worlds: Bedouin Stories*. Berkeley: University of California Press.

Aguilar, John: 'Insider Research: An Ethnography of a Debate. In Donald Messerschmidt (ed.), *Anthropologists at Home in North America*. Cambridge: Cambridge University Press: pp. 15–26.

Alarcon, Norma. 1990. 'The Theoretical Subject(s) of This Bridge Called My Back in Anglo-American Feminism'. In G. Anzaldua (ed.), *Making Face/Making Soul: Creative and Critical Perspectives on Women of Colour*. San Francisco: Aunt Lute Foundation: pp. 356–69.

Altorki, Soraya and Camillia Fawzi El-Solh (eds.). 1988. *Arab Women in the Field: Studying Your Own Society*. Syracuse: Syracuse University Press.

Appadurai, Arjun. 1988. 'Putting Hierarchy in its Place'. In *Cultural Anthropology*, 3:36–49.

_____ 1990. 'Disjuncture and Difference in the Global Cultural Economy'. In *Public Culture* 2:1–24.

1991. 'Global Ethnoscapes: Notes and Queries for a Transnational Anthropology'. In Richard Fox (ed.), *Recapturing Anthropology*. Santa Fe: School of American Research Press: pp. 191–210.

Behar, Ruth. 1993. *Translated Woman: Crossing the Border with Esperanza's Story*. Boston: Beacon Press.

Casagrande, Joseph (ed.), 1960. *In the Company of Man: Twenty Portraits by Anthropologists* New York: Harper and Row.

Clifford, James. 1986. 'Introduction: Partial Truths', in James Clifford and George Marcus (eds.), *Writing Culture: The Poetics and Politics of Ethnography*. Berkeley and London: University of California Press: pp. 1–26.

_____ 1988. *The Predicament of Culture*. Cambridge: Harvard University Press.

_____ 1989. *Firewalking and Religious Healing: The Anasteria of Greece and the American Firewalking Movement*. Princeton, N.J.: Princeton University Press.

_____ 1992. 'Travelling Cultures'. In L. Grossberg, C. Nelson and Paula Treichler (eds.), *Cultural Studies*. New York: Routledge, Danforth, Loring: pp. 96–116.

Dumont, Jean Paul. 1978. *The Headman and I*. Austin: University of Texas Press.

Dwyer, Kevin. 1982. *Moroccan Dialogues: Anthropology in Question*. Prospect Heights, Ill.: Waveland Press.

Fahim, Hussein. 1982. *Indigenous Anthropology in Non-western Countries*. Durham, N.C.: Carolina Academic Press.

Fahim, Hussein, Katherine Helmer, Elizabeth Colson, T.N. Madan, Herbert C. Kelman and Talal Asad. 1980. 'Indigenous Anthropology in Non-western Countries: A Further Elaboration'. In *Current Anthropology* 21:644–663.

Fernea, Elizabeth, 1965. *Guests of the Sheik: An Ethnography of an Iraqi Village*. New York: Doubleday.

Foster, George M., T. Scudder, E. Colson and R.V. Kemper (eds.) 1979. *Long Term Field Research in Social Anthropology*. New York: Academic Press.

Ginsburg, Faye. 1989. *Contested Lives: The Abortion Debate in an American Community*. Berkeley: University of California Press.

_____ and Anna Lowenhaupt Tsing. 1990. *Uncertain Terms: Negotiating Gender in American Culture*. Boston: Beacon Press.

Gold, Ann. 1988. *Fruitful Journeys: The Ways of Rajasthani Pilgrims*. Berkeley: University of California Press.

Gupta, Akhil and Ferguson, James. 1992. 'Beyond "Culture": Space, Identity, and the Politics of Difference'. In *Cultural Anthropology* 7:6–23.

Gwaltney, John L. 1981. 'Common Sense and Science: Urban Core Black Observations'. In Donald Messerschmidt (ed.), *Anthropologists at Home in North America: Methods and Issues in the Study of One's Own Society*. Cambridge: Cambridge University Press: pp. 46–61.

Hall, Stuart. 1989. 'Cultural Identity and Cinematic Representation'. In *Framework* 36:68–81.

Haraway, Donna. 1988. 'Situated Knowledges: The Science Question in Feminism and the Privilege of Partial Perspective'. In *Feminist Studies* 14:575–99.

Jackson, Michael. 1989. *Paths Towards a Clearing: Radical Empiricism and Ethnographic Enquiry*. Bloomington: Indiana University Press.

Jones, Delmos J. 1970. 'Toward a Native Anthropology'. *Human Organisation* 29:251–59.

Kondo, Dorinne. 1986. 'Dissolution and Reconstitution of Self: Implications for Anthropological Epistemology. In *Cultural Anthropology* 1:74–96.

———— 1990. *Crafting Selves: Power, Gender and Discourses of Identity in a Japanese Workplace*. Chicago: University of Chicago Press.

Kumar, Nita. 1992. *Friends, Brothers, Informants: Fieldwork Memoirs of Banaras*. Berkeley: University of California Press.

Lauretis, Teresa de. 1986. 'Feminist Studies/Critical Studies: Issues, Terms, and Contexts.' In Teresa de Lauretis (ed.), *Feminist Studies/Critical Studies*. Bloomington: Indiana University Press: pp. 1–19.

Lavie, Smadar. 1990. *The Poetics of Military Occupation*. Berkeley: University of California Press.

Limon, Jose. 1991. 'Representation, Ethnicity, and the Precursory Ethnography: Notes of a Native Anthropologist'. In Richard Fox (ed.), *Recapturing Anthropology*. Santa Fe, N.M.: School of American Research Press. pp. 115–36.

Lowie, Robert. 1937. *A History of Ethnological Theory*. New York: Holt, Rinehart and Winston, Inc.

Malinowski, Bronislaw. 1961 (1922). *Argonauts of the Western Pacific*. New York: E.P. Dutton.

Mani, Lata. 1990. 'Multiple Mediations: Feminist Scholarship in the Age of Multinational Reception'. In *Feminist Review* 35:24–41.

Maquet, Jacques. 1964. 'Objectivity in Anthropology'. *Current Anthropology* 5:47–55.

Messerschmidt, Donald. 1981a 'On Anthropology "at Home" '. In Donald Messerschmidt (ed.), *Anthropologists at Home in North America: Methods and Issues in the Study of One's Own Culture*. Cambridge: Cambridge University Press: pp.1–14.

Messerschmidt, Donald, (ed.) 1981b. *Anthropologists at Home in North America: Methods and Issues in the Study of One's Own Society*. Cambridge: Cambridge University Press.

Mohanty, Chandra and Ann Russo (eds.), 1991. *Third World Women and the Politics of Feminism*. Bloomington, Indiana: Indiana University Press.

Mohanty, Satya. 1989. 'Us and Them'. In *New Formations* 8:55–80.

Nakhleh, Khalil. 1979. 'On being a Native Anthropologist'. In G. Huizer and B. Mannheim (eds.), *The Politics of Anthropology: From Colonialism and Sexism to the View from Below*. The Hague: Mouton: pp. 343–52.

Narayan, Kirin. 1989. *Storytellers, Saints, and Scoundrels: Folk Narrative in Hindu Religious Teaching*. Philadelphia: University of Pennsylvania Press.

Ohnuki-Tierney, Emiko. 1984. 'Native Anthropologists'. In *American Ethnologist* 11:584–86.

Ortner, Sherry. 1991. 'Reading America: Preliminary Notes on Class and Culture'. In Richard Fox (ed.), *Recapturing Anthropology*. Santa Fe: School of American Research: pp. 163–89.

Rabinow, Paul. 1977. *Reflections on Fieldwork in Morocco*. Berkeley and Los Angeles. University of California Press.

Rosaldo, Renato. 1989. *Culture and Truth: The Remaking of Social Analysis*. Boston: Beacon.

Rose, Dan. 1987. *Black American Street Life: South Philadelphia 1969–71.* Philadelphia: University of Pennsylvania Press.

Said, Edward. 1989. 'Representing the Colonized: Anthropology's Interlocutors'. In *Critical Inquiry* 15:205–25.

Schutz, Alfred. 1973. *Collected Papers Volume I: The Problem of Social Reality.* The Hague: Mouton.

Shostak, Marjorie. 1981. *Nisa: The Life and Words of a !Kung Woman.* Cambridge, MA: Harvard University Press.

Spickard, Paul R. 1989. *Mixed Blood: Intermarriage and Ethnic Identity in Twentieth Century America.* Madison: University of Wisconsin Press.

Srinivas, M.N. 1952. *Religion and Society Among the Coorgs of Southern India.* New Delhi: Oxford University Press.

———— 1966. 'Some Thoughts on the Study of One's Own Society'. In M.N. Srinivas, *Social Change in Modern India.* New Delhi. Orient Longman.

———— 1976. *The Remembered Village.* New Delhi: Oxford University Press.

Srinivas, M.N., A.M. Shah and E.A. Ramaswamy. 1979. *The Fieldworker and the Field: Problems and Challenges in Sociological Investigation.* Delhi: Oxford University Press.

Stewart, John D. 1989. *Drinkers, Drummers, and Decent Folk. Ethnographic Narratives in Village Trinidad.* Albany, New York: State University of New York Press.

Stoller, Paul. 1989. *The Taste of Ethnographic Things.* Philadelphia: University of Pennsylvania Press.

———— 1992. *The Cinematic Griot: The Ethnography of Jean Rouch.* Chicago: University of Chicago Press.

Strathern, Marilyn. 1987. 'An Awkward Relationship: The Case of Feminism and Anthropology'. In *Signs* 12: 276–94.

Tedlock, Barbara. 1991. 'From Participant Observation to the Observation of Participation: The Emergence of Narrative Ethnography.' In *Journal of Anthropological Research* 47:69–94.

———— 1992. *The Beautiful and the Dangerous: Encounters with the Zuni Indians.* New York: Viking.

Among My Own in Another Culture: Meeting The Asian Indian Americans

MAITRAYEE CHAUDHURI

Introduction

This paper stems from my field experience in Cambridge, Massachusets in the United States of America carried out from September 1995 to the end of May 1996. The objective of my research was to look at the ways in which 'Indians' in Cambridge were defining their cultural identity. I use the term 'Indian' in quotes, for this paper is a story, in part, of the dismantling of the self-evident ease with which I once described myself as 'Indian.' In part it is the story of how I started off with the assumption that my subject of study were 'Indians' only to learn my first lesson in redefining them as Asian Indian Americans, a term completely alien to me, as un-Indian as anything else American could be. The term itself was entered in the American Census only in 1986. But it had its roots in the basic mode of classification of race and ethnic groups by the American state from its very inception. That is an American story within which I learnt to locate the Asian Indian. The moot question then was whether I was learning about my own culture or another culture. Put differently did my 'object' of study see me as one of their own, or as belonging to another culture. It is this process of mutual interpretation that I explore in the paper. What did they mean by 'Indian culture'? What did being 'Indian' mean to them? How does gender figure in the notion of 'Indianness'?

How different or similar was it from what being 'Indian' meant to me? Did I think of 'Indian culture' the way they did? What accounted for the sameness or difference? And why is 'culture' so central for them in defining their identity?

Since 'culture' is a key concept for this paper a clarification of the way the term is being used here may be in order. I recount two fairly typical uses. Narrating the kind of activities a South Asian student group in the Massachusets Institute of Technology (MIT) were holding, a spokesperson said 'We are interested in South Asian[1] culture and heritage', and 'We have speakers, sometimes first generation and sometimes second generation, who know a lot about their culture, to come and speak.' Responding to my query regarding the kind of events which they have organised in the past, he mentioned 'history of Bengal, food, music and Tagore.' The same kind of understanding of culture emerges in the following account of a second generation 'Indian.'

> ...the date of our parents' arrival in this country is important because it limited our cultural options. This slice of the second generation was raised without 'Indian friends, Bharatnatyam dance classes, Karnatic music recitals, Hindu temple societies, or Hindi films', because the large Indian communities of Los Angeles or the San Fransisco Bay Area, Dallas or New York, were not firmly established until the mid-seventies (Visweswaran 1995:301).

In this casual recounting of the elements that could collectively lead to learning 'culture' two meanings of culture emerge. The first is E.B. Tylor's 1871 formula as a group's total body of behaviour—both what one eats and how one thinks. The second is Matthew Arnold's version, in the 1860's, of a society's reservoir of the best that has been known and thought.

Within this broad context what appeared central to me was the way in which this 'culture', however understood, was being made and remade. I emphasise this 'inventive' aspect of culture. Indeed it has been argued that culture has been tied up with the 'invention' of anthropology (Wagner 1975). Unlike earlier generations of anthropologists who thought of anthropology in essentialist terms, it is widely recognised today that culture is a creation on our part. Cultures materialise in contradiction to one another and anthropology had tended to cement the exagerration, and to describe the other as everything we are not. This contrast was facilitated by the historical context within which anthropology emerged in an age of Western discovery and 'invention' of the others in the world. The world has vastly changed since then. The last two hundred years of history for the non-Western world has seen societies changing irrevocably, first as colonialism redefined economies and polities, law and culture, and second as anti-colonial nationalism initiated a process of creating a national culture.

I move from the more generic term 'culture' to 'national culture' for since the eighteenth century, one of the defining marks of modernity has been the use of two linked concepts of association—citizenship and nationality—to establish the meaning of full membership in society (Hoston and Appadurai 1996:187). This was a belief shared by both the subjects of my ethnographic focus, the Asian Indian Americans, and by me, the ethnographer defined as just Indian. As Ernest Gellner puts it:

> The idea of a man [sic] without a nation seems to impose a (great) strain on the modern imagination. A man must have a nationality as he must have a nose and two ears. All this seems obvious, though, alas it is not true. But that it should have come to seem so obviously true indeed is an aspect, perhaps the very core, of the problem of nationalism. Having a nation is not an inherent attribute of humanity, but it has now come to appear as such (Gellner 1983:6).

Against this background it is not surprising that culture is essentially national culture. And not surprisingly too, the idea of culture carries with it an expectation of roots, of a stable, territorialised identity (Clifford 1988:338). Since common notions of culture are biased toward rooting rather than travel, broken roots signal an ailing cultural identity and damaged nationality. Asian Indian Americans have travelled away from their land, their roots are broken, and their need therefore for a strong cultural identity that much more urgent. Culture is no longer available naturally to them from merely living in the nation. For

me it was my ethnographic encounter that prompted me to think
out what it is that Indian culture means. This is a theme which
repeatedly emerged. A young girl told me:

> What problem could you be having? Even if you do not wear
> Indian clothes it does not matter. I have to. You are naturally
> Indian. I have to learn to be one. And even if I wear Indian
> clothes, people in India immediately know I am not an
> Indian. I have travelled in a salwar kameez in a bus. I had
> not spoken a word. And yet at the end of the journey, the old
> woman sitting next to me asked me where outside India I
> was from.

If culture has to be defined nationally, what culture but Indian
culture can an Indian have. The problem is that national cultural
identities are not what we are born with, but are formed and
transformed within and in relation to representation. We only
know what it is to be 'Indian' because of the way Indianness has
come to be represented, as a set of meanings.

In this narrative the construction of history plays a pivotal
role. It may not be out of place here to mention that my main
area of academic research in the past was the interconnected way
in which Indian nationalism, communalism and the women's
issue defined themselves in colonial India. I was familiar with
the literature on the constructions of communalism and
nationalism, the dominant model of Indian womanhood,
inventions of tradition and the significance of reconstructing
history for the cultural and political agenda of the nation. But I
had not lived in that period to witness this process of invention.
In Cambridge however I found myself amidst a community
who were literally in the midst of creating for themselves a
cultural identity and thereby necessarily a history as Asian
Indian Americans, an identity closely interconnected to the roles
the community set for itself as a minority ethnic group within
the American nation state. Their history therefore could not be
mine.

The next section deals first with a very brief history of the
community and second with the making of their history as
identity, an identity linked closely with the future agenda of the
community in the United States.

History and the Asian Indian American in America

Before I begin on the history of the Asian Indian Americans,[2] I must mention that this is a beginning which I learnt in the field. I have often wondered, had the field encounter not been, where would I begin telling the story of Asian Indian Americans. Most likely with their departure from India. In America the story for everybody begins on arrival, a point I get back to later.

For most Indians the date of their history begins in the sixties, when Indians began migrating in large numbers after the passage of the Immigration Act of 1965, which ended the national origin quota system. This is actually the second wave migration for a first wave of migrants from India, predominantly Punjabi, reached the western shores of North America, a good hundred years earlier. Most post-1965 first generation immigrants knew next to nothing about them and more importantly saw little in common with them. A deliberate move however is underway to retrieve their history and merge the history of Asian Indian immigrants as one, for reasons which I go into later in this section. I thus begin a hundred years earlier.

A hundred years ago, Indians, mainly peasants from Punjab, migrated to the west coast of America, working initially in the timber industry and on farms. But by 1907, there was an association dedicated to organising opposition to Asian immigration. At first called the Japanese and Korean Exclusion League, the organisation was soon renamed the Asiatic Exclusion League (AEL) to include Indians among its targets. (Jenson 1988:44). Eventually immigration was virtually stopped from the subcontinent.

That was how it was until the United States law, fully implemented by 1968, allowed large numbers of Indians and other Asians to immigrate. The law gave preference to highly trained and educated professionals. Most were at least college graduates between the age of twenty and forty, urban educated and English speaking (Jensen 1988:281). Almost twenty years later, the children of the post-1965 immigrants have grown up and the community perceives a possibility that Indian culture may be lost to the wider American culture.

Cambridge is not like New York, in that it has no Indian locality nor any major presence of an Indian working class. Older

Indian residents told me that not too long ago spices had to be got from New York. The scene had changed in recent years. Indian shops and Indian restaurants were quite a few. But the professional middle class skew of the Asian Indian American population was still clearly marked. A young engineering student told me. 'Both my parents are Ph.D.s. Most of the Indians they mix with are equally highly educated. I know there are working class Indians, but I have never known one socially.' An Indian architect who had come as a student to the U.S. from Santiniketan in the 50s was puzzled as to why I should be interested to meet any but what he called 'the highly motivated Indian student at Harvard or MIT.' One morning when I chanced to meet him outside an Indian store run by a woman from Ludhiana, carrying on the conversation we had earlier, he told me: 'Things were different then. Indians were respected in the 50s.' Pointing to the store he said: 'People like them couldn't dream of coming here. Even now among the most motivated at Harvard are Indians. A professor was telling me the other day, "There is no challenge without Indian and Chinese students. They are the ones with brains." The WASPS were like that in the 60s, then the Jews. Whatever happened to them? They have become lazy.'

In this man's recounting of the past, the story of Indians begins with the 50s. And in their history they are placed with the history of the WASPS and the Jews. Neither the Asiatic Exclusion League, nor the history of the first wave of Indian migrants featured in it, nor even the history of the woman inside the store.[3] This is a perception not uniquely his. As I chatted with him in our common mother tongue, Bengali, I realised that though we may have similar territorial roots his history was not mine.

But that however was not always true. With most first generation immigrants I did share a past beyond a common growing up in middle class urban India. We were inheritors of Indian nationalist historiography. I understood when they spoke of the pride they had in India's 'ancient heritage', the disgust they felt at her contemporary slovenness, and the need to emulate the material achievements of the West with the spiritual strength of Indian culture.

Our differences as Punjabi, Bengali, Tamil, Gujarati and

Malayali... (incidentally there were seven Malayali organisations in Boston) were submerged in the 'we' feeling this invocation of the past provided us. This shared history of ancient India, our memory as a people, obviously comes up against a kind of impropriety for how can there be a history of ancient India when no India existed at that time. As Kaviraj writes,

> The lore of the Celts, to make the point with brutal simplicity, was nothing more than the Celt's lore, not the early history of the British people (Kaviraj 1993:16).

The history of the early Malayali similarly can only be theirs, neither mine nor India's.

This past, however improper, was dear even to the second generation, dearer perhaps, for the internal differences, contemporary hostilities, current tensions made little sense to them. Many indeed argued that as far as they were concerned, India was a cultural concept. They had little interest in the political entity. Indeed South Asia was a cultural entity, a view not often shared with non-Indian South Asians.[4] Pressing the point further a young scientist told me how particular the Indian association was in celebrating Independence Day and Republic Day, a practice he felt will not last. 'Diwali and Holi will. They have a long history. Independence Day is just 50 years old.'

For me, born only a decade after independence in India, 1947 cannot be so easily dismissed. His history of India goes much further back than the history of the modern Indian nation state. In this rendering of a 'time immemorial' cultural past which I repeatedly encountered the two themes which surfaced were the dichotomy of a 'spiritual us' and a 'material them' and the specific cultural and spiritual attributes of Indian women, both heritages of our ancient culture. Chatterjee has argued that this is the nationalist creation of its own domain of sovereignty within colonial society, its division of the world into two domains—the spiritual and the material, corresponding to the 'inside' and 'outside' of Indian life. The 'spiritual' inner domain bears the essential marks of cultural identity (Chatterjee 1994:6).

Women shoulder the burden of carrying on the cultural identity. Almost everyone mentioned how usually the girls could speak an Indian language while the boys could not, and how girls dressed in Indian clothes and learnt Indian music and dance. That of course did not stop the boys from wanting to return to India for an arranged marriage with their brides, their Asian Indian American women counterparts not being 'Indian' enough (read docile enough) for them. [5] This attempt to confine women to the 'inner domain' perceived as an Indian cultural space was a pivotal issue of generational conflict for the community.

Feminists from the community have been challenging such an interpretation and recasting their history to claim an identity of resistance:

> Whether deliberately or inadvertently, today's visible South Asian Immigrant community in the U.S. has propagated the idea that South Asian cultural heritage is antithetical to social change activism. By presenting itself as apolitical, the immigrant community is ignoring our rich political heritage both in the diaspora and South Asia. The 'first wave' Indian immigrants to this country, the majority of whom came as farm workers, were greatly involved in the labour, race and early immigrant politics of early twentieth century America. As modern South Asian feminists, we can look to this early community for strong female role models. Such activism can be traced throughout the South Asian diaspora, England, South Africa, Fiji, the Caribbean and South America. Women's participation in social change movements is a rich South Asian tradition (Dasgupta 1993:130).

As an Indian academic who had worked on the Indian women's movement, the South Asian feminists invited me to speak on some occasions. We came into close contact, I attended their regular meetings whenever possible, and met them individually on a regular basis. I felt more sympathetic to their recounting of history. Here was a history completely dissonant to the architect's who had felt nothing but shame at the sight of the non-professional, non-middle class kind of Indians. In both instances however a political project is underway. In the architect's history lies a belief that of the different immigrant groups. Indians are like the WASPS and the Jews. Less explicitly this is a denial of race, a point no second generation immigrant familiar with the epithet 'sand-nigger', ever failed to mention. In the feminist history is a conscious decision to break the hegemony of the middle class (caught in the image of a 'model minority') on the community, expresses solidarity with the increasing presence of working class Indians and the rest of the coloured populace. There was also a conscious decision to radicalise both 'Indian culture' and 'Indian women'. What struck me also was that by beginning with the story of immigrants from an undivided subcontinent, an attempt was also being made to erase the divided world of post-1947.

The feminists were however not the only ones to claim a shared past with the Punjab peasants. Another connecting to this past was made by small Indian businesses in San Francisco to avail of a ten per cent share of a minority bid. In order to avail of these economic advantages, they were willing to forge a shared history with the Punjab peasants. Interestingly, in order to qualify, the community had to present a case of historical discrimination in California in the early 1900s. Needless to say the descendants of the early immigrant community are not in a position to benefit from such Affirmative Action. Asian Indian American feminists told me disparagingly, that this very same group as NRIs (Non Resident Indians) was also awarded higher rates of interest to invest in India. This use of an identical piece of historical past for two very different agendas dramatically emphasises the issue of 'invention' which I had stressed at the start of the paper. It also brings me back to the issue of the boundaries which separated their history and mine.

My sympathies with the feminist rendering of history apart, it did seem a little unsettling to me that if I chose to migrate to the U.S. today, my history would begin with the Sikhs of Yuba Country and the Mexican Hindu community of the Imperial Valley, names unknown to me till yesterday. Yet my own biographical familiarity with a left, class history would make me more at ease with the same history rendered as an international history of the 'toiling people'. That leads us to the binding nature of the modern nation state in setting the stage for both issues of 'cultural identity' and 'history'. I argue therefore that the boundaries of the nation continue to play a critical role in defining culture and history even in today's global world. I argue also that the unequal power relations between the West and the others, and the special status of America in a uni-polar world make the American national context a very special one. In the following section I look at the very American cultural context within which the Asian Indian American formulates her/his history and cultural identity.

American Historiography and the Asian Indian American

American society was clearly an 'other culture' for me. Having reached America, for the first time, from a post-liberalised India, where the American presence, whether Kentucky Fried Chicken, or a Green Card holder, or prospective university admission or simply the media coverage of the American presidential election is omnipresent, it is a culture shock to see the world (not just India) recede to oblivion once one steps into America. For this is the country of immigrants. The story begins on landing. For me it meant learning not just about the community I wanted to understand but learning to locate it in the context of the American world they inhabited. Unlike the boundaries of the simple society which were clearly marked, here was a community (part of a community spread all over the United States) part of the larger Indian diaspora, part of the 'Indian heritage' and culture and an integral part of the American nation state. If I harboured any doubts about the increasing irrelevance of national boundaries in this global world, these were quickly dispelled as I learnt the overarching American context of the 'Indianness' which the Asian Indian Americans were representing.

America was a society that privileged the story of immigrants, of their life after reaching America, almost as though immigrants were not also emigrants. The disappearance of the world in everyday America can be explained at one level by the insular attitude which is a privilege of the powerful. 'Ideas, cultures, and histories cannot seriously be understood without their force, or more precisely their configurations of power, also being studied' (Said 1978: 5). This is very much like the invisibility of women in mainstream social science literature. The world simply cannot look the same from the centre as from the periphery. This is a

198 Anthropological Journeys

problem of the larger relationship between the West and the Rest, what Said succinctly describes as 'positional superiority' (ibid: 7).

Apart from the overall context of western hegemony, my contention is that there is something specifically American about the significance given to the unique and special nature of the American experience.

> Immigration not only has its history, it has its historiography. The writings of that great epic movement began almost as early as the movement itself. Every immigrant letter written from new shores was history, very personal and very uncritical. Every sheaf of reminiscences written by one of the participants in his later years was also history, a little more uncritical (Hansen 1996: 206).

This is the collective history of Americans. As Margaret Mead writes:

> We have our rituals of belonging, our DAR's, and our decendents of King Philip's Wars, our little blue book of the blue-blooded Hawaiian Aristrocacy descended from the first missionaries, and our 'Mayflower' which is equalled in mythological importance by the twelve named canoes which brought the Maoris to New Zealand (Mead 1942: 229).

To go back a little this positional superiority had of course ensured that the Mayflower is a myth larger than life even for us, here on the other side of the world. Speaking on a similar note in the context of postcolonial feminists Mary John writes:

> It probably goes without saying that the 'West' arrives on other shores in monochromatic terms; it travels elsewhere considerably whitened. Indian school and college students know of the 'discovery of America', but little else about the Conquistadores and their significance within a prior history of peoples native to the American continents. They will learn much more about Abraham Lincoln and George Washington than the American institution of slavery; and that Rev. Martin Luther King Jr. possibly plays the analogous role in India that Gandhi does in the United States. But the histories of

oppression of black women and women of colour on U.S. soil are nowhere to be found (John 1996:20).

Setting aside for a while this issue of positional superiority, I return to that sense of the 'special' and to the 'uniqueness' of the American experience to which I wish to return. Thanksgiving Day perhaps brings this feeling to the fore. Though multiculturalism now seeks to 'add some Native American touches to Thanksgiving' (The Boston Parents' Paper, November 1995), it remains a very American (read white) experience. Many second generation Asian Indian Americans mentioned the pain and humiliation they felt when friends in school looked shocked that they had not had the mandatory roast turkey for Thanksgiving. The pain no doubt was more acute when the 'melting pot' model was the norm where all differences were expected to cease. (This model has been increasingly questioned on the grounds that the non-white immigrants never really melted, and also that the cultural norm, which was supposed to be all American, was actually the culture of the dominant WASP.)

The multicultural reinterpretation of American history has sought to decentre American history and talk of many stories, not just one. But here too the American immigrant history occludes the world. In deference to multiculturalism the plural stories of different groups are projected. And yet it is the grand narrative of that singularly distinct American nation state that binds the rest. They celebrate what Ishmael Reed has described as a society 'unique' in the world because 'the world is here' a place where the cultures of the world criss-cross. (Takaki 1993:16).

I have a sense of deep discomfort here. Admittedly, nobody, least of all Takaki would deny the rest of the world its history. Yet such a statement reflects the self-centred obsession of a society for which the claim that it contains people from every culture may well mean that a knowledge of Asian Indian American, Chinese American or Korean America is as good as knowing India, China or Korea.

Articulation of a cultural identity for Indians had to be located in this context. I must mention here a reading session of Asian writers which I attended. An Asian Indian American woman writer when asked whether she read only American writers or also read Indian writers, said that she did indeed read 'Indian' writers, but then mentioned only Asian Indian Americans. Claiming that her feminist impulses were encouraged by her exposure to American literature I again felt that same consternation that I felt at the claim that 'the world is here'. She had read nothing written by Indians, not even in English. India meant the narrow world of her immediate family she had left behind in a little town in India when she got married and reached America. India meant unquestioned conformity and female passivity. And yet there she stood as a representative of 'Indian culture', a necessary component of an Asian American platform. As the discussion continued on minority literature, I increasingly felt that my 'Indianness' and her's had nothing in common. This 'Indianness' was an 'American' story.

> The heart of the matter is that in the present climate consent-conscious Americans are willing to perceive ethnic distinctions—differentiations which they seemingly base exclusively on descent, no matter how far removed and how artificially selected and constructed—as powerful and crucial; and that writers and critics pander to that expectation... and even the smallest symbols of ethnic differentiation... are exaggerated out of proportion to represent major cultural differences, differences that are believed to defy comparision or scrutiny (Sollars 1986: 7).

Multiculturalism or melting pot, it is extremely difficult to escape what I would call America's own form of Orientalism. The Orient is essentially an idea, or a creation with no corresponding reality. There 'were and are cultures and nations whose location is in the East, and their lives, histories, and customs have a brute reality obviously greater than anything that could be said about the West' but about this 'Orientalism has very little to contribute' (Said 1978: 5). The quest for cultural identity by the Asian Indian Americans is therefore quintessentially American. 'Indian culture' here is an idea, a representation that has little to do with the brute reality of India. The American discourse on multiculturalism and identity politics shape their pursuit of 'Indian culture and identity'. Significantly at Harvard there were more courses on what could be

Indological studies, Hinduism, Sanskrit and religion than on anything to do with contemporary India. An undergraduate student, intending to read medicine said:

I was not so interested in knowing about my religion earlier. When I came to Harvard I found that the Jewish and Christian students were well informed about their religion, even if they were going through a crisis of faith. I took Professor Diana Eck's and Professor Witzel's classes and was simply fascinated.

Similarly the tracing of the Asian Indian American's past to the Imperial Valley can also be seen as an affirmation of belonging to the American nation state. For by the acceptance of this particular form of imagining—what I had referred to earlier as the privileging of the story of the immigrant—we know that the Asian Indian is finally here to stay. I quote here from the *South Asia Journal* (a publication of the Harvard-Radcliffe South Asian Association):

Until college, I had never really considered myself Indian. Sure, I went to pooja and celebrated Indian holidays and was Hindu, but I never saw myself as Indian. I was an American through and through. When I came to college, I spent the first few months in a giddy whirlwind before coming down with a major case of homesickness. I missed everything about my home: my family, my friends, my car, my house, and...*aloo gobi!*

This was the first time she felt 'Indian' a feeling which visits her again on a trip to Paris with friends. Describing how tired and depressed they were feeling at the end of the journey she writes:

Suddenly, I noticed an 'India Quality' sign and looked up to find the ubiquitous Indian restaurant. I dashed inside, ate a *jalebi*, and found instant peace. My friend was shocked. In a split second, I went from crabby and whiny to upbeat and excited.

And then:

Until that moment, I had never realised what a comfort it is for me to be Indian. There are certain things that my friend will never be able to understand: how the smell of *jalebi* can make me happy, how much of a travesty certain nameless Indian restaurants are, how much fun Hindi film songs and techno rock, and bhangra are. Looking back on my life, I realise that so much of my identity is an Indian identity, or an Indian-American identity. For example as a child, I was an avid reader. My books of choice were always Amar Chitra Katha, though; I tore my way through Volume 1 to 10 like lightning.

Her American national identity however soon reasserts itself.

The day after the *jalebi* incident, we were walking on the Siene when we saw an American flag waving high in the sky. I felt an incredible sense of pride in my country of origin. That afternoon, we were in the Tuileries when we heard the unmistakable sound of an American high school band. We ran over to listen and almost burst with pride when we realised that we were right. I have never been so proud to be an American.

The truth dawns on her:

My heritage and my nationality combine to create my unique identity. No matter where I go, I can always feel at home. It took me awhile, but now I finally realise the truth. I am Indian. I am American. To deny one part of myself is to deny my identity. The two are inextricably intertwined and that is just the way I like it.

A distinct separation takes place between 'heritage' (cultural) and 'nationality' (political) allegiance. Indian 'heritage' is 'cultural' spelt in terms of 'food', 'family' and 'music'. America is the political nation state to which she belongs. India is 'cultural heritage' not the territorial, political entity which was 'India' for me. Such a possibility is also less common for her parent's generation. What we witness is yet another way in which the contemporary system of nation state composes a hegemonic topography, an ultimate verity (Herzfeld 1987:13). A related issue that emerges is that of categories and their aberrations which has, of course, a long history in anthropology. I look at this issue of categories and the overarching American discourse on race within which the hyphenated identity of the Asian Indian American has to be resolved.

Of Naming and Locations

I begin with my awkwardness in dealing with the term 'Asian Indian American'. A quote from my field diary written two months into the field reads:

> Belonging to a majority community in a nation state, having been born and bred there, I never felt any disquietude defining myself as an Indian. I should perhaps also add that belonging to a generation born just after a decade of independence, growing up in an atmosphere conducive to a healthy sense of self esteem, an atmosphere not yet vitiated with major challenges to the notion of an Indian nation state, I felt comfortable with my national identity.

I go on delving into my complacence with my identity and then write:

> A little unsure of the fixity of the category now, I however enter an entirely new discursive structure with my first visit to the United States of America. Learning the lexicon of American Asian Indian to define people who were just Indians back home opened up an entire new world.

I began my fieldwork with the idea that in the American context the category 'South Asian' made better sense. A very large number of associations existed with the same nomenclature. I soon realised that as an Indian I had particular problems with 'speaking' about 'South Asians'. There was a very embarrasing moment when I mistook a very old lady in a sari to be an Indian. I was admonished on the Indian belief that 'only Indians wear saris'. She was Sri Lankan and a Sinhalese. The category 'South Asian' was difficult because of a widely perceived view that Indians tended to displace others in the broad category South Asian. A Bangadeshi writer expresses this fear.

South Asian is a category fast catching on in academic and

204 *Anthropological Journeys*

literary areas. However, some of us have remained invisible in the new name and devoured by the multicultural zeal. The ideal of multiculturalism assumes that everything placed in these categories has equal space and voice within and between them. But a new hierarchy has emerged in which certain voices have been privileged and have developed their own hegemonic power.... India and Pakistan are the regional superpowers and play an active role in the struggle over distribution of resources and territory. We must examine how these regional political dynamics transplant and transform in the American context (Islam 1993:242).

The category of South Asia is problematic partly because of the politics of the South Asian region and also because of the representation of the region in America and within the American academia itself. Islam voices both these aspects below:

Despite the divisions into national boundaries, Bangladesh, Pakistan and India are in some ways perceived as larger (undivided) India. And Bhutan, Maldives, Nepal and Sri Lanka are either made invisible or seen in the context of the political and economic connections to India. For example, South Asia Studies departments in the U.S. focus their courses and research on India while claiming to 'study' the whole region. They are taught by predominantly white and male faculty (ibid: 242–43).

I was wary of a similar charge that my research may not be representative enough to be called South Asian. Though my fieldnotes on Bangladeshis are considerable I had decided against writing anything about them there.

I thus confined myself to the Asian Indian Americans. The first day in my son's school the Principal asked me which box in the form she should tick, Hispanic or Asian. His features were misleading. I had never before been identified as Asian. This was the beginning of my learning about the American census classification and the politics of ethnic enumeration.

I learnt that until 1820, ethnic data pertained mainly to the distinction between white citizens and groups with fewer civil rights like slaves and tribal Indians. I learnt that in 1850, the concept of colour was institutionalised as white, black, or mulatto. In 1930 the list expanded to include White, Negro, Mexican, Indian, Chinese, Japanese, Filipino, Hindu and Korean plus a space for other write-in-choice. Significantly the early migrants from the subcontinent were classified Caucasians. The only disturbing matter was that 'the Hindu resembles us except that he is black and we are shocked to see a black white man' (Jenson 1988:39). I could go on.

This initiation was important, for how else would I be able to comprehend a young girl's passionate explanation to me as to why the box brown should be added in the state's official forms when white, black, and yellow were there. This world of colour-based identity was new for me. A professor of sociology of Indian origin told me that the 'identity' of our children was really not such a contentious matter.

> Our children can be identified by colour, simply by looking at them. Society identifies them. I am an American citizen. I have been here 35 years. Still I am a foreigner. And when people ask me 'When are you going back' I say 'When are you going back?'

Though Indians are not refugees, yet it would not be to err to see them in Douglas's sense as a dangerous category because they blur national/natural boundaries, and challenge 'time-honoured distinctions between national and foreigners' (Arendt 1972:286). It can be argued that this view is not valid for an immigrant society. However notwithstanding the hyperbole on multiculturalism the view that the cultural core of America is white and western is a feeling that does not lack support. As the professor said: 'The European model is dominant, anything else is less than adequate.'

Colour in this context is critical. It is in America that the Sicilian learnt that he was white, not Sicilian, just as I learnt my son was Asian not Indian. It is another story that his classmates always pointed to him as native Indian when they had their social study class on the landing of the Pilgrim Fathers and their encounter with the Indians. Anthropological literature on classification has based itself primarily on the three phases of separation, transition and incorporation as delineated by Van Gennep. While the three phases help us understand the process of uprooting, transition and incorporation, we should be wary of applying the phases as an explanatory model. For there is a big difference between 'matter out of place' in the classification of plants and animals and 'matter out of place' when people are in question. For people categorise back ... (Tambiah 1985:4). In the story of census classification lies not only the moves of the state but the responses of different ethnic groups, mobilising, lobbying, campaigning to intervene in the classification system. For example when Asian Indian Americans were relegated to the category 'other' in the 1970 census and subsequently classified as whites as they had been since 1950 there was active lobbying by the Association of Indians in America (AIA) who lobbied to have Asian Indian Americans reclassified as Asian Americans. The reason was economic. Asians are officially recognised as minorities and therefore derive economic benefits in compensation for their past history of discrimination in the country (Fischer 1980: 135).

I had come a long way from the time I thought that being 'Indian' was a self-evident fact and that the 'Indian culture' the Asian Indian Americans were talking about was the same as mine. As I probed into the classificatory maze of the American census, read through American immigrant histories, sat through multicultural functions, I grew more and more sure that I was studying another culture. I grew more and more certain that it was my political identity as an Indian citizen in everyday, contemporary India that defined my 'Indianess'. My 'Indian culture' was embedded in my location in today's India, its changing economics and politics. Their 'Indian culture' was implicated in today's America, its discourse on race and multiculturalism, affirmative action and cuts in immigration, identity and lifestyle politics.

I have described the way my interrogation of the Asian Indian American's identity led to a tearing down of my taken-for-granted 'Indianness'. The story will however remain incomplete if I do not narrate how they in turn identified me. Central to my identity was my gender. I was a woman. I was married with two children. I wore saris and salwar kameezes. I was told I looked a typically Indian woman. I did not feel particularly comfortable with the epithet. Central to the mainstream self image of the community in North America, was the image of their women as virtuous and moral in sharp contrast to the decadence that marked white American society and, worse still, black America. From me (an Indian woman), they sometimes wanted confirmation of a view they held of India, or sometimes, a rebuttal. Especially with the second generation I was 'evidence' that India had not frozen in time somewhere in a distant small town from where their parents had come to America in the early sixties. I was a third point with whom they could converse about what they felt about their selves, their being 'Indian', their being 'American', their culture and the contentious issue of gender relations in their 'culture'. Often I sat through heated discussions of girls condemning the practice of the Asian Indian men going back to India to get a docile, typical Indian bride. This description never failed to agitate me. And I was shocked at the complete absence of knowledge of any form of political action in India. I understood better why feminists within the community (to whom I had become very close) repeatedly drew attention to the history of struggle and militancy of Indian women, a story invisible in the world of the middle-class emigré Indians.

Indian women stood for virtue. Change was against the grain of Indian culture. In his account of field experience in Malaysia, Jain remarks:

> The fact that I was married, my wife wore a sari, displayed all normal characteristics of an Indian wife (cooking, not participating in conversation between men, having many domestic issues of common interest to discuss with other women, etc.) led to easy adjustment with neighbours (Jain 1975:88).

I too found it easy to be 'normal'. Cambridge is a small town. As I went about my daily chores of shopping, going to school, children's get togethers, the public library, it was very simple to enter the world of women who were 'housewives'.

The younger generation found this 'normalcy' awkward and found me in my professional persona more reassuring. I also suspect that they shared the dominant perception that the Indian woman was docile, passive and uninitiated to the pleasures of being an individual which only the vibrancy of America can provide. In the latter part of my fieldwork, many young students, particularly girls visited me. They wanted to see my husband. They knew that he looked after the children when I went out. They found that strange, most un-Indian. One girl who had initially been very distant came home and told me about her mother. Her mother she said was very shy and timid and sad. But whenever she went back to India, to her small town in Madhya Pradesh, she was a different person. 'She was a queen. She even walked differently. She was so confident.' In this bare description the positional superiority of the West emerges sharply. The issue is not just of 'foreigners' but our historically constituted inadequacy with the West. And in the unequal gender relations within the household it is but inevitable that the women bear the brunt of the men's inadequacy.

This positional superiority of the West is not easy to dismiss. In a myriad way it shapes our everyday life and the academia where my central identity was that of a coloured woman. Whatever I said had to be interpreted from the context of the coloured women's experience in the U.S. Trinh T. Minh-Ha talks of the violent shuttling between two worlds and 'the challenge of the hyphenated reality' which lies in the 'hyphen itself: the becoming Asian-American' (Ttrinh T. Minh-Ha 1991:157). I was however not Asian-American. I was just Indian. But this identity was not easy to express.

While I affirm that my identity as a woman 'coloured' or 'typically Indian' was crucial for my field experiences, I distance myself from one of the earliest principles of a kind of feminist theory and research which was (and still is) generated from the idea that women have a particular way of knowing and seeing the world (Skeggs 1995:16). Experience can mean anything. Often it is used to refer to feelings, emotions, the personal, and to subjectivity. What is missed out is that our experience is part of our social, historical, political, cultural and economic process. It is not individuals who have experiences but subjects who are constituted through experience. I could only be a Third World woman and not a coloured one.

As I draw to the close of this paper, the one central point I wish to emphasise is that a wide gulf exists between the Western location and the Third World. The question of cultural identity is rooted within this unequal relationship.

The question has been posed: how does one 'know' when one is at home (Strathern 1987:16). It is argued that if we give up the idea of culture as essence and the other as an entity, 'Home' seems virtually boundless from the postmodern perspective. From my location in India where globalisation seems more of hegemony and hierarchy, exclusion and violence, more of IMF conditionalities and less of cultural fragmentations and hybridities, I argue that 'Home' does not seem virtually boundless. 'Home' did not seem boundless for the Asian Indian American as she strives to make space for herself.

Conclusion

A great deal of contemporary literature proceeds from the assumption that '[a] sense of rupture with the past pervades the public consciousness of our time' (Albrow 1996:1). It extends beyond national and ideological differences. Central to this global age is the construction of identity formations which cut across and intersect natural frontiers, and which are composed of people who have been dispersed from their homelands forever. People who belong to such cultures of hybridity have had to renounce their dream of recovering any kind of 'lost' cultural purity. They are irrecovably translated. Salman Rushdie notes that the word 'translation' comes etymologically from the Latin 'bearing across'. Migrant writers like him, who belong to two worlds at once, 'having born across the world... are translated men' (Rushdie 1991). They must learn to inhabit at least two identities, to speak two cultural languages, to translate and negotiate between them. This we are told is one of the distinctly novel types of identity produced in the era of late modernity (Hall et al 1992:310). I am a little confused as I read Nehru:

> I have become a queer mixture of the East and West, out of place everywhere, at home nowhere. Perhaps my thoughts and approach to life are more akin to what is called Western than Eastern, but India clings to me as she does to all her children, in innumerable ways.... I cannot get rid of that past inheritance or my recent acquisitions.... I am a stranger and

an alien in the West. I cannot be of it. But in my own country also, sometimes, I have an exile's feeling (Nehru 1947:596).

Or as I read about Rammohun Roy who lived more than a century before Nehru penned these feelings. Rammohun Roy maintained two houses in Calcutta, one for entertaining his European friends and the other for his family to live in. It is said that in the first house everything was European except Rammohun, and in the second everything except Rammohun was Indian (Panikkar 1995:1).

What is so new that makes the predicament of culture of such intense debate in the west? Is it the transformation of the west with the presence of the non-white enclaves embedded for 'good in an irrevocably changed West? Is it a case of the Empire striking back? For the colonised has for long been inhabiting this translated world. What is it that has changed for the anthropologist of 2020?

Anthropology in 2020, the argument is, will be conducted in a world of compressed cultures where the distinction (it was always unsatisfactory) of 'modern' versus 'traditional' is in shreds; so, too, is the Kiplingesque distinction—which Forster satirised in tragedy—of 'West is West and East is East' (and may the twain never meet, the West being Best). The question is, what of the anthropologist in this compressed world—is he or she (or they) not also 'compressed' culturally? For instance, 'he' could be a Fielding-Aziz. Put another way, what, by that date, will be the anthropologist's claim to 'privilege' as an observer? It will no longer be what it still usually is even today, namely, that the anthropologist is not a native; the category 'native' will long since have been muddled, culturally (Paine 1992:203).[6]

The native however continues to be the native. The gaze is not so easily reversed in a divided world. Just as the replacement of 'women's studies' by 'gender studies' does not reverse the patriarchal order.

James Clifford's seminal work tell us that the present predicament is linked to the breakdown and redistribution of colonial power in the decades after 1950 and to the echoes of that process in the radical cultural theories of the 1960s and 1970s

(Clifford 1988:22). The West can no longer present itself as the unique purveyor of knowledge about others. And that with expanded communication and intercultural influence, people interpret themselves and others in a bewildering diversity of idioms, a global condition of what Bakhtin called 'heteroglossia' (ibid:23). We have to now imagine a world of 'generalised' ethnography. Both the term 'generalised' and 'heteroglossia' convey a sense of easy shift from a hierarchical to a non-hierarchical plain of knowledge formation.

Modern or postmodern, colonial or postcolonial the desire of the West to slot the non-western 'other' into a pre-defined category is strong. As I spoke in seminars and workshops, I had little choice but to be an 'otherness machine' (Appiah 1992). I could either be, like Bharati Mukherjee,[7] the oppressed Indian woman who finds light on reaching America. Or I could be that authentic non-western voice[8] that would destabilise the culturally hegemonic Western discourses of nationalism, feminism and socialism. And what could be better suited than a woman for dramatising 'differences'. I failed to perform either of the roles expected of me. The feeling that the postmodern meets the postcolonial to create almost identitical polarities of the modern world grew stronger. There will always be differences within the erstwhile colonised experience of an India and an Africa but what Appiah has to say of the African experience will be no less true for the Indian:

> ...as intellectuals—a category instituted in black Africa by colonialism—we are always at risk of becoming otherness-machines. Its risks become our principal roles. Our only distinction in the world of texts to which we are latecomers is that we can mediate it to our fellows. This is especially true when postcolonial meets postmodern, for what the postmodern reader seems to demand of its Africa is all too close to what modernism...demanded of it (Appiah 1992:157).

Replace Africa with India and the story will not change much.

The postcolonial world continues to be a divided world. The hegemony of western capitalism continues. Indeed the post-cold war world is heralded as the era of unchallenged ascendancy of capitalism as a world system. As the imperatives of a global economy constantly demand the opening up of borders for free trade of goods and services, western states make stricter immigration rules, to close their borders to the flow of Third World migrants and refugees. The issue of immigration was central to the recently concluded Presidential election in the U.S., an issue which the Asian Indian community was raising even while I was there. I argue therefore that the category 'native' is not so muddled, the idea 'home' not so diffused, and cultures not so 'compressed' in a world which continues to be defined by the 'positional superiority' of the West. Significantly most flow of displaced people takes place within the non-western world. Significantly also the literature on their displacement has not acquired the same theoretical ascendancy in the Western academic world as the experience of the translated person has.

Notes

1. I will discuss the concept of South Asian in the section on 'Naming and Locations'.

2. There has been a steep rise in numbers of Asian Indian Americans. The 1990 census showed them to have grown 125.6 per cent in the 1980s, from 387,223 to 815,447. It is estimated to grow to one million out of a total Asian population of eight million by the year 2000, and to two million by 2050.

3. I must mention that she later told me that our conversation in Bengali confirmed what she had already suspected—that we were both from Bangladesh. It is outside the scope of this paper to deal with the different stories of different classes and communities.

4. I return to this point in the section on 'Locations and Naming'.

5. 'Arranged marriage' symbolised the docile, submissive nature of Indian women and the backwardness of Indian culture. I too have felt similarly at a point of time. What confused me was that most did not see any similarity between 'our' matrimonial columns and 'their' columns on partners and companions.

6. Robert Paine quoted by Sandra Wallman (1992).

7. I quote from the blurb on the back cover of Bharati Mukherjee's novel *Jasmine* (New York: Fawcett Crest, 1989): 'Poignant... Heart rendering... The story of the transformation of an Indian village girl, whose grandmother wants to marry her off at 11, into an American women who finally thinks for herself.'

8. My brief experience suggested that Ashis Nandy's critique of modernity or Vandana Shiva's eco-feminism fitted the bill.

References

Albrow, Martin. 1996. *The Global Age*. Cambridge: Polity Press.

Appiah, Kwame Anthony. 1992. *In My Father's House: Africa in the Philosophy of Culture*. New York: Oxford University Press.

Arendt, Hannah. 1972. The Origins of Totalitarianism. New York and London: Harcourt Brace Jovanovich.

Bhabha, Homi. (ed.). 1990. *Nation and Narration*. New York: Routledge.

Chatterjee, Partha. 1994. *The Nation and its Fragments: Colonial and Postcolonial Histories*. Delhi: Oxford University Press.

Clifford, James. 1988. *The Predicament of Culture: Twentieth-Century Ethnography, Literature and Art*. Cambridge: Harvard University Press.

Dasgupta, Sayantani and Shamita Dasgupta. 1993. 'Jowneys: Reclaiming South Asian Feminism.' *In Our Feet Walk the Sky: Women of the South Asian Diaspora*. Women of South Asian Descent Collective. San Francises: Aunt Lute Books.

Fisher, Maxine. 1980. *The Indians of New York City*. New Delhi: Heritage.

Hall, Stuart, David Held and Tony McGrew. 1992. *Modernity and its Futures*. Cambridge: Polity Press.

Hastrup, Kirsten. 1995. *A Passage to Anthropology: Between Experience and Theory*. Londoan: Routledge.

Hansen, Marcus Lee. 1996. 'The Problem of the Third Generation Immigrant'. In Sollors, Werner (ed.). *Theories of Ethnicity: A Classical Reader*. London: Macmillan.

Herzfeld, Michael. 1987. *Anthropology Through the Looking Glass: Critical Ethnography in the Margins of Europe*. Cambridge: Cambridge University Press.

Islam, Naheed. 1993. 'In the Belly of the Multicultural Beast: I am Named South Asian'. In *Our Feet Walk the Sky; Women of the South Asian diaspora*. San Fransisco: Aunt Lute Books.

Jain, R.K. 1975. 'Indians at Home Abroad'. In A. Beteille and T.N. Madan (eds.) *Encounter and Experience: Personal Accounts of Fieldwork*. New Delhi: Vikas.

Jensen, Joan M. 1988. *Passage from India: Asian Indian Immigrants in North America*. New Haven: Yale University Press.

John, Mary. 1996. *Discrepant Dislocation? Feminism, Theory and Postcolonial Histories*. New York: Oxford University Press.

Kaviraj, Sudipto. 1992. 'The Imaginary Institution of India'. In Partha Chatterjee and Gyanendra Pandey (ed.) *Subaltern Studies*. Vol. VII. New Delhi: Oxford University Press.

Malkki, Lisa H. 1995. *Purity and Exile*. Chicago: The University of Chicago Press.

Mead, Margaret. 1942. 'We Are All Third Generation Immigrants'. In Soolors Werner. 1996. op cit.

Nehru, Jawaharlal. 1947. *An Autobiography*. London. The Bodley Head Ltd.

Sandra Wallman (ed.). *Contemporary Futures: Perspectives from Social Anthropology*. London: Routledge.

Panikkar, K.N. 1995. *Culture, Ideology, Hegemony*. New Delhi: Tulika.

Rushdie, Salman. 1991. *Imaginary Homelands*. London: Granta Books.

Skeggs, Beverly. 1996. *Feminist Cultural Theroy: Process and Production*. Manchester: Manchester University Press.

Strathern, M. 1987. 'The Limits of Auto-Anthropology' in Anthony Jackson (ed.) *Anthropology at Home*. London: Tavistock.

Said, Edward. 1978. *Orientalism*. New York: Vintage.

Sollors, Werner. 1986. *Beyond Ethnicity: Consent and Descent in American Culture*. New York: Oxford University Press.

Takaki, Ronald. 1993. *A Different Mirror: A History of Multicultural America*. Boston: Little Brown.

Tambiah, Stanley. 1985. *Culture, Thought and Social Action: An Anthropological Perspective*. Cambridge: Harvard University Press.

Trinh T. Minh-Ha. 1991. *When the Moon Waxes*. New York: Routledge.

Urban, Greg and Joel, Sherzer. 1991. 'Introduction', in G. Urban and J. Sherzer. (eds.). *Nation-States and Indians in Latin America*. University of Texas Press: Austin.

Van Gennep, Arnold. 1960. *The Rites of Passage*. Chicago: University of Chicago Press.

Wallman, Sandra (ed.). 1992. *Contemporary Futures: Perspectives from Social Anthropology*. London: Routledge.

Section IV

Gendered Selves in Fieldwork

Dialogue as Method and as Text[1]

SARASWATI HAIDER

This paper has been written with a view to initiate a discussion on an approach to a method for collection of more 'authentic' data in 'women's studies' and in other studies also. It offers some thoughts on what needs to be debated, dialogued and questioned. It does not endeavour to come up with conclusive solutions. In the process I will deal with the questions this volume addresses on the relationship between the self and the other in fieldwork. I have tried also to explore whether the information received from my fieldwork method has generated more authentic, perhaps richer data.[2] I also ask whether such data helps us understand better the lives of women in *jhuggi-jhompri* clusters in our advocacy of issues relating to their problems. I have also tried to talk about my own self-questioning, and the self-discoveries that I made during my dialogues with women in the field.

Rationale for Use of Dialogue as a Two-way Interactive Method

Multifaceted Truths

All sciences, including social sciences, try to get at *the* truth of some reality. In social science, this becomes *the* truth of social phenomena. However, truth seems to be multifaceted, multiplex and polychromic. It appears that truth if viewed from different standpoints, takes on different hues, different meanings, different forms. If this is the case then there is a plurality of truths of a particular social reality. A social scientist then, perhaps, can never really get to *the* truth of any social reality or

218 Anthropological Journeys

phenomenon. He, or she can get at truth only as he or she sees it, as he or she wants to see it. The latter, moreover, can happen consciously or unconsciously.

In India we are faced with contested truths about the meaning of 'feminism' and how the reality of women can be constituted or reconstituted.[3] It is, therefore, not incorrect to proclaim that reality and truth are multifaceted and more importantly, multi-visional. They alter, change, take on new nuances and new contours from different standpoints and perspectives but each truth is grasped perhaps only approximately, not in toto. Nevertheless, each of the truth-views and reality-views from varied standpoints and perspectives, however approximate, contain within them some element of truth, some perception of reality and thus have validity. No truth of reality can perhaps be considered supreme unless so proved. Till such time all truths of reality perhaps have to be equally signified. 'Knowledge is in no case unitary and acquirable through one correct method, rather it is plural and heterogeneous, with truths being the norm, not Truth' (Kumar 1994:7). And, again, the social anthropologist has to learn to live with the plurality of truths of social reality, the latter, however, being itself, as per the above logic a truth from one standpoint only, valid, in the fluid situation that has been constructed, till replaced by a truth of more certitude—the option being quite open.

However, no matter what kind of truth the social scientist is trying to get at, he or she has to go about formulating a methodology to collect data which will make the social anthropologist get as close to his or her truth as possible. In this paper I try to push forward an idea which has now become a firm belief, related to the collection of data in fieldwork of the anthropological kind, which is not to act in 'bad faith' where my subjects of research are concerned and to approach them with full honesty, openness and forthrightness from my side in my interface with them. Only then perhaps, can one expect from the researched also, honest, open and forthright information about themselves. To receive such information, I feel, one should be prepared to allow the researched to question and query one with complete freedom. One should be ready to supply information to them with as complete candour as one expects from them. Not to do so would amount to an act of 'bad faith' and acting in 'bad faith' I am certain can never result in an egalitarian, subject-to-subject, two-way communication which is the only way that authentic data can be received.

Subjectivity and Objectivity in the Social Sciences
In this kind of give-and-take of information one will have to encounter the problem of subjectivity and objectivity in research. This is not a new discourse and it still continues.

The opinion voiced by Dipankar Gupta (1995) represents the opinion of the adherents of objectivity in social science research. Gupta writes:

> For in the ultimate analysis, a discipline can perpetrate itself as one only if its practitioners can rise above pure subjectivity. It is only then that minimum conditions of arriving at consensus are actually arrived at. In this sense the tendency that privatises the object of analysis can only do so on pain of undermining disciplinary specifics. No matter how attractive it might appear to knock down disciplines, the truth is that objective consensus cannot be arrived at without disciplinary grids…. This brings us to the next characteristic feature of contemporary feminist studies. This has to do with the tendency to make women so distinctly unique that general methods of intersubjectivity and enquiry are rendered meaningless. As feminist studies clearly privilege the female 'voice', intersubjectivity is methodologically and purposively curtailed. But intersubjectivity curtailed is intersubjectivity denied, which is why feminists have succeeded so well in converting the woman and her sex into a Derridian text (Gupta 1995:619).

It is however difficult to completely wrench out subjectivity from one's system as Gupta himself realises when he says 'nothing is objective in the absolute sense' (Gupta 1995:619). Consciously or unconsciously, subjectivity seems to pervade all our behaviour and actions in the 'disciplinary grid' that Gupta talks about. It is present in the way we formulate our hypotheses, the way we collect our data, make observations, analyse data, build theories, and in the way we present the findings of our data. No matter how much we may wish it, there is no escape from one's subjectivity.

The stress on objectivity is, in all probability, a hangover of the days when social science was trying to emulate the natural sciences. But it is necessary to recognise now that the forced creation of objectivity by a social scientist also involves his or her subjectivity. He or she creates objectivity subjectively.

The act of simulating objectivity cannot but end up distorting the subjective but rich, authentic experience of reality that the social scientist may have gone through. Srinivas, a firm adherent of objectivity in the interpretation and presentation of data, has proclaimed, that in anthropology, where collection of data is concerned '...subjectivity is not to be deplored but accepted as a condition of work when a human being is studying other human beings' (Srinivas 1992:150). And again:

A deep subjectivism is thus built into anthropology but this is not a condition to be deplored but accepted, if not rejoiced in. There is a difference between a human being studying rocks, plants or ants and another studying other human beings. The latter is in a sense studying himself—he is both the object and subject of his study (Srinivas 1989:170).

Authentic, reality-revealing, flesh and blood data is perhaps only obtainable when one is intimately, subjectively and personally involved with one's subjects, when one does not go to them like an inquisitioner or an aloof, distant, subjectivity-transcending enquirer, but tries to become a part of one's researched subjects's lives within certain limitations which, often, a social scientist cannot avoid.

The simulation of objectivity appears to be the brain child of an androcentric social science emphasising the higher value of reason and rationality over emotion and affectivity and hence objectivity over subjectivity. The so-called objective theory-building and 'disciplinary grids', even though they obviously cannot immunise one from subjectivity, seem to be games that male social scientists, and imitating them, some women social scientists, like to play to conform to their belief in deified reason. In these, emotions and affectivity which are considered to be an element of subjectivity are denigrated, and are required to be curtailed. But we need to ask why it is assumed that consensus can be arrived at only through a self-deceiving, simulated objectivity. Why cannot consensus also be arrived at when data are presented as subjectively as they were received?

The importance of intersubjectivity, however, cannot be denied. Indeed subjectively presented findings should most definitely allow scope for intersubjectivity. However, to believe that intersubjectivity is only possible by undergoing futile self-deceptive acts of transcending subjectivity is to pull the wool over one's eyes. Intersubjectivity *is* possible subjectively. But where the question of male social scientists researching women subjects, as well as the intersubjectivity of such social scientists with their female counterparts is concerned, the matter becomes a problem. Till the advent of 'women's studies', women were largely invisible in the work of social scientists. It is a fact that men and surprisingly, even some women have shown and continue to show a singular insensitivity to the presence of women subjects in social reality.[4] Women have been, and are still not assigned their due space in the research and writings of male social scientists. This one feels is because for centuries now women have been kept submerged in the 'culture of silence'. They have been, and continue to be rendered mute and/or subsumed under the generic term 'man' by male social scientists (Ardener 1986). Women's experiences have remained unexpressed and unarticulated, leading to the lack of recognition and comprehension of their being by men who did not feel the need to acquire such a comprehension; surprisingly some women do not feel this need either. 'Women's studies' seem to have been also designated by men, with their penchant for dualisms, as 'women's work.' In such a situation men will perhaps have to allow women to give voice to their pent up emotions, desires, hurts, suffering, pain and aspirations through 'women's studies' which are allowing them to do so. In this context it is apt to quote what Sangari and Vaid have to say about feminist historiography which can apply to all domains of knowledge concerning human beings:

> A feminist historiography rethinks historiography as a whole and discards the idea of women as something to be *framed* by a context, in order to be able to think of gender difference as both structuring and structured by the wide set of social relations. In this sense feminist historiography is a choice open

to all historians. Not as a choice of competing perspectives, or even as one among personal predilections of the sort which dictate interest in a particular region or a particular historical period. Nor is the issue here the tokenist inclusion of women as the numerical, even qualitative evaluation of their participation in this or that movement. Rather as a choice which cannot but undergird *any* attempt at a historical reconstruction which undertakes to demonstrate our sociality in the *full* sense, and is ready to engage with its own presuppositions of the social moments and movements it sets out to represent. The fact that this is a choice seldom exercised may perhaps even be partly ascribed to the emergence of women's studies in India which appears to be a convenience for mainstream historians who can now consign the onus on specialists in a 'separate' discipline and so recreate yet another gender-based division of labour within the rarefied world of academia (Sangari and Vaid 1993:3).

Research writings on women by women social scientists give out strong signals that women are different from men, that is, both the women social scientists and their women subjects researched: they feel differently about situations, speak differently, react differently, perceive differently, relate differently to people, and so on. This subject needs to be researched thoroughly in the Indian context. It might be more correct to say that women are indeed different, but this is perhaps because they have been an oppressed and marginalised group, and have been socialised as discriminated, subservient beings, within a patriarchal order. But different they are, and it is felt that to study them, different approaches, different methods and different forms of presentation of data about them are required (Duelli Klein 1983, Reinharz 1983, Du Bois 1983, Mies 1983, Stanley and Wise 1983a, 1983b).

Srinivas very strongly recommends that a social anthropologist should have empathy towards his subjects (Srinivas 1984, 1989, 1992). However, empathising means that one is still approaching the researched rather patronisingly, from a top-to-down position. Empathy carries with it connotations of largesse being bestowed, whereas I have in mind a stance in which the researcher is prepared to interface with his or her researched subjects on a more equal footing. That is, the researcher involves himself or herself in an act of mutuality, reciprocal sharing and give and take in his or her encounters with his or her protagonists so that an atmosphere of mutual trust and equal exchange of confidences can be created. The researcher, especially of women subjects, in order to relate with the latter, who are perhaps more emotional, more subjective and personal in their bonding, should respond with an equally deep, subjective and personal involvement which is only possible, again, if the researcher acts in complete 'good faith' and enters into dialogues and relationships with his or her women subjects on an egalitarian and scrupulously honest footing. That is what friendship, which Srinivas advocates with the researched (1992), is all about, not just empathy bestowed from an exalted position.

The Anthropology of Pain
Veena Das's advocacy of an anthropology of pain has great relevance to the study of women's situations (Das 1995). Pain can be a condensed expression of the trauma of individuals readable as a production of criticism by the body of injustices perpetrated. Das argues that in order to create a moral community through the sharing of pain, as was envisaged by Durkheim, individual pain must come to be collectively experienced. But she suggests that pain often strikes one dumb and destroys one's capacity to communicate. However, by deftly using Wittgenstein's arguments (1953, 1958, 1971) Das demonstrates that pain *can* be communicated and *can* be felt in another body; that there is no individual ownership of pain. This shows us the way in which relating to the pain of others can become witness to a moral life. Leder (1990 as cited by Das 1995) called this the moral significance of 'forming one body.' Das concludes that the healing force of social anthropology can come in if the experience of suffering that has been encountered does not become cause for consolidating the authority of the discipline but rather, an occasion for forming one body, providing voice to, and touching victims, so that their pain may be experienced in other bodies.

While Veena Das bases her conceptualisation of an anthropology of pain on sufferings inflicted by unprecedented havoc and man-made tragedies, the infliction of pain and suffering can also be a long drawn out and continuing process, as it is in the case of the oppression and exploitation of women. Anthropology should constitute the memory of the pain and sufferings of women as well with the social anthropologist feeling the pain of the mutilated women in his or her body first and then, making others feel the pain in their bodies. To do this, a different approach and different skills are needed.

A social anthropologist can only feel in his or her body the pain and sufferings that have been inflicted on women in their exploitation and oppression by a patriarchal set-up by becoming more intensely and more intimately involved in close pain-sharing relationships with his or her researched subjects and not acting as a still-distant, at-a-higher level, beneficent, sympathiser, empathic listener or munificent giver, which would in all probability alienate his or her subjects rather than create a milieu in which the pain and suffering of the latter can be expressed and articulated. It is by forging reciprocal, subject-to-subject, trustful confidences and pain-sharing, equal relationships with his or her women subjects that the researcher will succeed in giving back to the latter their silenced voices, and help form a moral community of the type envisaged by Durkheim. The kind of relationship being talked about cannot be built in 'bad faith' without the social anthropologist himself or herself being prepared to invest more of himself or herself emotionally and experientially. This increased investing of himself or herself by the researcher can only be accomplished if he or she is willing to share with the oppressed women subjects, pain and suffering which he or she is bound to have, at some point, in some way also undergone, honestly and with veracity. It is the only way to build bridges between human beings. In this paper, I, therefore, advocate a deeper, more intense and meaningful, self-involving engagement of social anthropologists to restore the voices of their protagonists who have been struck dumb by pain. The emphasis is on more honesty, genuineness, more giving, more sharing and more openness on the part of the researcher.

Research as Violence and Exploitation

Paulo Freire declared that 'the fundamental theme of our epoch is domination' (1978: 78). I would like to submit that another fundamental theme of our epoch is violence which coexists with domination.

In a world where human interaction is increasingly violent, investigation and research involving interaction with other human beings also appears to be a kind of violence. Such research appears as acts of aggression which violate the privacy and the established tenor of the lives of the investigated. Such research and investigation, if not connected with any action programme, can become exploitative acts in which the researcher stands to gain (professionally) while the researched are most often used as guinea pigs in this process of getting a degree, or writing a paper or a book which would further the researcher's career. Research thus is very often a selfish act of aggrandisement. It is often suggested that research should be made participatory. However, research cannot be made participatory with an initiation from the side of the researcher only. Those being researched should also be willing and their consent obtained. And why should they be willing to give their consent unless they stand to gain in some way? The only 'fair' behaviour in such a situation seems to be to make research more sincere and more honest on the part of the researcher involving a deeper and if possible more active engagement with the researched. The researcher should be willing to give at least as much information about himself or herself as he or she expects to get, to give confidences in return for confidence received, and to return trust and good faith with trust and good faith. This is the least that a researcher can do to make the act of research and investigation less violent and less exploitative.

The interview technique most often used is one in which the interviewer goes around with a lengthy schedule and a pencil in hand, fires a barrage of questions at the interviewee, and feverishly notes down the answers. I call this the 'inquisitorial concept of interviewing' (see Oakley 1981 for a critique of the classical interview method). On the other hand, in the dialogical situation that I used, I carried the schedule in my head as Srinivas has recommended (1988) and made notes after the dialogue in some place of privacy. I refrained from using a tape recorder because I found that it acted as a disturbing and intimidating intruder, especially for my women subjects; it had no part in a 'faithful' dialogue and friendship. I also refrained from calling my interface with my women subjects 'interviews', or calling my women subjects 'respondents' or 'informants.' The former gives the impression that they are mere response-giving machines, never allowed to ask anything from their side, with the conversation flowing from one side only—that of the researcher. I also do not call the researched women subjects 'informants' because this conveys the impression that the latter are informers of a spy or the police. I feel that perhaps it is a two-way, candid information exchange from both sides with the freedom given to both sides to ask questions and receive honest replies that can lay the plinth for an interactive and more democratic sociological method of data collection.

Such an interactive method with its emphasis on sharing and equal balancing of the power relationship that comes into being in a conventional interview situation with an inquisitorial interviewer 'self' and 'subject' and the inquisitioned interviewee 'other' and 'object' would perhaps change the whole process of research and result in a state of affairs in which both the interviewer and the interviewee become autonomous, self-determining, equal-level 'selves' and 'subjects.' The interview then becomes a dialogue and results in more authentic data being received and becomes an act of 'knowing' for both the researcher and the researched.

Presentation of Data and 'Voices'
Feminist researchers have increasingly advocated the use of the 'voices' of women subjects researched in the presentation of data concerning them. (Duelli Klein 1983, Kumar 1994, Reinharz 1983, Stivers 1993, Du Bois 1983, Oakley 1981, Stanley and Wise 1983a, 1983b, Karlekar 1991, Roberts 1981). It is important that women's narratives, and the voices in which they have been so trustingly recounted, be the vehicles to communicate directly the agony and the pain that women have been made to suffer. This should be seen as a methodological device to conscientise academics and others to women's brutalisation and dehumanisation which has been going on for centuries and still continues. Smothering these voices under a blanket of theory or 'using' them selectively to buttress the pre-conceived, self-believed theories of the academics amounts to betrayal and exploitation of the women studied.

Like their male colleagues, women social scientists often belong to different classes and different regional cultures or even other 'national' cultures, and are thus alien to the cultural milieu and psyche of many of their women subjects of research. There is always the danger that in their research, the women studied may be condemned yet again to becoming the 'other.' Women researchers as much as men can be guilty of using their subjects to serve the purpose of a patriarchal scientific model. That such models are adopted by many women academics proves that patriarchy has struck deep roots in the psyche of women researchers as well. If theorising and analyses are considered so necessary at all times that they cannot be refrained from for some time even, then, at present, in 'women's studies' at least, they should be appended to the narratives in received 'voices' and not allowed to subvert the communicative value of the latter.

Here, however, one must take cognisance of the fact that 'voices', that is, speech, is not the only means of self expression and communication. Silences and pauses, the latter often referred to as pregnant with meaning, also communicate and have their own language as do the eyes, gestures, face, hands—in fact the whole body (see Gal 1991) all of which may be culturally constructed. Therefore, the 'gaze' is as important as the 'voice' in the communication of one's subjects' state of being and consciousness and details 'gazed' at by the researcher (observation) should also form part of the narrative as produced in 'voices.'

The Social Anthropologist as an Ethnographic Field

In a recent article (1996b), M.N. Srinivas suggests that since Indian social anthropologists have gained considerable experience in the study of their own culture and society, the time has come for at least a few of them to move from studying the 'self-in-the-other', to studying 'the self' itself. Srinivas feels that every human being's life can be regarded, provided it is long enough, as an ethnographic field: individuals, each a product of a particular generic heritage and domestic culture, go through life reacting to various forces and events. Srinivas asks why a social anthropologist cannot treat his own life as an ethnographic field and study it? No outsider can know a person's life as the person himself. The social anthropologist moreover is trained to observe everything, including his own reaction to others. Every life mirrors to some extent the culture and the changes it undergoes. The life of every individual can be regarded as a 'case study.' And who is better qualified than the individual himself to study it? (Srinivas 1996b:657).

Such a self-analysis, perhaps, should be attempted by all those studying women's situation. This self-analysis can be appended to the text of their research outcome so that it can apprise the readers of the perspective, values, beliefs and attitudes of the researcher which surely must have gone into his or her research and production of the writing of its results and will make his or her standpoint clear to the readers. In fact, Freeman (1979) already laid the ground for such a practice in his classic biography of an untouchable. But how many social anthropologists will have the courage to make their self-analysis as truthful and forthright as it should be?

Dialogue as Method and Text

I have tried here, by recounting portions of some of my dialogues with Shanno, to bring out some of the flavour, the warmth, and the pain, and also the difficulties of researching in this fashion.

Shanno is one of the women I met and interacted with in the course of my fieldwork in a *jhuggi-jhompri* colony in Delhi. She is a well-built, woman of medium height, (5′ 4″) about 32 years old, though she looks older, about 45. She is ebony coloured, no doubt due to constant exposure to the sun in the course of the construction work she is used to doing. The skin of her face is wrinkled. Her face looks craggy and the corners of her eyes are marked with deep crow's feet. Her hands are small but dark and rough. Her nails are broken and lined with dirt. Her feet are large and flat. They are also dark and dirty with the skin broken not only on the heels but on all sides of the feet. The gashes are filled with grime. The toes are all spread out. She wears silver *jhanjhars*[5] on her feet and silver toe rings in one of the toes of each foot. Around her long neck which is marked by lines of dirt, she wears a silver *hansli*.[6] There are glass bangles on her wrists.

Shanno has a ramrod bearing, a rather superior, supercilious expression in her eyes, and a permanent sardonic smile on her lips. She lacks warmth, effusiveness and friendliness and, unlike the other *jhuggi*[7] dwellers, is short on hospitality and good manners.

Shanno wears a *lehnga*,[8] a *koti*,[9] and a *dupatta*.[10] But, it is obvious that Shanno cannot afford the yards and yards of material needed to make a proper *lehnga* and has substituted it with a readymade petticoat with frills at the bottom.

Shanno does not live in a real *jhuggi* but in two *pucca*[11] rooms with solid roofs. The rooms have mosaic floors and are about 8′ × 6′. The house has no WC and no water connection. The electricity is stolen by hooking a wire to the outside wires of the street light.

On some occasions when I had conversations with Shanno inside her house I noticed that the two rooms of her home were quite bare. There was practically no furniture. There was one flat, rectangular, wooden bed and two string cots. A string had been tied from one end of one of the rooms to the other end, on which hung clothes. There were several cannisters which most probably contained provisions. One corner of the front room which had a kerosene stove, served as the cooking area. Shanno possessed quite a number of stainless steel utensils. There was no bathing place. When I asked about this I was told that Shanno and her daughters, whenever they bathed, which was not every day, did so in a corner of the front room. Shanno's husband, and her sons, bathed at the hand pump, which was quite far from the house.

The first time I met Shanno she was sitting on a string cot in the alley outside her home. The alley was quite wide—about 4′—with open drains overflowing with slush on each side. Here and there were small piles of faeces obviously of little children. Shanno was busy sewing something on a sewing machine. She was surrounded by five or six women who were sitting on their haunches watching Shanno with unabashed fascination.

From the beginning, Shanno adopted a hostile attitude towards me and made me feel an unwelcome outsider and an intruder. This was perhaps Shanno's way of getting her back at one who she thought belonged to the enemy camp—the have's, with everything going well for them. Her cantankerousness was perhaps a 'weapon of the weak' (Scott 1990), a protest against the oppressor, the *oonche log*.[12]

I approached Shanno with folded hands and said 'Namaste, how are you?'

No reply. No raising of the head. No eye contact made. The sewing continued, perhaps a little faster.

'Can I sit down here?'

No reply. No looking up. No eye contact made. The sewing continued at a fast pace. Some of the women sitting around Shanno said 'Wait, we will get something for you to sit on.'

'No. That's not necessary. I will sit on the floor here. I sat down on the floor of the outer room which jutted out into the alley.

Shanno went on sewing.

'Well, what is your name?'

'Gita, as in *Sita aur Gita*.[13]

The women sitting around us giggled.

'*Mataji* (mother), said one, 'She is telling you a lie. Her name is Shanno and not Gita.'

Shanno remained impassive and continued sewing without lifting her head or looking up.

'Where do you come from Shanno?'

'Where do you think I come from?' asked Shanno without looking up. 'Can't you make out? You are from the *oonche log* and I am sure you have studied to a very high class. What is the use of all your *padhai* [reading i.e. education] if you can't even tell where I come from? Guess where I come from?'

'I think you come from Haryana.'

'Wrong. Your *padhai-likhai* [reading-writing, i.e. education]. is of no use. I come from a village in district Jaipur in the state of Rajasthan. I am a Rajasthani. Can't you make out? *Mera aadmi*[14] (literally, my man) also belongs to a village in Jaipur district. The name of his village is Dosa.'

'What *biradari*[15] do you belong to?'

'I am naturally not of the same *biradari* as you. Your *biradari* must be a high one. What *biradari* do you belong to?'

'I was born a Kashmiri a brahmin.'

'See, I told you, your *biradari* must be a high one. *Meri kismat itni achchi nahin hai* [my fate is not so good]. I belong to a *neechi biradari* [low community, i.e. low caste]. I am sure you have not even heard of it. We are *berwas*,[16] and you should not touch me otherwise you will become unclean. That is what your high *biradari* people say.' At last Shanno stopped sewing and looked up. There was a look of challenge in her eyes. Her body was taut.

'I don't believe in all that. Here, I will touch you.' I touched her on the head.

'Now you will have to go and have a bath. How can you not believe in *chhua chhoot* [pollution and contamination] if you have to live in your *biradari*? But the *oonche log* like you are free to do whatever they like. Nothing happens to you. But we *garib log* [poor people] have to live in our *biradari*. We have to do what the *biradari* says *nahin to hamen pareshan kar diya jayega* [otherwise we will be harassed]. I am sure you can't eat or drink anything from my house?' Again a look of challenge, the sewing abandoned and the body taut.

'Of course I can.'

'Our food is unclean according to your *biradari*. Also, it is bad food. You must be used to eating *halwa puri*.[17]

'What have you cooked? Let me taste it.'

For a moment Shanno was taken aback. 'Will you really eat what I have cooked? We don't have money to make many things. Today I only made *roti*[18] and *pyaz ka jhol*.[19] You will eat it?' The expression in Shanno's eyes changed from a challenging to a questioning one.

'Yes. Let me taste it.'

Shanno called out to a girl 'Aia Chitti, go and get half a *roti* and some *jhol* and give it to this *auntyji*.[20]

I asked Shanno 'What did you do in your village?'

'What do poor people do in a village? Don't you know? And you think you are *padhi likhi*. In a village people like us who have no land do *khet mazdoori* (agricultural labourer's work). My man's family had some land. Very little. About 2 *bighas*.[21] Suddenly she was pensive; the hostility disappeared for a while. But, again, she would not look at me. Her body was no more taut but a little hunched. 'There was not much *kamai* [earning] in doing *khet mazdoori*. This is why we came to Delhi. One of the relations of my man—his *dur ke mausa ka beta* [a far removed mother's woman cousin's son] told my man that there were good jobs available in Delhi. He worked here. He told my man to come to Delhi also. My man wanted to move to Delhi but we had no money for the *kiraya* [fare]. We worked very hard and tried to save money. You would not know what hard work it is to do *khet mazdoori*. You must be working in a closed room sitting on a chair with a table in front of you, writing on paper with a pen, not with your back bent for hours.'

Shanno looked at me. The look of challenge was back in her eyes but for an instant only and then the eyes seemed to look somewhere far into the horizon. 'What backaches I used to get. I could not sleep. When we had enough money we came to Delhi by *rail* [by train]. My man's relative met us at the station. I had not seen such a crowd before.' Now she looked at me directly; her eyes met mine. It seemed to me that she wanted to communicate with me. 'Not even in *melas* (fairs) is there such a crowd! So many people! So much noise! So many motor cars, and *rickshas* with wheels of motor cars [she meant the three-wheeled, covered, scooter rickshaws, which ply in Delhi]. *Mera to jee ghabra gaya* [my heart was greatly disturbed]! Shanno was animated. Her body and eyes were suddenly alive. 'How will we live here?' I thought.

While reminiscencing about her first impressions of Delhi, Shanno seemed to have forgotten that she was supposed to be hostile to me.

'My man's relation brought us here to this Rajpur [not the real name] *jhuggi-jhompri* cluster. It was so dirty. It was crowded with people. The houses were built so close together. There was no open space anywhere. I thought of our village and wanted to cry. But I was sure my man would have got very angry if I had done that, so I kept quiet. We stayed with my man's relation in his *jhuggi*. This relation got us jobs as *beldars* [building construction workers] with a *jamadar* [labour contractor]. That labour contractor was a wolf—a *bhediya*! He would take away so much of our money. I used to earn Rs. 20 per day and my man used to earn Rs. 30 per day.' Shanno is totally lost in giving information about herself which she does, not with much emotion, but rather detatchedly. 'We worked from 9 in the morning till 5 in the evening carrying bricks on our heads or mixing cement—really hard work it was. My head ached from carrying bricks. The *jamadar* took Rs. 5 from our earnings as his share.'

Suddenly Shanno stopped talking and went back to her sewing.

'Are you still doing the work of a *beldar*?'

'No. Now I teach.' All the women sitting around burst out laughing. Shanno smiled rather triumphantly. '*Auntyji*, she is telling you lies again. She still does the work of a *beldar* but at present she has no work. Her man does the work of a *raj mistri* [mason].'

'No. He doesn't,' said Shanno. 'He sings.

Peals of laughter. 'No *auntyji*. Her husband is a *raj mistri* and he also has no work just now.'

Shanno seemed to be enjoying playing to the gallery. She turned to me and asked, 'What does your man do?'

'My man is a writer. He writes for the newspaper and he also translates things from one language to another. If you write something in Hindi he will translate it into English.

'What kind of work is that?' asked Shanno looking at me directly. 'But I suppose it is not as hard work as *beldari*. You *oonche log* don't have to do hard work. I suppose your man gets much more money than *beldars*. Now the rate for doing *beldari* for women is Rs. 40 per day and for a man Rs. 60 per day.

'Why is there such a difference between what a women gets and what a man gets for the same work?'

'How do I know? That is how it is. I suppose it is because men are always supposed to be better than women.'

Meanwhile the *roti* and *pyaz ka jhol* was brought for me to eat. The *roti* was gritty and the *pyaz ka jhol* was full of chilly powder with a few pieces of onion floating in the watery curry. It was difficult for me to eat the food given but somehow I tried to swallow it. This was like a test for me, I felt. If I failed then I would lose all credibility.

While I ate everyone watched me.

One of the women asked 'How did you like it?'

I replied: 'Quite good.' But I felt the need to be more honest. 'You should be eating better and healthier food than this. This food will not make you strong. I know you all are poor and cannot afford better food. I sincerely wish it was in my hands to make better food available for you but I am helpless. I can do nothing.'

Shanno said, looking at me, 'Why don't you ask the *sarkar* [government] to get us good jobs so that we can eat better food?'

'I am not from the *sarkar*. I am studying. The *sarkar* does not do things because I ask them to.'

The women, including Shanno, looked at me with disbelief.

'You are so old and you are still doing *padhai*?'

'Yes. There is no age bar on studying.'

'You are not doing a *sarkari naukri* [government job]?'

'No. And I am not as rich as you think I am. Of course I won't say I am as poor as you all are but I don't have lots and lots of money. My man has to work also from 8 in the morning to 8 in the evening to earn enough money so that we can have enough to eat.' I turned to Shanno.

'Did you go to school, Shanno?'

'Yes. I went to school and I am very *padhi likhi*.'

Again laughter from the women and a supercilious look from Shanno plus a mocking smile.

One of the women said 'Why are you harassing mataji? Why don't you give correct answers?' And then, addressing me, 'She is not educated at all. She has never been to school. She is doing *maskhari* with you; she is joking. She cannot even sign her name. Her man also has not studied to a high class. He can't read or write either. But he can sign and count.'

Shanno did not say anything but continued sewing on the machine.

'Where did you learn sewing?' I asked.

'At Kiran.' She named a non-governmental voluntary organisation doing educational and social work in Rajpur.

'You must have children?'

'Naturally. Everyone has children. I have four—two daughters and two sons. You ask as if you don't have any children.'

'I have no children,' I said.

Shanno lifted up her head from her sewing and the hardness on her face and in her eyes, I felt, softened a little. 'You have no children? That's bad. People must be saying bad things about you. It is not good to be a *banjh* [a barren women]. Your man must be feeling very angry with you and also your *saas* [mother-in-law] and your *sasur* [father-in-law]. But you are rich. You could have shown yourself to a doctor and got yourself cured. Now, of course, you are too old and can't have children. In our *biradari* if a woman does not have children after she is married she is thought of as a very ill-fated woman. Her man can even go and marry again. You must be hearing a lot of taunts from your *biradariwale* [people of your community]?' There was a soft look of pity on her face.

'My mother-in-law and father-in-law are no more. But when they were alive they did not get angry with me. My *biradariwale* feel sorry for me but they don't taunt me. I am not barren. My man and I decided deliberately not to have any children and my man does not want to marry another woman.'

'You deliberately decided not to have any children!' Shanno looked shocked. 'What a strange woman you are! If you don't have any children, especially a son, who do you think is going to look after you in your old age? Your *saas* and *sasur* did not taunt you, you say. Strange people! Your *biradariwale* also do not taunt you. Your *biradariwale* are then different from ours. You should at least have had a son.'

'I suppose you think I should have had a son because a son is needed to light the funeral pyre of his father and carry the name of the family forward?'

Shanno was now talking to me freely and with interest. 'I don't know about lighting the funeral pyre or carrying the name of the family forward, but this much I know, that a son is needed to support one when one's *haat pair jawab de denge* [when our limbs will give up on one].'

'But what is the guarantee that the son will not turn out to be a good for nothing and does not look after one in one's old age? What then?'

'In your *biradari* you don't have respect for your elders, I think. In my *biradari* it is the son's responsibility to look after his old father and mother.'

One of the women sitting around us said, 'But *auntyji* is quite right. How can one be sure that one's son will look after one in one's old age? These days sons listen more to their wives who want to have nothing to do with their *saas* or *sasur*.'

'Do you want to have more children?' I asked Shanno.

'If I have more children who do you think will feed them? Will you feed them? I have had the operation [tubectomy] done after my fourth child was born. My man agreed and did not stop

236 Anthropological Journeys

me. I used to have great difficulty when my babies were being born. They were all born upside down and the *dai* [midwife] had a very hard time bringing them out. I used to shout and scream with pain and every time I felt I would surely die and gave my man a lot of *gaalis* [abuses]. You wouldn't know how painful it is to have a child.'

'What do your children do?'

'*Lo!* What do children do? If you had had children what do you think they would have done? The sons must go to school and then work. My eldest child, who is a boy— I don't know how old he is because I can't count—works in a factory which makes plastic bottles for putting in the water which turns into soap with which women of *oonche log* wash their hair, so my son tells me. He is a good boy and gives us money so that we can have *roti* at least once a day. If he was not working we would have had to ask for *bheek* [alms]. Your two meals a day must be assured, otherwise you would not be so fat.'

The other women tittered at this but one of them said 'Shanno, you are very bad. Mataji is talking so nicely to you and you are talking to her in such a shameless manner.'

'What do your daughters do Shanno?'

'You are really without any brains. In our *biradari* girls don't go running round with boys so freely as is shown in the films that I see on the TV. These films are not about people like us. I think they are about people like you. I suppose in your *biradari* boys and girls roam around with each other without any shame. This does not happen in our *biradari*. In our *biradari* we don't send girls to school. My daughter—the elder one—has never been to school but she knows how to do housework and to cook. What is the use of sending daughters to school? What good will it do to them because finally they have to get married and their work will be to look after their man, their children and their home. My elder daughter is now of marriageable age. In our *biradari* we marry our girls as early as we can. I suppose this does not happen in your *biradari*. It does not happen in the films that I see. In the films the boy and the girl are very grown up when they marry. My daughter should be married soon. I feel she should be sent to her *sasural* (in-law's house) as early as possible. A girl is a load on the heads of her mother and father [*apne ma-bap ke sar pe bojha hoti hai*]. The sooner one gets rid of the load of the daughter off one's head the lighter one feels. Amongst us, if we don't marry the girl early then people start talking ill about her. They think she must be having some *aib* [shortcoming] and the girl and her mother and father have to hear nasty things from everyone.'

'But do you know,' I said, 'there is a law that forbids the marrying of daughters before the age of 18. If you do so then you can be punished.'

'Is there such a law?' asked one of the women. 'We don't know about the law.'

Shanno asked, I felt, with great interest, 'How can there be such a law because everyone in our village, and even here, marries their daughters off at a young age and nothing happens to them?'

I said, 'There is also a law forbidding the giving and taking of *dahej* [dowry]. You can be sent to jail for taking and giving *dahej*.'

Shanno, now very much engrossed in the dialogue, asked, 'How can that be? If you want to marry your daughter to a good boy you have to give a lot of *dahej*. That is the custom. How can there be a law against custom? No *dahej* was given when I got married but nowadays the boy's father and mother want *dahej* and the better educated the boy is and the better his job, the more is the *dahej* asked for. Nobody is punished for that. At least I have not heard of anybody being sent to jail for that. I don't know where we will get money to give good *dahej* for our daughter.' Looking down, very thoughtful. 'I suppose we will have to take *karza* [a loan] and then it will take years to pay back the *karza*. But what can one do? Maybe we will marry off our son first and take *dahej* at his wedding which can then be used to give *dahej* for our daughter. My two other children are too young. Now you will ask if they go to school? They don't. We have no money to send them to school. I wanted that my sons at least should have become *padhe likhe* so that they could get a *sarkari naukri* but my eldest son studied only up to the sixth class and my younger son, as I said, does not go to school at all. I don't know whether we will be able to send him to school ever. If it is in his fate he will study to a high class otherwise not. Did you get married at a young age? You couldn't have because you must have studied upto a high class and when you study up to a high class you don't remain a girl, you become a woman by the time you finish.'

'I was 28 years old when I got married.'

There were sounds of astonishment from all the women who were sitting around us.

'You were 28 years old: *Hai bhagwan*! You were almost a *budhia*, [an old woman] when you got married. If you had been of my *biradari*, your ears would have become sore hearing people's taunts. Your father and mother did not get you married early?'

'They wanted to get me married early—not as early as girls get married in your *biradari*—but at about the age of 20. But nobody came forward to marry me, so I took up a job and started working.'

'You must have had a *prem vivah* [love marriage].'[22]

'Yes. I had a love marriage.'

'You married a man from your own *biradari*?'

'No. I did not marry a man from my own *biradari* though my father and mother wanted me to do so.'

Shanno's curiosity got the better of her and she forgot her antagonism towards me for the time being. 'You married a man out of your own *biradari*? Then your *biradariwale* must be having nothing to do with you or your mother and father. If such a thing happened in my *biradari* the *biradariwale* would not even drink water in our house leave alone eat anything. They would send the boy and the girl out of the village. It is better that our girls and boys marry in their *biradari*. They can never have a love marriage. They have to marry the person their mother and father choose for them to marry. Our children are not bold like you. They listen to their mother and father and think of the *izzat* [honour] of their elders and obey them which people of your *biradari*, it seems, do not do. Like you—you did not obey your mother and father. I could not even think of my daughter marrying anyone from any other *biradari* than mine and if she did so, or had a love marriage, I would ask her never to set foot in my house. These things are not done among us.'

'Not only did I not marry a man from my *biradari* but I married a man who was not of the same religion as myself.'

Shanno gaped at me. Her eyes were full of astonishment. 'What! You married a man who was not of your religion? You are a very *tez aurat* [fast woman]! You must have been a great headache for your mother and father. *Unki to naak kat gayi hogi* [their nose must have been cut—i.e. they must have lost face]! They must have turned you out of their house.'

'No. They did not. They were upset in the beginning but later gave in to my wishes and married me off from their house.'

'If you married someone who was not of your religion then by what ceremony did you get married?' asked Shanno who was by now totally engrossed in my life story, the sewing completely forgotten.

'We had what is called a civil marriage. In that a person from the court comes to the house or, you go to him, and you have to sign in a book, and you are married. There was no religious ceremony. We did not want any.'

'How can you get married by just signing your name in a book? If you did not have any *puja* [worshiping of God] then how can you call yourself married? In our *biradari* there has to be *puja* at the wedding and everything is done according to *riti rivaj* (customs). You have to have a *sagai* [engagement ceremony] first, then the *biyah* [wedding] and then the *gauna* [when the girl departs for her husband's house]. I had my *sagai* when I was very small. I don't remember anything much about it now. Then after a long time I had my *biyah* and *gauna* together. I was just a young girl. I had not started my *mahina* [month, i.e. menstruation]. You know, it is considered very bad if your daughter starts her *mahina* and is still sitting in her mother and father's house. You people have such different lives from us. You don't know anything of our lives and therefore you can't understand our worries. How can you, when you live so differently from us? You go and marry a man who is not of your religion. You have a love marriage and your *biradari* does nothing about it. People like you seem to do whatever you wish. There is no *lagam* [rein] on you. We can't do what we like.'

Speaking with Shanno on other occasions we talked about more personal subjects. These happened in private sessions inside her house, though it was difficult to keep her there.[23]

'Did you know about the *mahina*, before you started bleeding?' I asked.

'How could I know? No girl knows before-hand. I suppose you knew? We do not know about the *mahina* till we get it. No mother or anyone else tells the girl about it before it happens. But you *oonche log* are so lacking in shame that I am sure your mother told you.'

'No. My mother did not tell me about it either, I did not know anything about it also till I started bleeding. I remember I was playing a rough game of hide and seek with my *dadi's* [father's mother] sister's children—my *dadi's* sister was much younger than my *dadi*. My *dadi's* sister passed by while we were playing. She stopped in her tracks, came to me, caught me by the hand and said, "Come, you have to go home."

I was very irritated. "Why do I have to go home?"

"Don't ask questions" said my *dadi's* sister and took me to my house and to my *dadi*. My *dadi*, her sister and my mother, who had all had no formal education, took me to an inside room and started inspecting my underclothes. Then I saw there was blood on them and there was a large spot of blood on my frock also. They never said anything to me, but only made a pad out of old cloth and tied it with a string to me. I was very frightened but I did not ask any questions and they did not tell me anything. They changed my frock and told me to lie down. They said I was not to play hide and seek any more. They also told me that I was not to bathe for two days. On the third day I was to have a bath and wash my hair, when I would become *suchchi* [clean, i.e. non-polluting] again. Till then I would be *jhuthi* [polluted]. I was not to go near the place where gods were worshipped. I was not to go near the kitchen. I was not to let my shadow fall on the pickles kept out in the sun. I was not to play rough games. There were certain things I was forbidden to eat—some "cold" foods like curd and "hot" foods like meat.[24] I was miserable. I thought I had caught a disease. But no one else seemed to be bothered or upset and no doctor was called. In the evening everyone went to see a film in the cinema hall and took me along as though nothing had happened. I could not watch the film. I was so worried. What is this that had happened to me, I thought. I cried throughout the film but did not have the guts to ask anyone what had happened to me. I started my *mahina* when I was 12 yeas old. How old were you?'

'I can't tell you how old I was but I started bleeding when I was in my *sasural*' said Shanno. 'My father and mother saw to it that it did not happen while I was sitting in their house otherwise everyone would have started commenting. I discovered the blood on my clothes when I was drawing water from the well. I was very surprised. I thought I had hurt myself.

Shanno and I had suddenly developed a certain intimacy in our relationship because of our shared experience where the onset of menstruation was concerned.

'I went to my *saas* and showed her the blood. She also did not say anything. She also told me to tie a piece of cloth with a string and to tie another one when the first one got soaked. The stained cloths had to be washed secretly, away from the eyes of everyone. I was not to tell anyone what had happened to me and I was not to play with boys any more. I was also considered *jhuthi* [polluted] and was given instructions—you have to do this, you don't have to do this. All very confusing! But I asked why I was bleeding. My *saas* told me that all girls after a certain age bled. This was nothing unusual. I asked whether I was going to bleed all my life. She said yes, after every 25 to 30 days. I also cried a lot. I wondered why this had to happen to me. What a nuisance it was. My *saas* was a very strict woman. She had a very bad temper. My mother also had a very bad temper. She was always in a bad mood. I think because of her children. We were in all 8 children. We had no land and we were very poor. My father and mother and my elder brothers and sisters worked as *khet mazdoors* but the earnings were never enough. My mother was always worried and that is why I think she was always angry. She used to beat us up and also cry a lot. I think my *saas* also had a bad temper because of my man's family which was very big, eight people in all they were, and they were also poor *khet mazdoors*. Because I knew my *saas* had a bad temper I did not question her about the *mahina* too much, fearing she might beat me. But I worried inside. Then as time passed I discovered things about it by myself and stopped worrying. How can one keep worrying about something that one can do nothing about? I accepted the *mahina* as my *kismat*. I have not told my daughter about it. One doesn't tell these sort of things to one's daughter. She can learn about it when her *mahina* starts. Would you have told your daughter about it if you had a girl of your own?'

'Yes. I would have told her and now they also inform girls about these things at school. I was told about it at school later,' I replied.

'Did your mother tell you what a man and woman do after marriage? Were you told at school?' Shanno enquired avidly.

'My mother did not tell me what a man and woman do after marriage and I was not told about it at school.[25] I thought children just came of themselves when one got married. One day we went to see a film and in it a woman became pregnant before getting married. I could not understand how, but I could not ask my mother or my *dadi*. I don't know why. Somehow I felt that this was something which my mother and my *dadi* would not like me to know. I, therefore, asked my young teacher who used to come and give me tuition in English. It was she who told me about it and I was shocked. Then my friends and I discussed it at school but all of us were quite ignorant about the matter so we did not get to know much till we were in a higher class and read about it in books. We were also not told about it at school.'

Shanno said 'I think it is a very shameful thing men do to women after marriage. Maybe some boys and girls in your *biradari* do it even before marriage? In films boys and girls do all kinds of shameful things before marriage. I came near my man only after my *gauna* and then he started doing all sorts of dirty and shameful things which made me feel so ashamed. I was very upset. I had never imagined that men could do such things and it hurt so much. I did not like it at all and did not want my man to do it and so I used to try and push him away when he came near me. Then he beat me. I have suffered a lot of beatings because of that. Now things are better. The children are grown up and we all live close to each other. My man can't do it in front of the children, so it only happens once in a while. Also I am not so simple anymore. I fight with him and often manage to have my own way. He says "I will go to another woman." I say, "Go! I don't care." But he doesn't go to another woman. Earlier I used to obey my man in everything but now I don't want to obey him all the time. If there is something I don't want to do, I don't do it. I am not so frightened of him anymore.'

'Then you are not like Sita ji. Do you know who Sita ji was. It is said that every woman should be like Sita ji who obeyed her husband always, served him and looked after him? Don't you want to be like her? Have you listened to the Ramayana?'

'I know Sita ji was Ram ji's wife. I have seen her in Ram Lilas [the story of the epic Ramayan enacted on stage] in my village and also here and on the TV which I watch sometimes at the neighbour's. But I have never thought of becoming like Sita ji. My mother also never told me to be like Sita ji. I have never heard the Ramayana. It is never read in our *biradari*. I have only seen it on TV and watched the Ram Lila.'

'How did you get to know what a woman should do and what she should not do as a wife?'

'I can't tell. I just knew. I think I knew because I saw my mother and other women in the village and also I got advice in bits and pieces from my mother now and then. But I did not get any special instructions on what I should do and what I should not do as a wife.'

'If your man beat you why didn't you leave him?'

'Leave my man because he beat me? All men beat their wives sometime or other. If one were to leave one's man because he beat one, then all women would be leaving their men. They beat us when they tell us to do something and we do not do it. Sometimes we do not do things because they tell us to do bad things. But most often they beat us because they know more about the world than we do and we go and do foolish things because we don't know. Then I think it is all right for them to beat us. Now look. If a child does something you don't like, don't you beat him? But you don't throw the child out of the house because he has not listened to you, and the child also does not leave the house because he was beaten. So why does a woman have to leave her man if he beats her? He beats her because he is a man. That is how he shows that he is a man, and it is he who takes care of the family. I suppose your man does not beat you. If he beat you I suppose you would leave him?'

'My man does not beat me, and you are right—if he beat me I would leave him.'

'If I leave my man where will I go? How will I live alone? What will happen to the children? It is very difficult in our *biradari* to live alone if you are a woman. Everyone starts thinking badly of you. They think it is the man who must have left the woman because she must have done something wrong. They think she is a wicked woman. I am not educated. I won't get any proper work. How will I feed myself and my children? There is one woman here whose man has left her and she lives alone and all the men keep eyeing her. This is why I think if a woman becomes a widow, at a young age, she should be married off again, otherwise, she will have to bear a lot of difficulties. In our *biradari* widows are allowed to marry again.'

By this time Shanno had started talking to me with ease. Only now and then she would revert back to her hostile queries, perhaps to rile me, but the moment would soon pass.

'Does your man decide everything that has to be done or does he talk it over with you first?'

'I suppose in your house you decide everything that needs to be done? Your man must be a quiet mouse. I feel sorry for your man. Everyone must be calling him *joru ka gulam* [wife's obedient lackey]. In our *biradari* it is men who decide everything and that is how it should be. They are the head of the family. They have seen the world more than women and know more. I only decide what has to be cooked, what rations have to be bought, that's all. All the purchasing is done by my man. I am not allowed to go very far from my home. If I wander further away my man thinks I am up to some mischief. It is my man who will decide who our children should marry and what *dahej* should be given or taken and how long they should study. He also decides what changes have to be made in the house, what things have to be bought for the house, for the children and me. Now that I am older I sometimes argue with my man but I get a slap for it. No. Women are not as wise, or as strong, as men, that is why we have to obey our men and do what they tell us to do. Do you decide everything that has to be done in the house? You are a *sava mard* [one and one fourth man].

'No I don't decide everything that has to be done in the house. Some things I decide. Some things my man decides. Many things we talk about and then decide together. My man helps me a lot in doing the housework.

'My man would rather die than do any of the housework,' said Shanno. 'He thinks if he started doing housework people would laugh at him. He is right too. I am sure people laugh at your man behind his back. There are some things which are meant for women to do and other things that men should do. You and I do not come from the same *biradari* so what you do is different from what we do. Your women do whatever they feel like. Your men do not behave like men should. I don't think my *biradari* will ever become like your *biradari*. I can never be like you', summed up Shanno, very knowingly and decisively.

Speaking Pain

Dialoguing with women in the *jhuggi-jhompri* cluster has been a most interesting, informative and also a rewarding experience for me. I have found the women easier to approach, not so bitter as the men, and in many ways very child-like, especially the younger women. What has been most educative for me has been the discovery that each of the women with whom I dialogued was unique. Simultaneously, while in some respects they are all so different from each other, in several respects their experiences, their attitudes and their behaviour patterns are similar. A common thread is definitely woven in the warp and the weft of the lives of all the women.

Shanno was not the only woman that I found who displayed hostility towards me. There were some others who were also antagonistic and sometimes ruder to me than Shanno. However, on the whole, the women in the *jhuggi-jhompri* cluster were never openly hostile and were always hospitable and well-mannered. It was amazing that even though they lived in such difficult circumstances under, most probably, great stress and strain, both physically and psychologically, they could still display such fine good culture in their behaviour to an outsider whom, more often than not, they treated as an honoured guest.

Many of the women, however, seemed to live in silence and seemed to have lost their power of speech to a large extent. Even when they talked it was of trivial superficial things, never about their real being. No doubt a response to the continued sufferings that they have been made to endure which can strike one dumb as Veena Das has so perceptively surmised (Das 1995).

Suffering, the Body and the Dialogue

Signs of suffering and pain are definitely visible on the bodies of the women as Veena Das professes they are apt to be (Das 1995). They were 'gazed at' by me in the case of Shanno, during the dialogues, in her older-than-her-age body, her wrinkled, craggy, sun-burnt face, the deep crow's feet on the corners of her eyes, her calloused hands, broken nails full of grime, large, unshapely, ugly feet with broken skin all round, the gashes filled with dirt. These features of Shanno's body are starkly visible signs of her suffering as a woman—the constant struggle, and the back-breaking work in the house and outside. These features of her life are painful and agonising, not only physically but psychologically.

The marks on Shanno's body and heart, and indeed on the bodies and hearts of the other women in the *jhuggi-jhompri* cluster, certainly stand out as a critique of the social reality to which the women belong. They are also signifiers of the membership of the women, including Shanno, to a particular community and gender. In Shanno's case they signify her membership to the sub-caste of the *berwas*, a scheduled, untouchable caste, marginalised, oppressed and at present, largely employed, either as agricultural labourers in their villages, or, as building construction workers, in urban areas, as well as Shanno's identity as a woman—all-enduring, all-suffering, in all probability full of pain and sorrow.

Shanno does not dwell in silence. This aspect of her personality I think emerged primarily as an outcome of the kind of dialogue that I tried to initiate, making myself open to attacks and questioning by Shanno. She may perhaps have remained quite silent after an initial show of hostility in a conventional interview or a non-equal dialogue situation which would probably have cramped her style. A freer dialogical encounter and my willingness to allow Shanno to be a full and equal participant in it, gave her the confidence to express her hostility openly.

Reactions to Pain and Suffering

There is, perhaps, not only one reaction—that of being struck dumb to pain and suffering. One could also become immune to pain, get resigned to it, justify it and get on with life as best as one can. This seems to be the case where Shanno is concerned. Shanno is not silent but quite vocal. She blames her misfortune on destiny. She does not go on bearing pain stoically but has sort of got over the traumas that come in its wake. She has learnt to cope with pain and suffering. She has got used to them and they seem to have ceased to matter in her life with which she carries on from day to day without, it seems, really living it.

Shanno's vocality perhaps is also due to the fact that she has been a wage-earning working woman. My experience in the *jhuggi-jhompri* cluster, in which I am doing fieldwork, has been that more often than not, women who are doing some remunerative work outside their home are more vocal and articulate than those who are housewives.

The younger men in the *jhuggi-jhompri* cluster, react to pain and suffering very differently. Their behaviour is marked by a smouldering anger. Their conversation is full of bile, venom and rancour. The women were never angry in quite the same way.

The Dialogic Encounter

Honesty in the Dialogical Encounter

Being fully honest with my women subjects in a dialogical encounter was the ethically 'correct' stand. It was not a strategy. That word contains within it connotations of conspiracy and manipulation. Fortunately my ethically 'correct' stand provided me a glimpse into lives of women in the cluster. As a result of their curious questions, which I entertained freely and answered with veracity, their own notions of those they perceived as *oonche log*—the resentment that my women subjects had towards them, their ideas of the world in which they thought such *oonche log* lived, how they behaved, the attitudes and their beliefs about the lifestyles of *oonche log* were revealed very tellingly. In my dialogues with Shanno, her conception of *oonche log* and their world, which she equated with the world shown on television, was exposed very vividly. Her interest and curiosity-aroused questioning of me somehow made her drop her self-consciousness a lot more easily because of the kind of dialogue that I initiated. Perhaps, she would not have been so unselfconscious if she had been asked direct questions on what she thought of the *oonche log*.

My sincerity in my effort to be honest and patient finally communicated itself to Shanno and slowly and gradually she did develop a certain trust in me and was able to open up and dialogue with me in a free and honest way. Shanno, who was hostile to me in the beginning, by and by began to soften and feel that I was not trying to exploit her in some fashion. (I am still not sure whether I was not being exploitative. After all, I stood to gain a lot from the encounter, and what Shanno would gain is not all that clear.)

Shanno is a talkative woman and seems to be as prone to chatter about herself, whine and grouse, especially about her struggle and her deprivation, as any other person, would be. Perhaps, for her, our dialogues were a kind of cathartic relief for she was at least able to talk about her difficult life to someone, especially an outsider, willing to listen to her and not mind too much her cussedness, which emerged from the dialogues as quite an important trait of her personality. My encounters with Shanno with the resolve that I would be scrupulously sincere and frank in my relationship with her finally were able to establish a common bond between us especially at the particular moment when we found out that our experiences at the onset of menstruation were more or less similar.

Self and Other in Dialogical Encounter

The discourses between Shanno and myself were such that sometimes I became the interviewer and Shanno the interviewee and at other times Shanno became the interviewer and I the interviewee. The focus kept continuously shifting as it should in an egalitarian dialogue. I must admit, to my disappointment, that the moments of sharing were negligible. I tried on my part not to patronise or hegemonise; I tried to allow Shanno to be a Self and Subject and not become the Other and Object for me—the Other who is often assumed to be alien, unlike one, unequal and at a lower level. However, since Shanno was not a social anthropologist nor was she making a deliberate effort to make the discourses democratic and egalitarian, in perhaps, a large part of the dialogues, she treated me as the Other and displayed towards me all the attitudes that I was trying to curb in myself, i.e. a sense of superiority, better-than-you, different-from-you, and a stance of condescension.

For a large part of the interface that I had with Shanno, Shanno was very much the Self and Subject. I do wonder, however, if Shanno had been the Other and Object in the dialogues how she would have responded. Would she have displayed the same aspects of her personality as she did while being the Self and Subject or not? Would Shanno not have allowed herself to be treated as the Other and an Object? Which out of the two—the Other/Object and the Self/Subject—would one consider to be the real Shanno? Or would qualities displayed both as Self/Subject and Other/Object be considered part of Shanno's personality.

Even though 'for Shanno I became the Other/Object and she treated me as such, I did not allow myself to be cast in that role and throughout the dialogues tried to remain the Self/Subject. To maintain this state of autonomy, in the kind of dialogical situation that I was trying to create self-assurance and self-confidence on the part of the researcher are very necessary in order not to allow the researched person to completely colonise the researcher and thus create an inegalitarian relationship in reverse.

The Dialogue: Understanding Resistance

Shanno's 'anger' is different from that of the angry young men of Rajpur. Her hostility appears to be more like what James Scott calls 'weapons of the weak' (1990). Does the dialogic method help us uncover and understand this different anger, these 'weapons'?

The theoretical debates of the 70s were dominated by concepts of conflict, power and agency located in their socio-historical moorings and seen to be a part of social and economic processes. The studies focussed on cultural hegemony as a historic process. On the other hand, post-modernism locates agency at the individual level. Post-modernism's reconstituting of culture seems to have no moorings in history and is confined to time-bound discourses of resistance at the individual level. Shanno's anger certainly resembles Scott's 'weapons of the weak'. Scott speaks of the prosaic but hesitant struggles, those forms of resistance between the peasantry and those who seek to extract labour, food, taxes, rents and interest from them. Here Scott has in mind the ordinary weapons of relatively powerless groups: foot-dragging, dissimulation, desertion, false compliance, pilfering, feigned ignorance, slander, arson, sabotage, expressions of hostility and so on. These Brechtian—or Schwekien—forms of class struggle have certain features in common. They require little or no coordination or planning; they make use of implicit understanding and informal networks: they often represent a form of individual self-help; they typically avoid any direct symbolic confrontation with authority—and an investigator is often presumed to be authority. To understand these commonplace forms of resistance is to understand much of what the peasantry has historically done to defend its interests against both conservative and progressive orders and it is Scott's guess that such kinds of resistance are often the most significant and the most effective ones over the long run. What Scott holds true for the peasants is also true for first generation peasant migrants to an urban area—people like Shanno. Shanno's weapons—bluster and rudeness, are but a defence mechanism and run only skin deep. Shanno's behaviour does not have as its base the kind of anger that is the potential for revolutions. Shanno's hostility towards the *oonche log* was tellingly revealed in our dialogical encounters. She found here the freedom to display her, perhaps rather impotent, resentment. This display of resentment seemed to be more to lighten her heart than to be related to any collective form of protest. Shanno was able to express her hostility because perhaps she got the signal from me that I was willing to allow her to do so. In a conventional interview or an unequal dialogue Shanno would surely have been more on her guard and more reticent.

However the concentration of resistance at the individual level draws attention away from oppression and exploitation operating on a much wider scale and reifies an individual's mostly futile acts of protest. These facts have to be kept in mind while analysing Shanno's mode of resistance. To understand Shanno, it is necessary also to understand the socio-economic and political forces that have led to her resorting to these 'weapons'; her resistance needs to be grounded. But this is beyond the scope of this paper.

Dialogue and Impression Management

The dialogues with Shanno also reveal aspects of her behaviour that can be analysed from the point of view of what is referred to as the 'dramaturgical school of interactionism' (see Goffman 1959, 1967) which focusses on the ways human beings manipulate gestures to create an impression in a particular social scene as actors do in theatre. Goffman very insightfully analyses how actors validate self-conceptions, how they justify their actions through gestures, how they demonstrate their membership in groups, how they display social distance and how they interpersonally manipulate many other situations. Shanno's life is also a grand performance like the lives of most of us and in her dialogues can be discerned all the above acts that people resort to when presenting their selves. Shanno's masks became visible in the kind of dialogues we were involved in. In a conventional interview, or even a dialogue which was unequal, Shanno would surely have felt more inhibited. In our dialogues she was bolstered to reveal herself more readily for I think she came to believe that she could do so because I would not take umbrage. Shanno most probably unconsciously, if not consciously, gauged, that in our kind of dialogical situations she could be herself because I would allow her to be so.

Shanno, like most of us, also has her masks which she puts on for others—her mask of self-confidence when perhaps she is quailing inside, her supercilious attitude, her attention-getting devices to boost her self-esteem, like the quips directed at me which make her companions laugh and mark her out as a heroine. Our dialogues also revealed Shanno's off-the-stage face which is different from her many masks. She is vulnerable, is obviously envious of me; of my being better-off, as she feels, than her; of my being a representative of *oonche log*; of my high education. Shanno tries to hide her real self in mockery and derision but in the dialogues her reality continually keeps peeping out from behind the masks. What is also evident is her very natural desire to communicate the pain and suffering that she has endured, her proclivity to talk, and her, again, very natural, curiosity, which often gets the better of her. This reality keeps showing itself from behind the masks because Shanno is not really a consummate actress; she cannot hide herself very effectively behind them.

Shanno seems to have transcended her pain and suffering and to some extent seems to have found her equilibrium by providing for her own conviction, according to her, plausible, justifications. However, I feel, that her equanimity is more due to her alienation. (I use this word in the Marxist sense.) She carries on with the motions of living almost like reflex actions and is not really deeply involved in committed way in any activity or endeavour. She stands aloof and alone from all, even perhaps from herself, in spite of all her sound and fury. Most probably defeated, accepting her defeat, she has ceased to struggle. She has laid down her arms and finds nothing very deeply engaging. She has no hopes, no dreams. She just carries on from day to day, perhaps, only from moment to moment, uttering thoughts which do not have any deep convictions behind them. She skims on the surface of life. In short, she exists in a state of alienation from everything and everyone including perhaps herself, despite all the surface sound and fury.

Class, *Biradari* and Dialogue

One very significant fact that emerges from my encounters with Shanno is the all-pervasiveness of class and caste differences. That I belong to a different class and caste is easily perceived by Shanno and most of the people in the cluster and it is difficult to bridge this chasm even in easy and equalitarian, informal communication.

It is difficult to say what effect class and caste differences must have on the reception of accurate data. Even after working and mixing with the dwellers of the *jhuggi-jhompri* cluster for a considerable time I found the class and caste barrier persisting. There is very little one can do about this situation.

It is very difficult to live down one's class and caste in a milieu like that of the *jhuggi-jhompri* cluster. The cluster is inhabited by people from the scheduled untouchable castes, who have come to Delhi from the countryside. They are very sensitive and touchy about their *jati* (sub-caste) and their class position perhaps because these are much more marked and accentuated in rural areas and the *jhuggi-jhompri* dwellers have as yet not been able to develop a more permissive and less rigid outlook and behaviour. Linked to the above is the important information received of the indigenous categories which are used by the *jhuggi-jhompri* dwellers, at least of the *berwa* caste, to designate class and caste differences which researchers should seek to discover. For instance Shanno uses the term *oonche log* as a blanket term to refer to all the classes who are above her in status and wealth and *garib log* to refer to her own class which seems to imply that class is seen by Shanno more in terms of differences in wealth. For caste Shanno uses the term *oonchi biradari* for all castes that are above her own caste and *neechi biradari* for the caste of *berwas* i.e. her own caste and in all probability for other castes falling below her own caste. The term *biradari* is often used coterminously with *jati* but in common parlance it is used more to refer to community.

Shanno emerges from our encounters, at least at the level of discourse, as a person who is totally bound up and swamped by her *biradari's riti-rivaj* (customs) which she seems to follow like an automaton and which seem to be sacrosanct and unbreakable for her. She gives in to them without any questioning. Shanno seems to follow the *riti-rivaj* of her *biradari* also like reflex actions in her state of alienation. She is so much influenced and overawed by the inflexible norms and sanctions of her *biradari* allowing no development of individuality that she finds my flouting of my own *biradari's* norms shocking and reprehensible. She abides by the norms of her *biradari*, and she sees this as something to be proud of; it is, for her, a sign of superiority over me. Perhaps in her heart of hearts Shanno too would have liked to break out of her *biradari's* mould but finding herself unable to do so, conveniently converts her weakness into an admirable and exalted quality which the *oonche log* lack. The grip that the *biradari* has on Shanno came into bolder highlight as a counterpoint that I provided with my own freedom from such a grip. This could only happen because I was willing to give honest information about myself to Shanno in our dialogues. However, whether in her behaviour Shanno allows herself to be so ruled by her *biradari's* norms and sanctions needs to be observed.

Women's Situation and Dialogue
There are three main features that stand out, again at the level of discourse which may not be cosubstantiated by actual behaviour, from the dialogues between me and Shanno related to women's situation in the *jhuggi-jhompri* cluster that are also signifiers of Shanno's own thinking and which too, I feel, emerged in bold relief because of the kind of encounters I had constructed with Shanno. First of all is the fact that patriarchy has the mind of Shanno and, as I have found, most women in the *jhuggi-jhompri* cluster, totally under its sway (see Sangari

1992). Shanno, for instance, believes that girls should be married early before the onset of puberty; that girls are a burden on the family; the preference in children is for boys but not for any ritual and religious purposes which, it seems are considerably underplayed in lower caste communities but for a very practical reason—to look after parents in the latter's old age (see Haider 1996a). Shanno believes that girls should not be highly educated; that the main work of girls is to become good housewives and mothers and that *dahej* is now necessary to be given at a girls's wedding and so on. In no way does Shanno reveal that she considers the discrimination against girls unfair. One point to note here is that Sita seems not to be a role-model for lower caste women (for Sita as role-model for women in India see Nabar 1995:108–113, 120–122, Mukherjee 1994, Kakar 1990:66) who naturally have not read the Ramayana because they were not allowed to do so and also because they are mostly illiterate (see Ilaiah 1996, Dube 1996:10). They were only familiar with the Ramayana through the watching of Ram Lilas (see Haider 1996a) and now because of the telecasting of the television serial of the epic. My data on this does not support Kakar's analysis of slum women. From the narratives of two of them, he surmises that even slum women see Sita as a role-model. But then Kakar does not state the caste of the women which makes a lot of difference as far as being aware of Sita, leave alone making her a role-model, is concerned (Kakar 1990).

The second feature of the women's situation in the *jhuggi-jhompri* cluster that emerges from my dialogues with Shanno is the wife beating that she is subjected to. This is a quite a common feature in the cluster but what is most disturbing is that many of the women, instead of feeling that their dignity and self respect have been mauled, actually find suitable, convenient justifications for their men for the violence perpetrated on them (the women), as does Shanno. Perhaps they resort to justifications in order to excuse their own selves for their inability to protest against the violence that they are made to endure. It is far easier to submit to oppression and exploitation passively than to carry out a persistent long-drawn out struggle, which is bound to go against them. Shanno seems to see her relationship with her husband as that of a debtor and creditor. She feels she is in debt to her husband because he gives her food and clothes and protects her and her children and she has to repay the debt by complete obedience and subservience—even suffer his beatings. Shanno, and most of the women in the *jhuggi-jhompri* cluster, are not willing to leave their husbands, who perpetrate violence on them because they are afraid, and perhaps rightly so, that they will not be able to live in peace alone; there is also the very real worry as to who would look after the children? The women seem to see the upbringing and looking after the children as solely their responsibility and not that of their husband's.

The third feature about the women's question in the *jhuggi-jhompri* cluster that seems to emerge from my dialogues with Shanno is related to the lack of control of women over their sexuality. Sex is forced on Shanno and obviously she does not enjoy it. Surprisingly almost all women in the *jhuggi-jhompri* cluster do not enjoy sex and have to submit to what one might call rape in marriage (see Haider 1993, 1996b). This situation I think has a lot to do with the social construction of the attitude towards sex and the part that women are supposed to play in the sexual act in India. Sex is never talked about in India. In fact there seems to be no word for sex or normal sexual intercourse in colloquial Hindustani. Perhaps this is because the activity is never talked about and named. It is kept shrouded in mystery. Girls are never told about it. When they overhear something it is always in negative terms—that it is a shameful, loathsome act which is liked only by men, and meant only for their pleasure. There is no question of women getting any pleasure out of it or initiating the act and playing a lead role in it. This social construction of the attitude towards sex in all probability ends up in women finding the act disgusting, degrading and shameful, meant only for the pleasure of men, to be passively submitted to and endured. For Shanno too this has perhaps been the case. Here I would like to clarify that there seems to be a misconception about so-called slum women, among the middle class and also it seems among academics and well-educated persons, who assume that slum women are quite lax where sexual morality is concerned. This is not what my experience has revealed to me. I have found that women in the *jhuggi-jhompri* cluster where I am working are, generally speaking, quite prudish and conservative about their sexual morality.

An important point which deserves attention here is that Shanno after having four children took the bold decision to have tubectomy performed on herself. This is the case, I have found, with many women in the *jhuggi-jhompri* cluster (Haider 1993, 1996b). Men agree to the women going in for tubectomy but almost never go in for any family planning method and certainly not vasectomy. It is strange that Shanno could take a bold decision where family planning methods were concerned but seems to succumb to her husband's commands where practically all other decisions, even minor ones, are concerned inspite of her, I think, rather hollow boast, that now that she has become older she does not always listen to her husband and often does not do what she does not want to do.

Shanno revealed to me intimate details of her sexual behaviour because of our mutual sharing of experiences. She built up enough trust in me to repose her confidences in me. I must confess here that though I was absolutely honest with Shanno in my revelations, I have withheld some information about myself in this paper for with Shanno and the other women of the *jhuggi-jhompri* cluster I somehow felt that my confidences would not be misconstrued, whereas I am not so sure that this would be the case if I go public about certain of my life's experiences in a paper of the present sort with its varied readership. In this perhaps I am being unfair to Shanno and do candidly admit that inspite of thinking myself to be a very progressive, modern, liberated woman, it seems, I am still shackled by tenacious, conservative inhibitions. This has been a rather unsettling self-discovery.

The discourses between Shanno are myself are interesting in that from them emerge comparative silhouettes of a woman like me, born in a conservative, high-caste, upper middle class, fairly well-off family, highly educated and to a large extent liberated, and Shanno, a woman belonging to a scheduled untouchable caste coming from a low class family, illiterate and still very much caught up in the patriarchal bind. The pictures that filter out are of two dissimilar types of women, and there may be other types—the in-betweens or the even-more-liberated, to be found in India. The problem that surfaces is whether one can spin feminist theories and organise a women's movement that can arch over all these types of women in India as well as include within its orbit, personal uniquenesses and similarities that exist side by side within the disparate groups of women in the country differentiated by ethnicity, class, caste and other categories. In such a situation theorising about gender becomes problematic in view of the presence of 'multiple patriarchies' (see Sangari 1995) which it has thus to confront.

Indian Women's Movement and the Dialogue

What relevance does the Indian women's movement have for women like Shanno and others like her? What implications does the interactive, equal-level, dialogical method, that I have employed in my research work have for the Indian women's movement.

First of all, I feel, there does not really exist a well-coordinated, all-India, coherent, specific-goals oriented, Indian women's movement in the country though claims have been put forward to prove that this is not true (see Gandhi and Shah 1991, Calman 1992, Kumar 1993, Desai 1988). There are very many autonomous women's groups and organisations which are working with women in several small pockets in India (Patel 1988, Datar 1993, Desai 1988) especially in rural areas and in some urban areas as well. Their aim is mostly to help women become earning members of the family, to become self-sufficient financially, and to participate in struggles against other kinds of oppression, apart from gender, being waged by other exploited and oppressed sections of India's population (see Desai 1988, Rose 1992, Sen 1990, Jain 1980, Caplan 1985). Other women's issues are addressed only tangentially. These autonomous groups and organisations have become wary of getting involved in the struggle against women's oppression in the family. Moreover, there is no formal national level organisation that binds the autonomous women's groups and organisations together and guides them in their activities towards consensually decided goals. In actual fact the Indian women's movement was at its strongest during the 1980s especially in its initial sustained campaigns against violence perpetrated on women in public and in the family but the ardour soon died down (Agnes 1993). At the present juncture the so-called Indian women's movement is at a somewhat critical juncture, face-to-face with rising communalism and casteism in the country which are splitting women's solidarity, if it ever existed, along religious and caste lines. In such a situation the women that are becoming visible are those that belong to the middle class (see Tharu and Niranjana 1994, Sarkar and Butalia 1995). Political events as they are unfolding in India have put the Indian women's movement in a quandary and the need is felt for a new discourse (Agnes 1995, Agnihotri and Mazumdar 1995).

The dialogical method does have implications for the Indian women's movement. The information I was able to glean from my dialogues seems to point to the fact that the pain and suffering of the women in the *jhuggi-jhompri* cluster have not been articulated; they have not found expression in speech. To find such expression is one way of becoming conscious of oppression. So this process of allowing women's voices to be heard is a major task for the Indian women's movement at the present juncture and also for the disciplines of social anthropology and sociology. The biggest challenge before the Indian women's movement, I feel, is to weld women together on the basis of the pain and sufferings that they have commonly endured into a moral community that could act as a protest group and aim to change the structures of patriarchy in cooperation with men and not see men as their enemy. In fact I think one of the main drawbacks of the Indian women's movement has been its ignoring of the fact that perhaps one of the important aspects of their agenda should be changing the patriarchal attitudes of men. This can only be done if men are also encouraged to realise how patriarchy dehumanises them as well and prevents them from leading a richer and fuller life. Men too should be encouraged to participate in the struggle against women's oppression.

Activists involved in working with women like Shanno will understand the need to establish dialogical relationships of the kind that I tried to establish with the women in the *jhuggi-jhompri* cluster. They will also realise that if they put forward a top-down agenda they would be seen as the Other perhaps more markedly, as women like Shanno seem to be prone to see members of the classes that are above their own class. Establishing a two-way communication with their subjects, on the other hand, earns the latter's trust and confidence. Activists and researchers may find too that what they think are crucial issues are not priority issues for women like Shanno. The significant issues for Shanno and her sisters may be different from what the activists have in mind. For instance, Shanno seems to feel the difference of class more deeply than gender inequality. It might also be revealed to the activists, as it was revealed to me, that women like Shanno are completely in the thrall of patriarchal norms which have colonised them and which have been totally internalised by them. This means that the task of the activists would be first to help women like Shanno to reflect on their situation critically and become conscientised to the fact that they are being exploited and oppressed and that this is an injustice to them as Paulo Freire has advocated (Freire 1972). Only after such a critical reflection can women like Shanno be really helped to take any action to change their condition.

Self Discovery and Dialogue
My special kind of encounters with Shanno and other women in the *jhuggi-jhompri* cluster have been a voyage of self-discovery both personally and intellectually. My encounter with Shanno was one of the several difficult ones and was fraught with anxiety and tension and also required great determination on my part to keep my cool. At many points I felt I was getting nowhere with Shanno. Her hostility and rudeness often made me feel like terminating the dialogue. I did lose my patience with Shanno sometimes and in some cases it was of help and in others it was not. I did, however, manage to somehow continue my dialogues with Shanno. The difficulties with her were more in the beginning. Later, however, it became much easier to talk to her and as bits of her life were revealed to me I tried to develop an understanding of her behaviour and attitudes. I will not say I pitied her or I was sympathetic towards her. I was overcome more by a feeling of helplessness. This has been the uppermost emotion that I have felt as I have got to know my protagonists better. The feeling of helplessness has been accompanied by a feeling of guilt.

My resolve to conduct dialogues with my women subjects on the basis of complete honesty on my part brought in its wake the establishment of close bonds with the latter—so close that it made me feel even more of a predator than I would have perhaps felt if I had carried on the dialogues keeping myself

260 Anthropological Journeys

closed up—aloof and distant, up on a pedestal with my lofty empathy. My decision to reveal quite freely as many details about my life as far as possible when questioned has led me to a far deeper involvement with my women subjects than I thought it would. And as they in turn revealed details of their painful and agonising lives I returned home each day after my fieldwork heavy of heart with a great sense of depression. This in turn has led me to question myself as to what I am doing to remove even a little of the misery and squalor that I have seen so closely. The answer seems to stare me in the face. Research has got to be linked with action programmes, otherwise it remains an exploitative act. At the very least, the findings of the research should be made to reach the corridors of power that have to do the planning for the eradication of poverty. I am however unable to make grand resolutions and thus feel just helpless and wretched.

My resolve to be honest in my dealings with my women subjects has been able to get me valuable authentic data. It has also made me wonder time and again whether the truth can ever be received from the persons being researched without deep and sincere involvement. I think not. I think I have learnt a very important lesson which all researchers must be learning in their own ways, that even in research work, as in theatre work, if one wants to get under the skin of the role, or as in the research situation, under the skin of the role of the researched, one must learn to be humble. Then only will one be able to get close to the truth.

Notes

1. I would like to extend here my thanks to Dr. Patricia Uberoi, my former teacher, who created in me an abiding interest, that has now become a commitment, in gender studies. I would also like to express my deeply-felt gratitude to my supervisor for my Ph.D. dissertation, Prof. M.N. Panini, Centre for the Study of Social Systems, School of Social Sciences, Jawaharlal Nehru University, New Delhi, who is also a friend, for his continued, experienced guidance, immense patience and understanding. I also thank Dr. Meenakshi Thapan and Ms Vidya Rao for painstakingly reading through my earlier manuscripts, making many insightful, very professional suggestions and doing the excellent job of editing which have all lent greater focus and coherence to the

paper. Last, but not the least, I extend my heartfelt thanks to my husband and friend, S.T. Haider. My Ph.D. project is more his dream than mine, and I have received support from him in so many ways that it is difficult to enumerate them all. I shall remain indebted to him always.

2. I am conducting fieldwork for my Ph.D. dissertation on 'A Sociological Study of a *Jhuggi-Jhompri* Cluster in the Indian Metropolis, Delhi', of which the study of women forms an integral part.

3. See also the debate on the supposedly close fit between feminist studies and post-modernism (Gupta 1995, John 1995, Thapan 1995, Karlekar 1995, Dasgupta 1995, Poonacha 1995, Chakravarty 1995, Ganesh 1995, Haider 1995, Gupta 1996).

4. See for instance Veena Das's assertion that the question of gender in the constitution of the subaltern studies series has been largely absent except for one exception till the time of her review (Das 1994:323). Also, in recent volumes on caste by Fuller (1996), and Srinivas (1996a), except for a token inclusion of a paper on gender, in other papers written mostly by males (three in Srinivas's volume are by women social scientists apart from the one on gender; in Fuller's book two are by women social scientists apart from the paper on gender), but for tangential references, here and there, women remain quite invisible. The same is the case in Volume 3 of the series *Social Structure and Change* brought out by Shah et al (1996a) where even a token paper on gender does not find space. The editors of this series have devoted another Volume 2 to *Women and Indian Society* (1996b) but here all the papers except one have been written by women social scientists thus constructing a gender division of labour leaving men social scientists free to make women invisible in their research and writing.

5. *Jhanjhars* are thick anklets.

6. A *hansli* is a thick necklace.

7. A *jhuggi* is a makeshift hut.

8. A *lehnga* is an ankle-length skirt made of many yards of material.

9. A *koti* is a tight blouse that comes to just below the midriff.

10. A *dupatta* is a long piece of cloth worn to cover the bosom which Indian women are supposed to hide and also the face whenever it is required to hide that.

11. *Pucca* rooms are rooms made of concrete.

12. Literally 'high people.' Shanno called people above her in status and wealth, of whom most probably she thought I was a representative, '*oonche log*.'

13. The name of a popular Hindi film. Sita is the name of a docile, meek, submissive, all-suffering girl in the Hindi film *Sita aur Gita*. Sita is treated like a doormat by everyone and is always taken advantage of. Gita is the name of her identical twin sister, a girl who is the exact opposite of Sita—assertive, confident, self-assured, a girl who demands and gets her right. The film *Sita aur Gita* had recently been shown on the television. Shanno had obviously seen the film. Sita is also the name of Rama's wife in the Indian epic *Ramayana*. She epitomises the good, virtuous, chaste, obedient, husband-worshipping wife which all Hindu wives are supposed to aspire to be.

14. Shanno, like a majority of Hindu wives, does not take the name of her husband. *Mera aadmi* (my man) is a term used to refer to the husband by lower class women.

15. *Biradari* is a community of several lineages of the same sub-caste which could be spread over several villages and has a *panchayat* or a local dispute-settling body comprising five elders.

16. *Berwas* are a sub-caste belonging to the *Chamar* untouchable scheduled caste who cure and prepare leather.

17. *Halwa* is a rich sweet dish made of wheat flour and sugar cooked in butter oil. *Puri* is a small round thin bread of wheat flour deep fried in oil. *Halwa-puri* is considered to be rich food, a food of the rich.

18. *Roti* is a round thick tortilla-like bread made out of wheat flour.

19. *Pyaz ka jhol* is a gruel made of onions.

20. Aunty is the kinship term in English which has come into common use, especially in Delhi, in place of indigenous kinship terms which were used earlier to address and to refer to even acquaintances. Now everyone calls elderly people *auntyji* and *uncleji, ji* being a suffix of respect in Hindustani.

21. A *bigha* is approximately one quarter of an acre.

22. Here Shanno uses a Sanskrit word because in colloquial Hindustani there is no word for love marriage. The Sanskrit word Shanno has most probably picked up from Hindi films which she apparently sees quite often on the television.

23. Shanno tried to dodge me several times but I persisted and finally she did give me information in bits and pieces during two sufficiently long private sessions that I had with her. On one occasion when I pinned her down she was cooking and could not escape, and on the other she was picking out lice from her daughter's hair and could not leave the job unfinished. However, I got the impression that inspite of her hostility Shanno had started liking her discussions with me especially getting to know details about my life that apparently intrigued and interested her. I reproduce portions of the two long private sessions here which helped in getting data about Shanno's sexuality.

24. According to the Unani indigenous system of medicine, foods are divided into 'hot' or 'cold' foods and are thought to have 'hot' or 'cold' effects.

25. In colloquial Hindustani there is no word for sexual intercourse.

References

Agnes, Flavia. 1993. 'The Anti Rape Campaign: The Struggle and the Setback'. In Chhaya Datar (ed.) *The Struggle Against Violence*. Calcutta: Stree. pp. 99–150.

―――― 1995. 'Redefining the Agenda for the Women's Movement Within a Secular Framework'. In Tanika Sarkar and Urvashi Butalia (eds.) *Women and the Hindu Right: A Collection of Essays*. New Delhi. Kali for Women. pp. 136–57.

Agnihotri, Indu and Mazumdar, Vina. 1995. 'Changing Terms of Political Discourse: Women's Movement in India: 1970s–1990s'. In *Economic and Political Weekly*. Vol. XXX No. 29, July 22, 1995, pp. 1869–78.

Ardener, Shirley. 1986. 'The Representation of Women in Academic Models'. In Leela Dube, Eleanor Leacock and Shirley Ardener (eds.) *Visibility and Power: Essays on Women in Society and Development*, New Delhi, Oxford University Press pp. 3–14.

Calman, Leslie J. 1992. *Toward Empowerment: Women and Movement Politics in India*. Boulder. San Francisco and Oxford: Westview Press.

Caplan, Patricia. 1985. *Class and Gender in India: Women and Their Organisations in a South India City*. London: Tavistock.

Chakravarti, Anand. 1995. 'Selective Readings of Feminist Scholarship'. In *Economic and Political Weekly*. Vol. XXX, No. 27, July 8, 1995, p. 1706.

Dasgupta, Susmita. 1995. 'Redeployment of the "Feminine"'. In *Economic and Political Weekly*. Vol. XXX, No. 25, June 24, 1995, p. 1529–31.

Das, Veena. 1994. 'Subaltern as Perspective'. In Ranjit Guha (ed.) *Subaltern Studies VI: Writings on South Asian History and Society*. Delhi: Oxford University Press. pp. 310–24.

_____ 1995. 'The Anthropology of Pain'. In Veena Das. *Critical Events: An Anthropological Perspective on Contemporary India*. Delhi: Oxford University Press. pp. 175–96.

Datar, Chhaya. 1993. 'The Women's Movement in Maharashtra: An Overview'. In Chhaya Datar (ed.) *The Struggle Against Violence*. Calcutta: Stree pp. 1–50.

Desai, Neera (Coordinator). 1988. *A Decade of Women's Movement in India* (papers presented at a Seminar organised by the Research Centre for Women's Studies, S.N.D.T. University, Bombay). Bombay: Himalaya Publishing House.

Du Bois, Barbara. 1983. 'Passionate Scholarship: Notes on Values, Knowing and Method in Feminist Social Science'. In Gloria Bowles and Renata Duelli-Klein (eds.) *Theories of Women's Studies*. London: Routledge and Kegan Paul pp. 105–16.

Dube, Leela. 1996. 'Caste and Women'. In M.N. Srinivas (ed.) *Caste: Its Twentieth Century Avatar*. Delhi: Viking, Penguin India pp. 1–27.

Duelli Klein, Renata. 1983. 'How to Do What We Want to Do: Thoughts About Feminist Methodology'. In Gloria Bowles and Renata Duelli Klein (eds.) *Theories of Women's Studies*. London: Routledge and Kegan Paul pp. 88–104.

Freeman, James M. 1974. *Untouchable: An Indian Life History*. London: George Allen and Unwin.

Freire, Paulo. 1972. *The Pedagogy of the Oppressed*. Harmondsworth: Penguin.

Fuller, C.J. (ed.) 1996. *Caste Today*. Delhi: Oxford University Press.

Gal, Susan. 1991. 'Between Speech and Silence: The Problematic of Research on Language and Gender'. In Maria di Leonardo (ed.) *Gender at the Crossroads of Knowledge: Feminist Anthropology in the Postmodern Era*. Berkeley, Los Angeles, Oxford: University of California Press pp. 175–203.

Gandhi, Nandita and Nandita Shah. 1992. *The Issues at Stake: Theory and Practice in the Contemporary Women's Movement in India*. New Delhi: Kali for Women.

Ganesh, Kamala. 1995. 'Feminism at the Margins of Anthropology' In *Economic and Political Weekly*. Vol. XXX, No. 34, August 26 1995 pp. 2146–2148.

Goffman Erving. 1959. *The Presentation of Self in Everyday Life*. Garden City, New York: Doubleday.

Goffman, Erving. 1961. *Encounters*. Indianapolis, Ind: Bobbs-Merrill.

Goffman, Erving. 1967. *Interaction Ritual*. Garden City, New York: Anchor Books.

Gupta, Dipankar. 1995. 'Feminification of Theory'. In *Economic and Political Weekly*. Vol. XXX No. 12, March 25 1995, pp. 617–20.

Gupta, Dipankar. 1996. 'Feminification of Theory and Gender Studies'. In *Economic and Political Weekly*. Vol. XXXI, No. 24, June 15 1996, pp. 1546–47.

Haider, Saraswati. 1993. 'Women's Oppression and Their Reaction in a *Jhuggi-Jhompri* Cluster'. Paper presented at the XX All-India Sociological Conference. Mangalore, 29–31. December 1993.

Haider, Saraswati. 1995. 'Once More to Feminification of Theory'. In *Economic and Political Weekly*. Vol. XXX, No. 36, September 9 1995.

Haider, Saraswati. 1996a 'Women and Religion in a Squatter Settlement'. Paper presented at the National Seminar on Women and Religion. Kurukshetra Women's Research Centre, Kurukshetra University, 29 Feb.–1 March 1996.

Haider, Saraswati. 1996b. 'Lifting the Veil of Silence: Jumuna's Narrative of Pain'. In *Sociological Bulletin*. Vol. 44, No. 2, September 1995 pp. 241–54.

Ilaiah, Kancha. 1996, *Why I Am Not a Hindu: A Sudra Critique of Hindutva Philosophy, Culture and Political Economy*. Calcutta: Samya.

Jain, Devaki. 1990. *Women's Quest for Power: Five Indian Case Studies*. Ghaziabad: Vikas.

John, Mary E. 1995. 'Indisciplined Outpourings: Myth and Bathos of Male Exclusion'. In *Economic and Political Weekly*. Vol. XXX, No. 22, June 3 1995 pp. 1333–36.

Kakar, Sudir. 1990. *Intimate Relations: Exploring Indian Sexuality*. Delhi: Viking.

Karlekar, Malavika. 1991. *Voices from Within*. Delhi: Oxford University Press.

Karlekar, Malavika. 1995. 'Feminification of Theory'. In *Economic and Political Weekly*. Vol. XXX, No. 24, June 17 1995 pp. 1464.

Kumar, Nita. 1994. 'Introduction'. In Nita Kumar (ed.) *Woman as Subject: South Asian Histories*. Calcutta: Stree, pp. 1–25.

Kumar, Radha. 1993. *A History of Doing: An Illustrated Account of Movements of Women's Rights and Feminism in India 1800–1990*. New Delhi: Kali for Women.

Leder, Drew. 1992. *The Absent Body*. Chicago: University of Chicago Press.

Mies, Maria. 1983. 'Towards a Methodology for Feminist Research'. In Gloria Bowles and Renata Deulli Klein (eds.) *Theories of Women's Studies*. London: Routledge and Kegan Paul, pp. 117–39.

Mukherjee, Prabhati. 1994. *Hindu Women: Normative Models*. Calcutta: Orient Longman.

Nabar, Vrinda. 1995. *Caste As Woman*. Delhi: Penguin India.

Oakley, Anne. 1981. 'Interviewing Women: A Contradiction in Terms'. In Helen Roberts (ed.) *Doing Feminist Research*. London: Routledge and Kegan Paul, pp. 30–61.

Patel, Vibhuti. 1988. 'Emergence and Proliferation of Autonomous Women's Groups in India. 1974–1984'. In Rehana Ghadially (ed.) *Women in Indian Society: A Reader*. New Delhi: Sage Publications, pp. 249–56.

Poonacha, Veena Ravi. 1995. 'Feminification of Theory'. In *Economic and Political Weekly*. Vol. XXX, No. 26, July 1 1995, pp. 1617.

Reinharz, Shulamit. 1983. 'Experiential Analysis: A Contribution to Feminist Research'. In Gloria Bowles and Renata Duelli Klein (eds.) *Theories of Women's Studies*. London: Routledge and Kegan Paul pp. 162–91.

Roberts, Helen. 1981. *Doing Feminist Research*. London: Routledge and Kegan Paul.

Rose, Kalima. 1992. *Where Women Are Leaders: The Sewa Movement in India*. Delhi: Vistaar.

Sangari, Kumkum. 1992. 'Consent, Agency and Rhetorics of Incitement', Second Series, Number LIX. New Delhi: Nehru Memorial Museum and Library.

Sangari, Kumkum and Sudesh Vaid. 1993. 'Recasting Women: An Introduction'. In Kumkum Sangari and Sudesh Vaid (ed.) *Recasting Women: Essays in Colonial History*. Delhi: Kali for Women pp. 1–26.

Sangari, Kumkum. 1995. 'Politics of Diversity: Religious Communities and Multiple Patriarchies'. In *Economic and Political Weekly*. Vol. XXX, No. 51 and 52, December 23 and 30 1995 pp. 3287–310, pp. 3381–389.

Sarkar, Tanika and Urvashi Butalia. 1995. *Women and the Hindu Right: A Collection of Essays*. Delhi: Kali for Women.

Scott, James C. 1990. *Weapons of the Weak*. Delhi: Oxford University Press.

Sen, Ilina. 1990. *A Space Within the Struggle: Women's Participation in People's Movements*. New Delhi: Kali for Women.

Shah, A.M., B.S. Baviskar, and E.A. Ramaswamy (eds.). 1996a. *Social Structure and Change*: Volume 1. *Complex Organisations and Urban Communities*. New Delhi: Sage.

Shah, A.M., B.S. Baviskar, and E.A. Ramaswamy (eds.). 1996b. *Social Structure and Change*: Volume 2: *Women in Indian Society*. New Delhi: Sage.

Srinivas, M.N. 1984. 'Some Thoughts on the Study of One's own Society'. In M.N. Srinivas. *Social Change in Modern India*. New Delhi: Orient Longman, pp. 147–64.

Srinivas, M.N. 1988. 'Social Anthropology and the Study of Rural and Urban Societies'. In M.N. Srinivas. *Caste in Modern India and Other Essays*. Bombay: Media Promoters and Publishers Pvt. Ltd. pp. 136–47.

Srinivas M.N. 1989. 'The Observer and the Observed in the Study of Cultures'. In M.N. Srinivas. *The Cohesive Role of Sanskritisation and Other Essays*. Delhi: Oxford University Press pp. 160–71.

Srinivas M.N. 1992. 'Studying One's Own Culture: Some Thoughts'. In M.N. Srinivas. *On Living in a Revolution and Other Essays*. Delhi: Oxford University Press pp. 132–50.

Srinivas, M.N. (ed.). 1996a. *Caste: Its Twentieth Century Avatar*. New Delhi: Viking.

Srinivas, M.N. 1996b. 'Indian Anthropologists and the Study of Indian Culture'. In *Economic and Political Weekly*. Vol. XXXI, No. 11, March 16 1996, pp. 656–57.

Stanley, L. and S. Wise. 1983a. 'Back into the Personal or: An Attempt to Construct "Feminist Research"'. In Gloria Bowles and Renata Duelli Klein (eds.) *Theories of Women's Studies*. London: Routledge and Kegan Paul.

_____ 1983b. *Breaking Out: Feminist Consciousness and Feminist Research*. London: Routledge and Kegan Paul.

Stivers, Camilla. 1993. Reflections on the Role of Personal Narrative in Social Science. *Signs*. Vol. 18, No. 2, Winter pp. 408–25.

Thapan, Meenakshi. 1995. 'Partial Truths: Privileging a "Male"

266 *Anthropological Journeys*

Viewpoint'. In *Economic and Political Weekly*. Vol. XXX, No. 23, June 10 1995 pp. 1399–400.

Tharu, Susie and Tejaswini Niranjana. 1994. 'Problems for a Contemporary Theory of Gender'. In *Social Scientist*. Vol. 22, Nos. 3–4, March-April. 1994 pp. 93–117.

Wittgenstein, Ludwig. 1953. *Philosophical Investigations*. (Eds.) G.E.N. Anscombe and R. Rhees. London: Basil Blackwell.

_____ 1958. *The Blue and Brown Books*. London: Basil Blackwell.

_____ 1971. *The Private Language Argument*. (Ed.) O.R. Jones. London: Macmillan.

Gender in Field Research: Experiences in India[1]

LOES SCHENK-SANDBERGEN

Introduction

In 1979 I did fieldwork in Alleppey, a medium-sized town in Kerala.[2] The purpose of my research was to focus on women domestic servants, and to study and analyse their poverty and household survival strategies (Schenk-Sandbergen 1988).

As the women resided in three locations in the town at rather far distances, and because local transport did not reach those places, I decided to buy a cycle. My husband, who also did research in Alleppey (Schenk 1986), suggested that we should buy a ladies cycle so that we could both use it.

It seemed that it was not possible to buy a ladies cycle in Alleppey. I have to admit, that so far I had not seen any woman cycling in the town: but friends assured me that there were *some* girls and women cycling in Alleppey. Besides, I assumed that as a foreign woman it would be all right for me to ride a cycle. So my husband and I went to Cochin-Ernakulam, a more modern and economically better-off port city, and we succeeded in buying a beautiful red ladies cycle. When I started cycling in front of our house however, there was a minor furore. Children ran behind me, pushing and pulling the cycle. On the whole there was great deal of commotion. As I had one of our children riding pillion, this was quite an unpleasant experience. However, my husband could cycle everywhere without any problem on our red-for-danger cycle. This reaction to my cycling went on for several weeks. I continued, however, undaunted.

One day, as I was cycling, a man suddenly gave me an

enormous blow, and my small son and I fell from the cycle. The reason for his behaviour it seemed was that he was so angry at my violating the gender rule of restricted mobility for women, that he wanted to teach me a lesson. The fact that I was a foreigner and therefore, as I had thought, outside of these circumscriptions—was not an issue. From that moment on I decided to conform to the ascribed gender role regarding mobility in Alleppey.

This small example from my own fieldwork experience illustrates that gender may play an important role for male and female researchers in the fieldwork setting. It is on that subject that I will focus in this article. I shall first introduce some very important and interesting studies that have been published on the role gender plays in anthropological and sociological fieldwork; I shall then explore how far the findings and topics raised in those studies are also described, elaborated and/or characterise the research of western, female anthropologists and sociologists who have conducted fieldwork in the Indian context.[2]

Methodological Feminocentrism

Carol Warren has stated very clearly that

> The myth of the researcher as any person, without gender, personality, or historical location, who would objectively produce the same findings as any other person has been increasingly challenged (1988: 8).

The development of an epistemology of fieldwork has made both women and men more aware of the influence of the personal characteristics of the fieldworker, the methods and objective of the study, and the context (Golde 1970, Roberts 1981, Harding and Hintikka 1983, Bowles and Klein 1983).

These studies show clearly that gender is only one of many personal characteristics shaping the course of fieldwork; age, social class, and race or ethnicity are other obvious influences. Still the fascinating question remains: in what way does gender—as the most obvious ascribed factor, and one that is visible to everyone—shape access to the field, the collection of data and the interpretation of the findings.

It is remarkable that considerably more women have tried to understand the role played by a fieldworker's sex and gender: in comparison fewer men have written on the subject (see especially Bowen 1954; Golde 1970; Papanek 1964; Wax 1971, Cesara 1982). Carol Warren gives a plausible explanation for this phenomena. She assumes that this methodological 'feminocentrism' (which contrasts with the 'androcentrism' of theoretical concerns) arises from the paradoxical situation of women field researchers:

> From the entrance into fieldwork in anthropology in the early twentieth century, women scholars did their research against the background of taken-for-granted *androcentric* assumptions about social life. Over time, these assumptions became the object of inquiry, resulting in a self-consciousness about issues related to women in the field (Warren 1988: 8).

I remember that my first encounter in the field was not so much a confrontation with androcentric theoretical concepts, but more a question of what was generally understood, and perceived by me, to be a 'scientific' methodology: or rather, an androcentric research methodology.

In 1971 I started my Ph.D. research on living and working conditions of sweepers (Scheduled Tribe, the Kuknis) and scavengers (Scheduled Caste, the Bhangis) in a very poor slum in Bulsar, or Valsad, an economically stagnant town in South Gujarat (Schenk-Sandbergen 1975, 1979 a, b). My university education was very much determined by the left-wing student movement of the sixties and its related struggle against elitist hierarchical structures and the war in Vietnam. At that time I had written an article to protest against the kind of anthropological research, conducted in Thailand and Vietnam by American social scientists, which helped the whole industrial-military complex destroy the people of Vietnam (Schenk-Sandbergen 1971) Students of my generation had studied the works of Habermas and others of the Frankfurter Schule. Inspired by the Chinese Cultural Revolution, we had animatedly debated and discussed the idea of a 'science for the (oppressed) people' and the concept of 'integration between theory and practice'. But although I participated actively in these debates that critiqued established social science research methodology, yet, I was not aware of the problems related to gender aspects, and in particular of their methodological consequences.

It took only a few days after my arrival in Bulsar for me to become very aware of it. That happened when accompanied by a male interpreter, I entered, very nervously, the first hut in the slum area of Bulsar. There were five people in the hut: the father, blind and without work, his daughter, lying on the floor with her first baby, born just two days ago, and his two younger sons. The father showed me a dirty piece of newspaper with some left-overs of rice in it. This was the only food he had got by begging that day for his whole family. For two days before this they had no food at all. He urged me to give him money to buy some good food for his daughter. And being a young woman myself with a daughter of just one year, with memories still fresh of the days just after my delivery when I had been looked after so well, the other woman's condition affected me emotionally. It was at that moment, in those few seconds that I realised that despite my education as a critical sociologist, and my strong social and political commitment with the poor and oppressed in India, from a methodological point of view I was conditioned by the androcentric methodology. I had internalised this androcentric view that held that the researcher should remain a neutral observer, and not intervene in local conditions. The androcentric view would have us believe that intervening would affect one's objectivity; one's conclusions therefore would not be 'scientific' any more.

I remember very well that in those few seconds, in which my heart was beating very fast, I realised what for me was the right thing to do. I never regretted my action. I gave the man money to buy milk and fruit for his daughter, and I told him I would come back the next day to see how things were with them.

When we came outside the hut, my male assistant was very angry with me, because besides the gender aspects in this encounter, there was the complication of community. He shouted that I had spoiled everything by giving money—and moreover, support, to that particular family. They were, I was told, Muslims and the majority of the other families in the slum were Hindus: the community would now suspect me of Muslim sympathies. And since this was the autumn of 1971, with an Indo-Pakistan war looming on the horizon, this was hardly the best start to my fieldwork.

For my part, I felt both relieved and guilty. Relieved because I realised that for me, as a woman, fieldwork methodology require me to intervene and to be concerned with the people involved. Guilty, because I had acted against the academic rules. It took several months during that research, in which I encountered many other such situations, to overcome my feelings of guilt. But struggling with these ambivalent feelings, I understood the human and scientific dimensions and meaning of what later was called a 'feminist' methodology of conscious partiality, a view from below, research 'for' people (and in particular women), and not 'on' people.

I agree with Peggy Golde (1970) who states that the women contributors to her volume were more sensitive to the role gender plays in fieldwork, because of their socialisation process as women and professionals. She writes:

> Simply growing up as women in American society would have made the contributors [who were all women] aware of the kinds of subtle and conflicting pressures that may be exerted on women. Their own personal adaptation as professionals would have demanded that they develop heightened sensitivities about sex role, and I believed that this awareness, including an acceptance of 'perceptiveness about feelings' as appropriate to the feminine role, would make the assessment of the influence of sex easier for women than it would have been for men (1970:3).

The Advantages of Being a Woman Fieldworker

There is a vast and growing literature on gender and fieldwork relationships. The generalisations found in this literature concerning the advantages and disadvantages of women versus men in cross-cultural fieldwork indicate that besides restriction to particular worlds within settings, women fieldworkers are portrayed as more accessible, person-oriented, communicative and less threatening than men. This makes the interaction of fieldwork easier (Warren 1988; Golde 1970).[3] There is a remarkable cross-cultural similarity in these generalisations.

However, as talks and observation in the field in India taught me, we have to be cautious with these kind of generalisations because, as Margaret Mead indicates, there are different types of women fieldworkers. She divides women fieldworkers into those

> with deeply feminine interests and abilities, who in the field will be interested in the affairs of women, and those who are, on the whole, identified with the main theoretical stream of anthropology in styles that have been set by men (1970: 323).

Mead sketches a black-and-white dichotomy. The 'feminine' type of researchers she sees as oriented toward feminine concerns, and generally working with their husbands. The 'masculine' oriented women she sees as independent, bored by babies at home and abroad; they work alone, and use male informants. I think that this dichotomy has to be replaced by a more subtle differentiation in categories of women field researchers who are in different degrees, and dependent on the setting, more feminine or masculine oriented. Such a categorisation will also apply to male fieldworkers: I know male fieldworkers with more feminine than masculine personalities and interests. There are thus no homogeneous or monolithic categories.

Maria Mies does not differentiate categories of women and men fieldworkers in relation to their gender orientation. However, she makes firm statements on the extra quality and capacities of committed women social scientists (e.g. women who want to contribute to the cause of emancipation). She expands upon this and says that this extra quality comes from the fact that

> women and other oppressed groups, out of their subjective experience, are better sensitised towards psychological mechanisms of dominance.... Due to this inner view of the oppressed ... women social scientists are better equipped than their male counterparts to make a comprehensive study of the exploited groups. Men often do not have this experiential knowledge, and therefore lack empathy, the ability for

identification and because of this they also lack social and sociological imagination (1983: 121).

Maria Mies's analysis of the cause of women's extra qualities as fieldworkers is similar to that of Peggy Golde: women's socialisation. But, in the interpretation of the effects of this socialisation, Mies states that women should realise that their own existence as women and scholars is a contradiction. Out of this contradiction grows a double consciousness which must be taken into account, not as an obstacle but as a political and methodological opportunity to do committed action-research. Mies recommends that the special talents of women fieldworkers should be used to contribute to the cause of emancipation of women.

The fieldwork context is, however often more complicated and that raises the point Carol Warren (1988) makes that women's special talents for fieldwork can also be seen from a different perspective: as a feature of the 'politics of gender dominance and submission' that characterise so many cultures. Thus, the very positive characteristics of women as accessible, person-oriented, communicative and less threatening are also the ones which make women very vulnerable and allow for stereotyping.

Gender as a Negotiated Role

The previous perspective relates to the debate on the gender politics of fieldwork. Some western feminist women researchers perceive the trade-off between accepting certain degrees of sexism on the one hand, and the acquisition of knowledge in the interest of furthering their careers on the other hand, as distasteful. It is unavoidable that while doing research in a patriarchal society, such as India, the woman fieldworker comes across certain forms of sexism hitherto unknown to her: she may be a witness, or become involved in situations in which other women suffer from male dominance.

For example: the problem of the dinner-parties in middle and upper class families in which the women of the house served the men and the guests and did not eat with them at table. When I came across this situation for the first time in 1971 in Bombay, I was very upset that our hostess, an academic colleague and a woman like me was treated differently from me. I suggested that I would eat only when our hostess did not play the role of the waitress or servant, but also joined us at table. Alternatively, I would eat in the kitchen with her, later. But, these suggestions were kindly waved aside, and our hostess said with a smile, that she liked to serve us and eat afterwards. I had no choice but to adjust to—in my eyes—this ritual of subordination of women. In 1993 it is still the same, and I have stopped protesting against this feature of the politics of male-gender dominance.

Sometimes I have the feeling that it is part of the 'sexist ritual' of powerful male government officials and professors to show, now and then, in an unpredictable way, their male superiority by displaying a complete lack of interest in what a woman has to say. However accepting a certain degree of macho showing-off during fieldwork may have its positive side. Sometimes, feminine features (probably together with being a foreigner), can manipulate male decision-makers in government and development circles to get things done.

There is another interesting point of debate in the discussion on the role of gender in field research, and this reflects the development in a time-perspective of feminist anthropology. There is an obvious change in perspective that frames gender not as an 'ascribed' role, but, as Carol Warren calls it, a 'negotiated' one, based on both the gender features of the setting, and the interactions of fieldworker and respondents over time. For the early feminist anthropologists—when the androcentric roots of science were being discovered and dug out, and when many women had started to do studies aimed at making women visible in all respects, gender was such a serious ascribed component, that it was not possible to challenge the role it played in different conditions. The current phase in feminist anthropology however focusses on showing and explaining the differences of gender roles and gender relations in relation to class, caste, status, ethnicity, historical dimensions etc. as a result, the role of gender has become more flexible and open to modification (Moore, 1988).

Three studies in the field of gender and research reflect these changes in the discourse of gender over the past twenty five years. The first, published in 1970 (and then reissued in 1986) is *Women in the Field: Anthropological Experiences* edited by Peggy Golde. A collection of fourteen essays by women anthropologists, this volume deals with the experiences of women fieldworkers. As such it reflects the first wave of feminist concern with the androcentrism of earlier fieldwork.

The second volume, *Self, Sex, and Gender in Cross-Cultural Fieldwork* edited by Tony Larry Whitehead and Mary Ellen Conaway, and published in 1986, is a collection of sixteen essays. The volume contains essays by both women and men about their experiences in the field, and reflects not only a continuing concern with women's issues, but also a new awareness of problems and processes in the field. It considers, for instance, the husband-wife relation of anthropologists in the field where the wife is the main researcher. And on the understanding that 'gender' includes the male gender, it deals with the problems of men. The volume is structured around three components: the role gender plays in field adjustment, information gathering and interpretation. The third volume, is the excellent state-of-the-art study by Carol Warren (1988): *Gender Issues in Field Research*. Warren summarises and gives an overview of all the findings, views, components and aspects in both anthropology and sociology. She warns against the 'focal gender myth' of field research and encourages young researchers to find the 'social facts' and to avoid allowing voices of the past generation to become the shapers of the new one. However, it should be kept in mind that these three studies are mainly based on the experience of western social scientists.

What are the common experiences of female fieldworkers that might stand as generalisations? Which experiences might be framed as hypotheses for future testing in the Indian setting?[4]

Four major themes were brought up in every discussion I had on the subject with my co-researchers. They are as follows:

1. Western women fieldworkers are allowed greater freedom in crossing local gender boundaries than are male fieldworkers.
2. Women fieldworkers are under greater pressure to conform to local gender ascriptions than are male fieldworkers.
3. Women fieldworkers are allowed less mobility and are

> under pressure to provide for chaperones and
> 'protection'.
>
> 4. Women fieldworkers are under greater pressure to
>   provide all kinds of support, help and assistance than are
>   male fieldworkers.

Experiences of Western Women Fieldworkers in India

Access to Two Worlds

In a seminal article, Wax states (1986), that women
anthropologists from the Western world have an advantage over
their male colleagues in that, as women, they have access to the
women's world of the culture they study, while as Western
outsiders they can also maintain contacts with the men. Also
Wertheim had indicated, in his preface to Vreede-de Stuers' book
on *purdah* (1968), that women fieldworkers have an immense
advantage over the male researcher when they use the technique
of participant observation: female sociologists can enter both the
women's and the men's worlds (Vreede-de Stuers 1968). This
view seems to be confirmed by statements from several women
anthropologists working in India. Men did not, and could hardly
get in touch with women, while women researchers did conduct
studies among men (Du Bois, 1970, Sharma, 1980, Pettigrew,
1975, Bellwinkel, 1979). The one exception to this is Brouwer,
whose study focusses on craftswomen in South India (1987).
Unfortunately, he does not discuss his methodology at all. It is
also unknown to me how Mandelbaum collected his material on
such a gender-sensitive topic as 'seclusion of women and men's
honour' (1988).

My experience in field settings in Bengal and Mirzapur was
that it was very difficult in areas with a strong *purdah*-ideology
for men to communicate with women. Women (in particular the
younger ones, the daughters-in-law) immediately withdrew
when they saw me entering the area accompanied by a male
colleague: that never happened when I came with another
woman. However, one of my male colleagues working in the
southern districts of West Bengal, did not face problems when
talking with women on very intimate matters. It would also be

an oversimplification to assume that women fieldworkers can easily get access to the world of both sexes.

Women's Access to the World of Woman

The problem of doing research in a patriarchal society, in combination with the polarised society, has however, as far as I know, never been analysed.[5] The consequence of the patriarchal society is that it is often very difficult for women sociologists, to get access to women of certain castes and tribes. The main reason is that the male leaders and other men consider themselves as the head of the household or the community, therefore the spokespersons of the community or household. Women are not considered capable of giving replies; it is therefore not easy, even for a woman to speak in private with women.

This happened during my investigations in villages in tribal areas of Orissa in 1990. Men and women of the Gond tribe sat in groups and in response to each question directed to the women about their living conditions and role in agricultural production, the older male leaders gave the reply. After many efforts I succeeded in breaking through the 'culture of silence' of the women a bit. An older women leader started to talk, but she spoke for the collective, and she also looked better-off than the rest. During this stay it was also difficult to get access to women because the male staff worker of the NGO, with whom I visited a couple of villages in order to assess the impact of the activities of the NGO, was always present—his presence was also a constraint on the women.

I experienced the same male dominance in slums in Bangalore. The male leaders would immediately be around when the researcher arrived in the slum with the representative of the involved NGO; the leaders would reply to all questions.

I developed several strategies to get rid of the men. The best was to start talking about things perceived by men as trivial women's talk—deliveries, health practices, or to ask to see the cooking arrangements and *chulha* and then to stay on in the kitchen. It would be interesting to know how other women fieldworkers have developed strategies to escape patriarchal dominance in interview settings.

Wieke van der Velden argues (1991) that access to the women's and men's world is a problem especially when the subject of the research is more related to the women's world. She felt the push directing her into the women's world, and out of the men's world of politics which she also wanted to study. It was half-way through her fieldwork that she fully realised the disadvantage of being confined to women's and children's worlds. She also emphasises that women's worlds are not necessarily open to all women. Gender alone is not enough to win full acceptance into female concerns especially those related to sexuality and reproduction. She writes:

> Not being married did have one clear disadvantage: matters of sexuality and childbearing were out of bounds for me. As it is, matters of sexuality are not easily discussed (other than being joked about) all over the Gangetic plain ... and certainly not with one who is unmarried. Only towards the end of my research, and with a few women with whom I had become close friends, was I able to talk about such matters to some extent (1991: 17).

One student told me that during her fieldwork, a young, poor, married woman heard that she was unmarried. The woman could not stop laughing. The reason for her amusement was expressed thus: 'I may be poor, but at least I am married'. After that she did not take the researcher's questions at all seriously.

Women's Access to the World of Men

Other women field workers confirm the advantage of having access to the worlds of both men and women. However this general statement should be modified. In many cultures women fieldworkers never get access to male domains, such as cockfights, rum bars, mosques etc. In India women often do not get access to all fields of the men's world that they want to study: this restriction reflects their age, marital status, their personality and the setting. The fieldworker's martial status is of particular significance to anthropological informants, since most cultures take kinship bonds as the fundamental source of social structure and social order. It is my experience that my conformity to that pattern—it was said 'your family is just like an Indian family'—helped me greatly.

Marriage to an Indian man seems to confer a kind of 'insider' status with its advantages and disadvantages. Ursula Sharma is very positive on the easy access she could get to people via her in-laws (1980: 1). Joyce Pettigrew, a British anthropologist, who married into a rich landowning Jat family belonging to Ludhiana district, wanted to do research in 1971 on the role played by rural factions in building up the power of state level political leaders. In rural Punjab women are usually secluded and conduct their lives separately from men. The reputation of the family depends on the behaviour and conduct of the women. Pettigrew describes how—because of her affinal connections— she had an enormous advantage in being able to meet and speak to many political leaders. However, certain persons e.g. prominent male members of the faction opposing her relatives, were not accessible to her because they were considered 'bad characters'. And meeting these 'bad characters' would lower her status and that of her affinal family.

Cora du Bois has an exceptional story to tell about her long stay in a comfortable guest house in Bubaneshwar. She describes that she had excellent relationships with Oriya men (though not with women, because they did not speak English) who frequently dropped in to chat with her on the neutral ground provided by the guest house.

She suggests that it is the sympathetic stranger to whom Indian men speak frankly of matters they would hesitate to discuss with their families, their peer group, or their working colleagues. She senses that her age, in India at least, facilitates rather than inhibits confidences. She writes: 'Grandmothers in India are, stereotypically, loving and indulgent figures' (1970: 229). Probably her case illustrates the point that older women are culturally androgynised; they are allowed 'male' privileges.

Carol Warren points to the important fact that both whiteness and foreignness permit women field researchers more cross-gender behaviour than is allowed to native women (1988: 26). This perspective is also suggested by Leela Dube (1975) who makes the very remarkable statement that, western women, are able to relate to people better than western men, but that with reference to Indian women this statement must be made with caution. Because of the constraints of the social structure under which the latter are brought up and in which they function, they face difficulties in relating and communicating with all kinds of people. Dube goes on to say however that once an Indian woman fieldworker 'overcomes these limitations of her upbringing she can use her life experiences to full advantage while doing fieldwork' (1975: 175).

Conformity to the Situation

Women fieldworkers have maintained that female fieldworkers are under greater pressure to conform to local gender ascriptions than are male fieldworkers. This view is expressed by both Golde (1970) and Whitehead and Conaway (1986), and finds a place in many of the contributions in Golde's volume. My colleagues and I tend to agree with this view in the Indian setting, but as I will show there is also scope for negotiation on gender role expectations; there is a lot of flexibility, depending on the character of the research, the rural, or urban context, the methodology followed, etc.

Dutch women fieldworkers I spoke with expressed that they feel confronted by a whole range of gender ascriptions that they had to either follow, or negotiate by making some compromises. Adjustment or conforming to gender roles prevalent in the field setting may have advantages and disadvantages. The advantage can be easy access, it may facilitate the gathering of material. The disadvantage is that the flexibility in adapting to a variety of gender roles, and the flexibility in adopting a somewhat neutral stranger role, if necessary, are more difficult.

Should the field worker conform to the culture of the field area? This question focusses our attention on the different expectations a society may have of women from different cultures. It focusses too on the fact that sometimes *not* conforming to the dominant cultural practice can uncover submerged patterns, behaviour, voices and ideologies. And therefore it brings us to the realisation that 'conformity' itself is often only a 'conformity' to the dominant, androcentric mode. In this context, Gail Omvedt's discovery of a counter-culture that viewed marriage as a prison is significant. At the time of her research, she herself was unmarried and therefore not in conformity with the dominant view of women. Did the non-conforming status particularly encourage or influence her findings?

The subject of conformity relates to many aspects of Indian

gender ascriptions: dress/appearance; restriction of mobility/protection/ chaperones; marital status, division of labour; showing respect and subordination to men etc.

I shall first consider visible aspects of conformity to local gender ascriptions: dress and appearance. In India physical appearance is very important. In particular for women the size and shape of the body, hair and skin, clothing and jewellery, denote her place in the social structure. It is expected of the foreign fieldworker that she refrain from violating these norms.

It is my experience, and that of my students, that conformity in this area is highly appreciated, and facilitates a woman fieldworker's access to the field. There is, however, a certain class aspect to this observation; it is the middle class which appreciates this kind of conformity the most. People of this class will pressurise the woman fieldworker to wear a blouse and *sari*, to wear bangles and other jewellery, and, in the case of a married woman, to wear a red *tika* and *mangalsutra* or *tali*.

In general it was indicated in our talks that compromises in dress and appearance were made, in order to conform somewhat to the gender dress norms of modesty: long dresses, or *salwar-kameez*—the latter even without the *dupatta* that hides the contours of the body—were an acceptable in-between solution. However, flexibility was essential: on other occasions such as visits to high government officials it was wise to dress up in as western a manner as possible to get things done.

One of my male colleagues working in West Bengal stated that conformity in dress is equally important for male fieldworkers. He reported that the state of his clothes—whether washed or not, whether ironed or not, how they were stitched etc.—was subjected to constant scrutiny and comment.

In this subject of conformity regarding dress and appearance we can also distinguish, as Laurie Krieger does in her fieldwork in Cairo (1986), between the crucial, and not so crucial, gender expectations. In Kerala there were so many questions every day, as to why I was not wearing gold earrings and a gold chain that I decided to buy very small ones to fit into the culture's gender role. While we were in Alleppey, friends from Holland came to stay with us. They were wearing old jeans and shorts, and since it was very hot, exposing a lot of white skin. Our Indian friends and neighbours were shocked by the 'bad habits' of our friends.

They expressed their astonishment and disapproval and for a while, our own status was challenged. Thankfully, with the departure of our Dutch friends, our status was restored.

On another occasion, one of my students felt pressed to adopt the Indian hairstyle because her loose hair was not considered appropriate. Other Dutch women researchers told me that they would not drink beer or smoke in public, and, that they learned to use the Indian form of greeting. They said too that they would lower their eyes when being introduced to a strange man, and in general, would simulate more shyness and hesitation in discussions with males than they would have done in the Netherlands. However, they admitted that this behaviour was often a strategy to manipulate male respondents in order to get relevant data at a later phase.

Many women found themselves being pressured to avoid the sun, and to protect their fair skins—a middle class symbol of beauty. It would be interesting to know how far this pressure applied to male fieldworkers. Finally, a point that came up frequently in our discussion—cleaning and sweeping. According to the sexual division of labour in the West these are, along with other household chores, female tasks, but in India they are part of class/caste roles. Most Western female fieldworkers I spoke with did not like conforming to Indian culture in this matter. We learned a lot however, about social stratification and the position of scheduled castes from our experiences in this area.

A few examples of this.

In 1979 my husband and I arrived in Alleppey with our three small children, one of whom was a baby of six months. We rented a few rooms in the house of a Tamil Brahmin family. The family continued to live at the back of the house. When we entered the house, I was concerned because the rooms were dusty, and, in particular the wash-basin and bathroom were dirty. My first reaction was to clean everything up thoroughly before unpacking our suitcases or arranging our furniture. I managed to get the cleaning material but before I could get much cleaning done, the broomstick was snatched out of my hands by my Indian friends who shouted: 'Stop it, the sweeper will come; the sweeper will come tomorrow'. I understood the situation. In their eyes I was lowering my status. But I, on the other hand, was thinking of the health of my small children, and in particular of my baby who had just started crawling and tended to put everything he found in his mouth. But there was no escape. I was not allowed to clean and sweep—of course the sweeper did not come as promised. It took weeks before any cleaning was done and when it was, it was certainly not up to the standards of a Dutch housewife.

Similarly, one of my students told me that during dinner, one night a bat flew into the electric fan which was turning at a high speed. The bat was beheaded, its head fell next to my colleague's plate. She wanted to remove it immediately because otherwise she was afraid that she might vomit. But she was not allowed to do this. This was considered the sweeper's work, and the sweeper, she was assured, would come the next day. Dinner continued, with the bat's head left exactly where it fell. My student realised that she was forced to conform to the norms and that it was not her work to remove the corpse. Clearly here too, it is caste and class rather than gender that determine attitudes behaviour, and expectations.

Restriction of Mobility
The ideal that a woman has to be protected is very strong in Indian culture. Situations should be prevented that might provoke others to exploit women—and this includes the possibility of sexual exploitation. Women who get into difficulties are not supposed to have the skill, or knowledge, to defend themselves. Many Indian women have however worked out culturally acceptable strategies to avoid personal sexual harassment and molestation by adopting behavour that evokes the powerful Hindu goddesses like Kali and Durga, or by speaking to the offender as if she were a powerful mother (Kishwar 1992).

The assessment of the vulnerability of women in terms of physical weakness and openness to sexual attack are some of the assumptions behind the strict rules of chaperoning of women. Even in a modern city like Bangalore, when we had to go to our hotel by autorickshaw at eleven o'clock at night (not late at all for us) our very friendly host insisted that his son chaperoned us on his motorcycle, following the autorickshaw all the way.

It is not only the need for a chaperone but also the company of one's family that is considered normal and desirable. I remember when my daughter and I made plans for her to help me in one of my projects, the problem we faced was getting permission from my Dutch employers. In India on the other hand, everyone was delighted and liked it very much that I had brought my daughter with me.

From my talks with Dutch women researchers, I found that most women were uneasy about travelling and staying alone. We were all aware of the stereotypical image of a foreign woman travelling alone, or sitting alone in a restaurant, as a 'loose woman'. Therefore most of the women had made arrangements to have the company of another person—an assistant, interpreter or counterpart.

The mobility of women fieldworkers is of course restricted by the fact that travelling in buses, trains and public boats is often a hazard for women. Public transport is monopolised by men. In big cities such as Bangalore, some seats at the front of the bus are reserved for women but in many other public transport facilities it requires inventive strategies or a lot of elbow work to travel. In Kerala I worked out a strategy where an Indian male friend jumped onto the public boat from the edge of the boat jetty, and occupied a seat, even before the boat had entered the jetty. I got on the boat later and took the seat he had 'reserved' for me.

Does this mean then than certain types of studies cannot be conducted by women sociologists? Jan Breman (1983) used a regional study methodology which required him to be very mobile. Within a short period, he slept in a modern and comfortable farmhouse, a 'brits' (some kind of field-bed) under a roof of a hut, or in the open sugarcane field along with migrant labourers. He reports feeling like a 'chameleon' in the necessity to adjust to many different environments (1983: 8–14). We do not know whether Jan Breman did all his travelling by motorcycle, or whether he travelled alone or with company. But we do know that for most female researchers travelling alone would have been impossible. One of my female junior fieldworkers also moved around with considerable speed on her 'moped' in sugarcane fields, camps and factories but she was always accompanied by her female field-assistant. But, even in that case, people often remarked that they did not understand the parents of the girls who allowed their daughters to roam around like that. Another experience of a young unmarried student was that she was constantly watched and controlled by men. Others were not allowed to travel by bus but were urged to take a reliable taxi.

This notion of protection and escort applies much more to Indian women fieldworkers. Leela Dube did her first fieldwork among Gond women because her father-in-law was in charge in the area as a civil servant and he took care of her. She went to the field as a well-protected daughter-in-law accompanied by a maid-servant and escorted by a peon (1975: 160). The experience of Joyce Pettigrew who had cousins and nephews of her affinal family as chaperones around her all during her research makes a very amusing and interesting story. She realises through this experience that she was perceived primarily as the wife of a Jat, subordinated to patriarchal norms, rather than as a professional anthropologist (1981: 76).

Questions of Reciprocity
According to Peggy Golde, the issue for the researcher is 'how can I repay these people who give me so much'? (1970: 10). The issue for the community is: 'What does she give that makes up for the trouble she causes'? Do female anthropologists feel the need to 'repay' to a greater extent than do males? In the Indian context other considerations are at stake as well: the day-to-day confrontations with hunger, poverty, serious illnesses, inhuman living conditions, discrimination, violation of human rights, are so intense that the fieldworker inevitably and spontaneously offers help and support.

Another important question is, do informants consider women fieldworkers more accessible than their male counterparts when support and favours are sought? And what pressure, time constraint and dilemmas arise from that? It can be supposed that women, and in particular fieldworkers with a clear identity of being a mother, are perceived as caring, committed persons who will protect, comfort and support others. When the woman fieldworker is foreign—and in the eyes of the involved people in the research area, rich and powerful—they will expect in line with patron-client relations, something in return, So the pressure comes from both gender and the class components, with the fieldworker being perceived as nurturant and also, rich and powerful.

Male sociologists have told me that they were approached

during their fieldwork in Indonesia and the Philippines to arrange for improvements of the conditions of the people. Jan Breman mentions in his report that he did not hesitate to offer help in case of emergencies (1983: 22). Similarly many people in India asked my husband to help them arrange or organise something. Willem van Schendel was approached many times by people for support, information and help during his long fieldwork in Bangladesh and West Bengal. But he noticed that when women asked him for medical help, it was generally for a more serious problem and a genuine one. (Personal communication.)

There is however a gender-specific condition which puts women under more pressure in this respect than men. Men hardly can approach, or have intensive contact with women of poor households who are most in need of everything. Male fieldworkers simply do not do this type of research because of gender-segregation, and do not know, and are not aware of the serious implications women fieldworkers face in view of these types of studies. Women fieldworkers interact and communicate with this category of women, which creates a situation in which, from both sides, the pressure for the fieldworker to do things will increase. She will do things because she feels it as an absolute gesture of concern and solidarity, and the women will approach her as they would a powerful sister or rich mother. Let me present one illustration:

My student and I were conducting interviews in one of the poorest slums on the outskirts of Bangalore. The people were shifted here from their original place which they had to vacate because a market was to be constructed on that location. They had been relocated in a desert-like surrounding, far away from anywhere that they knew. A few hundred families in make-shift huts had to fetch water from only one handpump. The women had to walk a long distance over hilly and rocky terrain. There was no other water nor any sanitary facilities at all. But, worse, the people had to walk more than six miles over a sandy track to reach the main road to catch a bus. This was the main reason that most of the people had lost their jobs. In particular, the women who worked as domestic servants and construction labourers had perforce to give up their jobs. We came across blind and handicapped people living in some shabby tents, and we wondered how they survived in the middle of nowhere. We became very depressed seeing so much suffering and such inhuman conditions. During one of our interviews, a young woman with a badly undernourished baby in her arms became unconscious. The baby was crying loudly and we feared that the mother had died. Nobody took action and we were not allowed to touch her. We were very relieved when the mother opened her eyes after a few minutes and became conscious again. She told us her sad story. She had five small children. Her husband, an alcoholic, had abandoned her for another woman. She showed us big burn wounds on her whole body and open wounds on the head and belly of the baby, caused by the fact that she often had these fainting spells when cooking and then she and the baby would fall into the fire. At such times, her toddlers of two and three years old would help revive her by sprinkling water on her. She had no money at all. She survived because her mother occasionally brought her some money which she had earned by selling sweets at the nearest bus station. My student and I looked at each other, and we started to organise a visit to the nearest hospital in an autorickshaw. We also gave her some money for several medical examinations.

It is my observation that women fieldworkers spend a lot of energy and time on support and help, out of a sense of a deep identification with the problems of the poor women in their research area. Equally this is so because the claim on them relates to their gender role. Many told me that they gave information on family planning, menstruation and in particular, on how to avoid pregnancies, spent many days in taking people to the X-ray departments of hospitals, provided all kind of medicines, gave food, small loans, photographs, taught lessons in English, or collected money for sewing machines in the Netherlands, or were desperate because they did not know what to do with requests of a more political nature such as making a speech at a political meeting, joining in demonstrations, collecting money for religious purposes etc. And, what is one to do on the many occasions when people offer their small children to the researchers as servants. I watched one of my students during her departure at the airport for a revisit to her fieldwork area: she had two big bags, 25 kg of luggage: 23 kg of presents and gadgets ordered by people in the field, and 2 kg of personal belongings for her long stay. She is not an exception.

It is my experience that in comparison with my male colleagues I am much more approached, in particular by women, with requests for support and help. In fact on several occasions. I could compare the role of gender in accessibility. When I stay with my male colleague in the villages of Bengal (Schenk-Sandbergen, 1991), people come to me and ask for ploughs, bullocks, tiles for the roof of their hut. Is this only a question of 'personality', of being 'a softy'? Can it be denied that it has to do with gender?

The support and activities I could realise for practical improvements for the women in my research location have helped me very much to deepen my insight and understanding of their lives, and to collect material which really reflect the problems and priorities of the women. In view of that experience I prefer to be involved in projects and programmes in which committed action research 'for women' and not 'on women' can be conducted. However, the implications of that choice and related methodology are far reaching and deeply pervade not only the personal life of the researcher, but even into the lives of the researcher's family.

Gender and Development

It is my experience that gender plays probably an even more significant role in development work. In practical work such as consultancies, advice, evaluations, impact studies, participatory rural appraisals, in the field of 'Women (gender) and Development' there is a more condensed confrontation with different arenas of participating people and counterparts in a short period. This concentrates and accelerates, so to speak, the above discussed gender-specific conditions for women researchers. To be confronted in all types of projects (bi-lateral, multi-lateral, voluntary agencies, etc.) with the immense poverty, obvious needs, interests and demands of tribal and scheduled caste women in slums and rural areas, evokes strong gender-internalised feelings 'to care and to support'. Equally contacts with middle and upper-class women create commitments and obligations in other different ways. Interacting with local male policy makers, planners, government officials, NGO leaders, technical consultants, implementers etc. requires skills in the field of social gender engineering. As time is short, optimal interaction is necessary for full rapport. In turn, intense communication increases the depth and quality of the relations, which make them less casual and professional, but more personal and private. Consequently, apart from the pursuit of the project objectives, there will be other personal relations and expectations. These too will have to be maintained and fulfilled. Women will be inclined to look after these personal or more private ties and relations more carefully. It is often taken for granted that this may shape the success of a development project. Yet, the time, costs and energy involved in it are invisible in the project documents, and even unnoticed, denied and ignored by project officials and bureaucratic procedures. This is reflected in the fact that consultants in projects may find themselves replaced by others for reasons of transfer, availability or economic reasons.

It seems very urgent to stimulate publications, similar to those of the experience of women anthropologists, of women social scientists actively involved in women and development programmes and projects, in which they analyse how their gender role has shaped the project performance. It is my contention that gender plays an even more important role in the success of a development project than is described by female anthropologists. The tremendous 'costs' however of those efforts have to be borne privately, and are not acknowledged. We are back then to the debate on the sexual politics of fieldwork: we should be cautious that the exploitation of gender by gender-specialists themselves is not perpetuated.

Notes

1. This paper is a revised version of a paper published in the series: Occasional Papers and Reprints of the Indo-Dutch Programme on Alternatives in Development (IDPAD) 1992–2. I want to thank my husband, Hans Schenk, and the following colleagues and students for the sharing of experience on what role gender played in their fieldwork in India and Asia: Mirjam Letsch, Kristoffel Liteten, Anne-Marie Loeber, Rensje Teerink, Maaike van Vliet, Jyotsna Gupta, Hanneke Meyer, Ot van den Muijzenberg, Janet Rodenberg, Willem van Schendel, Hein Streefkerk, Wim Wertheim.

2. The material in this paper is based on my own fieldwork experience and the experience of my husband, of male and female colleagues, several junior

researchers and students who have recently conducted fieldwork in India in different settings—the remote rural area in the North of West Bengal, a more advanced rural and urban region in South Gujarat, a small town in Uttar Pradesh, tribal areas in Andhra Pradesh and Orissa, the metropolitan setting of Bangalore, etc. So, when I write 'we' and 'our' in this article, it relates to the talks I had with my husband, colleagues and students. For comparative reasons, I will now and then refer to the experience of Leela Dube, who is one of the few female Indian anthropologists who has written about her fieldwork experiences at three different stages of her life (Dube 1975).

3. See in particular the papers by Margaret Mead and Ann Fischer in Golde's volume (Golde 1970).

4. Peggy Golde summarises the following five common themes which were made explicit in the contributions of the 14 female fieldworkers as having gender-specific components: protection, initial suspicion, conformity, reciprocity and culture shock.

Whitehead and Conaway focus on a number of views regarding the role of fieldworker sex and gender identity that are worthy of further exploration and debate. Such views include. 1) Female fieldworkers receive greater pressure to conform to local gender ascription than do male fieldworkers. 2) Female fieldworkers receive greater pressure to have sexual relations than do male fieldworkers. 3) Female fieldworkers are allowed greater freedom in crossing local gender boundaries than are male fieldworkers (Cesara 1982, Papanek 1984, and Golde 1970.) 4) Females are more sensitive than males to the field situation and are therefore more likely to attempt to understand the systemic relationship between the fieldwork process and the fieldworker's sense of self. 5) Sharing the field site with a spouse, children, or a colleague can be prohibitive to the fieldwork process and to the type of introspection necessary for the growth of self and objectivity, particularly for women.

References

Bellwinkel, Maren. 1979. 'A Slum in Kanpur'. In M.N. Srinivas, A.M. Shah and E.A. Ramaswamy (eds.): *The Fieldworker and the Field. Problems and Challenges in Sociological Investigation*. New Delhi: Oxford University Press.

Bowen, Elenore Smith (pseudonym). 1954. *Return to Laughter*. New York: Harper & Row.

Bowles, Gloria and R. Duelli Klein (eds.). 1983. *Theories of Women's Studies*. London, Boston, Melbourne and Henley: Routledge and Kegan Paul.

Breman, Jan. 1983. *Veldwerk in een gepolariseerde samenleving*. Rotterdam: CASA serie werkdocumeten 5.

Brouwer, Jan. 1987. 'An Exploration of the Traditional Division of Labour Between the Sexes in South Indian Crafts'. In Andrea Menefee Singh and Anita Kelles-Viitanen, *Invisible Hands: Women in Home-based Production*. Delhi: Sage

Cesara, Manda. 1982. *No Hiding Place: Reflections of a Woman Anthropologist*. London: Academic Press.

Dube, Leela. 1975. 'Woman's Worlds—Three Encounters'. In Andre Beteille

Gender in Field Research 291

and T.N. Madan (eds.). *Encounter and Experience: Personal Accounts of Fieldwork*. Delhi: Vikas.

Du Bois, Cora. 1970. 'Studies in an Indian Town'. In Peggy Golde (ed.): *Women in the Field. Anthropological Experiences*. Chicago: Aldine Publishing Company.

Fischer, Ann. 1970. 'Fieldwork in Five Cultures'. In Peggy Golde (ed.): *Women in the Field. Anthropological Experiences*. Chicago: Aldine Publishing Company.

Golde, Peggy (ed.). 1970. *Women in the Field. Anthropological Experiences*. Chicago: Aldine Publishing Company.

Harding, Sandra and Merill B. Hintikka (eds.). 1983. *Discovering Reality, Feminist Perspectives on Epistemology, Metaphysics, Methodology, and Philosophy of Science*. Dordrecht, Holland: D. Reidel Publishing Company.

Kishwar, Madhu. 1992. 'Sex Harassment and Slander as Weapons of Subjugation'. *Manushi*, 68, Jan-Feb 1992, pp. 2–15.

Krieger Laurie. 1986. Negotiating Gender Role Expectations in Cairo. In T.L. Whitehead and M.E. Conaway (eds.) *Self, Sex, and Gender in Cross-Cultural Fieldwork*. Urbana and Chicago: University of Illinois Press, pp. 117–29.

Mandelbaum, David G. 1988. *Women's Seclusion and Men's Honour. Sex Roles in North India*. Tucson: University of Arizona Press.

Mead, Margaret. 1970. 'Fieldwork in the Pacific Islands, 1925–1967'. In Peggy Golde (ed.) *Women in the Field, Anthropological Experiences*. Chicago: Aldine Publishing Company.

Mies, Maria. 1983. 'Towards a Methodology of Women's Studies'. In Bowles, Gloria and R. Duelli Klein (eds.): *Theories of Women's Studies*. London, Boston, Melbourne and Henley: Routledge and Kegan Paul.

Moore, Henrietta. L. 1988. *Feminism and Anthropology*. Cambridge: Polity Press.

Omvedt, Gail. 1979. 'On the Participant Study of Women's Movements: Methodological, Definitional and Action Considerations'. In G. Huizer, and B. Mannheim (eds.): *The Politics of Anthropology*. The Hague: Mouton.

Papanek, Hannah. 1964. 'The Woman Fieldworker in a Purdah Society'. *Human Organisation*, 23, 161.

Pettigrew, J.J.M. 1975. *Robber Noblemen*, London: Routledge and Kegan Paul.

Pettigrew, Joyce. 1981. Reminiscences of fieldwork among the Sikhs, in Helen Roberts (ed.), *Doing Feminist Research*. London: Routlegde and Kegan Paul.

Roberts, Helen (ed.). 1981. *Doing Feminist Research*. London: Routledge and Kegan Paul.

Schenk, H. 1986. 'Views on Alleppey, Socio-historical and Socio-spatial Perspectives on an Industrial Port City in Kerala, South India'. Ph.D, Nederlandse Geografische Studies, 4. Amsterdam: Koninklijk Nederlands Aardrijkskundig Genootschap, Instituut voor Sociale Geografie, Universiteit van Amsterdam.

Schenk-Sandbergen, Loes. 1971. 'Sociaal-wetenschappelijk onderzoek in Zuidoost-Azie in dienst van de Amerikaanse Regering'. In *Wetenschap en Samenleving*, 25e jrg, no. 4, pp 98–110; en in; Ledenbrief Bond van Wetenschappelijke Arbeiders, 26 Juli 1971 en 1 Sept. pp 7–13 en pp 22–28.

_____ 1975 'Vuil werk, schone toekomst? Het leven van straat-vegers en vuilruimers: een onderzoek in Bulsar (India), verkenningen in Peking, Shanghai, Tientsin en Tangshan (China)' Diss. Ph. D. Amsterdam: Van Gennep, pp. 402.

_____ 1979a 'The People of Dhobi Talav: Poverty and Solidarity'. In

S. Devadas Pillai and C. Baks (eds.). *Winners and Losers, Styles in Development and Change in an Indian Region*. Bombay: Popular Prakashan, pp. 141–63.

_____ 1979b 'Caste, Poverty and Disease. Some Observations in an Indian Town'. In J.v. der Geest and K.v. der Veen (eds). *In Search of Health, Essays in Medical Anthropology*, University of Amsterdam, CASA, Amsterdam. pp. 131–45.

_____ 1988 *Poverty and Survival: Kudumbi Female Servants and their Households in Alleppey (Kerala)*. New Delhi: Manohar, p 108.

_____ 1991 'Empowerment of Women: What is its Scope in a Bilateral Development Project? The Case of the Small-scale Irrigation Project in North-Bengal (Terai Area)'. In *Economic and Political Weekly*, Vol XXVI, No. 17, April 27.

_____ 1992 India: Van spelen tot beleven: met kinderen op veldwerk, LOVA.

_____ and H. Schenk. 1979. 'The Setting of Polarity. An Introduction to the Research Area'. In S. Devadas Pillai and C. Baks (eds.). *Winners and Losers. Styles in Development and Change in an Indian Region*. Bombay: Popular Prakashan, pp. 13–27.

Sharma, Ursula. 1980. *Women, Work, and Property in North-West India*. London: Tavistock Publications.

Van der Velden, Wieke. 1991. *Silent Voices: Gender, Power and Household Management in Rural Varanasi, India*. Amsterdam: Centrale Huisdrukkerij Vrije Universiteit.

Vreede-de Stuers, Cora. 1968. *Parda, A Study of Muslim Women's Life in Northern India*. Assen: Van Gorkum & Comp.

Warren, Carol A.B. 1988. *Gender Issues in Field Research* . Qualitative Research Method Series 9. Newbury Park: Sage.

Wax, Rosalie H. 1986. '"Not Any Good Thing is Done by Man Alone": Gender and Age in Fieldwork and Fieldwork Education'. In T.L. Whitehead and M.E. Conaway (eds): *Self, Sex, and Gender in Cross-Cultural Fieldwork*. Urbana and Chicago: University of Illinois Press, pp. 129–51.

Whitehead, T.N. and M.E. Conway (eds.) 1986. *Self, Sex, and Gender in Cross-Cultural Fieldwork*. Urbana and Chicago: University of Illinois Press.

Learning to Take People Seriously[1]

Madhu Kishwar

Introduction

One of the most important things I have learned from my experience as a researcher and activist intervening in social issues is that even the most well-meaning efforts to help improve people's lives can end in disaster if you do not take people's own lives and perceptions sufficiently seriously, or if you fail to understand the effects of any particular effort at change on other parts of a complex situation and society. Contributing to social change involves deliberate attempts at mobilising opinion in a particular direction. If the conclusions, however, are predetermined by the activist's own predilections and ideas, without taking into account the situation, perceptions, and wishes of those on whose behalf we seek to help bring about change, we can easily end up either being irrelevant, pompous impostors or authoritarian manipulators. One reason for the failure of the anti-dowry campaign during the years since independence, for instance, is that it was a well-intentioned effort at social change based on an inadequate understanding of social reality.

Before we can effectively intervene to help bring about the social change, we need to understand why things are as they are and not as some group or theory tells us they are. Only a more accurate understanding of what is really going on can enable us all to help concerned activists create a relevant and meaningful agenda for improving the lives of women and other oppressed groups. The task, though not easy, requires us to maintain a degree of scepticism regarding predetermined explanations and political formulae. Reality rarely matches available preconceived notions, whatever their origin.

The researcher needs to be sensitive to unexpected information and to what may appear to be puzzling contradictions. If the people who could provide first-hand information of the situation are unwilling to talk to the researcher, this must be seen as a sign that greater care and effort is required to make sense of the situation. The researcher has to be alert not only to explicit cues but also to implicit ones regarding people's experience, and the conclusions they have drawn from their experience.

A common dilemma relates to how much one should tell one's informants in advance about what one is trying to do. By withholding one's assumptions from them, is one acting under false pretences? I remember being greatly aggravated by this dilemma when I was assisting a colleague with a Punjab-based village study documenting the lives of women of peasant and landless poor households. One important aim of our study was to try to explore the reasons for the unnaturally low sex ratio in Punjab, and to find out how this was connected to women's status in the village (see *Manushi* No. 11, 1981).

The investigators found that the villagers were extremely cooperative and helpful. This was chiefly because a revered local leader had introduced the investigating team to them. The team gathered detailed information that included the daily caloric intake of male and female members of a small sample of households, and surveyed a larger sample about facts such as the hours of work put in by women, the nature of women's labour contribution, marriage practices, dowry practices, decision making in the household, domestic violence, and women's mobility. Apart from an overall census and detailed interviews with a sample of women, the investigators spent a substantial part of their time in the village recording and discussing women's situation with knowledgeable villagers not included in the formal sample.

However, when we came to interpreting the information, we faced serious dilemmas to the point of almost abandoning the report. The overall picture that emerged portrayed the village as abounding in wife beaters, drunken husbands and opium addicts. Daughters appeared somewhat less likely to survive than sons. Very few positive features emerged in our description of women's status. Clearly, this was not the whole truth about the community, although the team had been fairly careful in gathering the information.

We had relied principally on information from discussions with women, without men ordinarily being present, on male-female relations within the family. This was necessary since we feared we would fail to get much of the information we sought if men provided or monitored the answers. Objective information such as the exact caloric intake of males and females, and the body weights and measurements of men and women belonging to different strata of the society, was collected by actual observation and measurement. Yet we could not escape the feeling that in a few important areas our results read like an oversimplified version of a complex reality.

We were left with many unresolved questions. Did women view their relations with men in their families as merely exploitative? Would they recognise our picture of women's place in the village? If not, what would be the reasons for any divergence between their version and our interpretation? Also, we realised that if they did not agree with our description of their reality, they were less likely to agree with our prescriptions for changing it.

Further, could the men's version be totally dismissed? Were there not fathers who became heavily indebted to raise dowries for their daughters, and did not they and their daughters genuinely believe that this was done out of love? Could we dismiss altogether the image of a fair number of these Punjabi farmers as industrious, good-natured, warm-hearted, supportive and family-minded men? Did not the generosity, hospitality and openness that we observed and benefitted from reflect an aspect of reality and of interpersonal relations that had not emerged in our study? Our study depended to a great extent on prestructured questions addressed to the women alone. No doubt, this particular effort made to obtain the women's version of reality helped us get important glimpses of village and family life which are often overlooked. But a more authentic version would need to be far more complex, and derive from many additional sources of information.

One way of combating the tendency to impose one's preconceptions on the facts is to make a special effort to elicit as many versions or interpretations as possible of a situation from the different persons involved in it as participants or observers. The realisation that there are usually a variety of versions that may be relevant, some easily available and others that require more probing, will determine how carefully we weigh, sift, crosscheck, and give meaning to what we hear and see. It is true that no matter how careful we try to be, it is still likely that a lot will be missed. Nevertheless, in general, the more sources we are able to query on the same issue or a set of known events, the more likely we are to get a more sensible view of the situation.

Which Women, When?

While in some ways women's lived experience may be said to be different from that of men as a group, it took me a long time to realise how diverse women's perceptions are. A woman's version of social reality varies substantially depending on where she is placed. These are not just differences in caste and class, which do matter a great deal, but also the differences that separate women within the same family. For instance, when gathering information about women's labour contribution, one must clearly assess who is talking about whom. A woman often describes her own workday very differently from that of her daughter or daughter-in-law.

So also, a woman is likely to give one sort of description of how much dowry was given at her daughter's marriage, and another of how much dowry her daughter-in-law brought. This is not to suggest anything so simplistic as that her account will be more accurate for her own dowry, exaggerated for her daughter's dowry, and underestimated for her daughter-in-law's. The description one gets in any one of these three situations, however, is likely to be influenced by a complex set of criteria related to family politics, status considerations and numerous other factors.

Woman to Woman

For years, as an activist, I had simplistically assumed that women's experiences would be more accessible to me because I am a woman who professes to be sensitive to women's predicaments. I continue to believe that, as a woman, I have certain advantages in gaining access to a woman's world. However, these advantages can be offset by several limitations.

In a society like ours, where women's subordination and exclusion often assumes fairly extreme forms, women are frequently not allowed to share their experiences, perceptions and opinions with other women, particularly those who are seen as outsiders to the family. Such sharing is seen as a kind of defiance and therefore a threat to family honour. Women are required to funnel their opinions and experiences to outsiders through the men of the family.

For instance, when conducting a survey of marriage practices in a Madhya Pradesh village, I found that women very often answered my questions regarding the amount and items given and taken at their children's marriages with the remark: 'I don't really know. Ask the men—they arrange it all. They know.' This could easily be interpreted as duplicity, since I know they were not really so ignorant. It could also be seen as their ignorance, springing from their isolated housebound role, which prevented them from acquiring basic information regarding their own lives. This perception was doubtless part of their own self-view too, linked somewhere to the sentiment that respectable women do not engage in economic deals pertaining to the public arena, that being men's domain. One reaction to these problems in investigation might be to stop asking women, and ask only men, since men tend to be more forthcoming. This, however, does not mean they are necessarily more accurate. One could also choose to see the woman's response as meaningless stupidity, and hence neglect to report it at all in one's writing.

It took me a while to figure out that even in not divulging information, the women were in fact revealing an important aspect of their situation within marriage and the family. This aspect was that of their lack of authority to decide on their own whether I, a stranger, should be told anything at all about complex internal interrelationships and economic matters. Even if it were all right to say something, it might be even harder for them to take responsibility for how much I should be told, and in what ways. Men took these decisions without consulting women and gave me a version which was carefully tailored in different ways. But women did not feel certain that they could undertake to do this tailoring without the men's approval. Hence they felt it safer to refer me to the men even though most often they did have the details themselves.

It is significant that the only woman who was forthcoming was a woman who had entered into an open confrontation with the men of her marital family. She had been able to do so because she had the backing of the men of her natal family who were powerful and wealthy and lived in a nearby village.

Men may not be physically present but the fear of their power often acts as an effective censor in women's minds. My initial access to women's lives is almost always in some important ways determined by how far the men of the community decide to cooperate. There is rarely any way I can reach women by bypassing men. This is especially the case in rural areas.

The hold that men have over women's minds and over women's perception of their subjective experience does tend to get weakened under certain circumstances. It has often been observed that women's participation in political movements tends to get a fillip during phases of repression, because that is when men feel compelled to bring the women out. In their own interest, they often loosen the traditional bonds, so as to better combat outside forces such as the repressive arm of the State.

Similarly, men are compelled to loosen their control over what women will say and how they will describe their experiences to each other and to outsiders, during phases of extreme crisis. I have noticed this during different investigations of massacres, whether unleashed by the State or by other forces.

After the November 1984 anti-Sikh pogrom in Delhi, I began to interview members of the Sikh community. This was within three of four days of the events. The entire community, including the men, was in a state of trauma. Therefore, I did not once face a situation of the men of a family saying: 'Why ask women? We'll tell you better.' Women poured out their experiences of personal humiliation, sexual assault, and gangrape, even in the presence of men.

However, whenever I have investigated such atrocities a couple of weeks or a month after the event, women's voices are always more subdued. Men take over literally as well as in women's minds. The male-defined censorship norms of the community are imposed again once the men have regained some of their lost composure. Women's experiences are pruned and edited automatically without any formal decisions necessarily having been taken in this regard.

In Meerut, which in 1987 witnessed a large scale massacre, our team, which arrived a couple of weeks after the violence, did not find any women narrating their own experiences. Women would tell how male relatives had been killed or arrested and tortured, or at most how the police had beaten, shot or killed a particular woman.

Is one then to assume that women were not sexually assaulted because they did not talk about it? I think that assumption would not be justified. The one woman who described to us the sexual brutality she had suffered was lying wounded in hospital. She had lost all the members of her family. Her vagina had been ripped with a knife up to her stomach and her intestines had spilled out. I recalled the very telling comment of Gurdeep Kaur, a woman victim of the November 1984 violence in Delhi: 'Why should I hesitate to tell? I have no one left.' She meant that all the men of her family were dead and there was now no one for the sake of whose 'honour' she should censor details. The female members of her family had all survived.

On another occasion in 1980, when investigating cases of police atrocities in a tribal area, we were baffled by the fact that the political activists at district level who had invited us to the area to conduct an investigation were full of stories of police and Bihar Military Police (BMP) gangrapes of women. Yet in the villages hardly any women or families stated that they had been victims of such assault. They would always evade the question by saying it happened in other neighbouring villages. From that response some of the members of our team concluded that all the stories about police rape and atrocities were politically motivated and, therefore, needed to be discounted. I was also puzzled and felt that the silence on the subject of rape needed to be further investigated, especially since all of the other allegations of police atrocities had been corroborated by the victims without any hesitation.

Upon our persevering with the investigation, one episode did shed some light on the situation. At one of the villages on the Gua-Manoharpur road we interviewed a group of women who all denied that they had suffered any personal indignity but told us in detail about the beatings and arrests of the men and the looting indulged in by the BMP. At the next village, the account was the same. We expressed our confusion and inability to write the report we had come prepared to write, since no woman was forthcoming about what had happened to women. As we were leaving, a young man quietly came up and said he would take us to meet his sister. He brought us back to the village we had left and introduced us to one of the same women who had denied being molested. He was at least ten years younger than this sister of his, but when he told her to tell all, she did so, not just about herself but also about other women.

She said the reason she had withheld this information earlier was that she feared that her husband, who had been arrested and for whose release she had sold her jewellery and her family's animals, would ask her to leave his house if he found out that she had admitted to being raped by BMP men. Yet, even the support of a younger brother was sufficient for her to risk talking about her experience to us.

In this area, only two other women were also willing to describe their experience. They did so because a revered trade union leader of the village persuaded the men of the family that the women should be allowed to speak of this to our team.

My woman-to-woman communication thus has limited possibilities, because it is almost always the men of a community who directly or indirectly decide how much of a woman's experience is allowed to be expressed. This is primarily because the collective and individual power of men comes to determine what the consequences of that talking will be for women.

The Ideology Trap

Let me give an example of the limitations of viewing reality through the prism of ideology and thereby distorting it. This can happen even if one is a quite knowledgeable local observer. In the course of a village study on women's land rights, the woman social worker who was helping me gather data informed me with great enthusiasm that for the first time in the 12 years that she had lived in the village as a social and political activist she had witnessed a spontaneous case of 'class struggle.' She was referring to the case of a tribal man, who, along with his sister, niece and other relatives, had beaten up a tribal woman of the same village who had worked as the recruiting agent for a contractor who supplies tribal labour to brick kilns around Calcutta. The reason for the outburst was that the niece of this man had returned pregnant from one of her migration trips to Calcutta and the recruiting agent who took her from their village had not helped or protected this young woman. The political activist who informed me of the case interpreted the man's beating up of the agent as a case of revolt against capitalist exploitation. She saw the village-based recruiting agent as a symbol of the system—the last and lowest link in the chain of exploiters.

When I talked to the wife of the man who had given the agent a beating, she saw the matter very differently. She had always complained that her husband was a good-for-nothing who beat her up often and snatched away the little she earned. While she toiled and starved, he drank rice beer and had fun at the weekly market. Others confirmed her description. Now that he had got into a fight, a police complaint had been made against him and he had to pay a bribe of Rs 1,000 or else go to jail. Much against his wife's wishes, he had mortgaged a part of their agricultural land in order to pay the bribe. His wife said she would rather he went to jail for a few months than that the family land be mortgaged. How would they survive if they lost part of the little land they had? She saw the beating as another example of her husband's irresponsible behaviour.

The woman who was beaten up, and her mother, were angry and bitter at being thus assaulted. Part of their anger arose from their perception that this man would only dare beat them up because they had no adult males in their household—they were three sisters living with their widowed mother. Like most such female-headed households, they had hardly any land. The mother had been widowed when her daughters were small, therefore she had not able to retain her share of the family land which was grabbed by her husband's male kin.

The other villagers saw the affair as a family matter springing from the outrage felt against the woman contractor who, although she belonged to the same *killi* or clan as the young woman, had not adequately protected her. But they were not as perturbed by the pregnancy or the beating in themselves. They were much more perturbed that the beating had led the woman to go and lodge a police complaint. The villagers panicked lest the police descend on the village. Police entry into the village signified for them indiscriminate extortion of bribes from all and sundry. Therefore, the elders got together and prevailed upon the accused man to go to the police station and voluntarily surrender before the police came to the village.

The man who did the beating did it because he felt his family honour was involved. He had expected a member of their *killi* to take special care of his niece while she was working away from home. It was not as if he had any grouse against the contracting system. Far from leading any 'class struggle' against the system, in all likelihood, he would not have been averse to acting as a recruiting agent himself.

Thus, the imposition of a formula, in this case that of class struggle, acts as a distorting rather than an illuminating factor, and can lead one to adopt inappropriate political strategies.

Keeping Prejudices in Check

All writing is inherently selective and interpretive. However, interpretation is different from distortion. One needs to be careful that prior to offering an interpretation one does not distort facts, for instance by leaving some out, in order to reach a conclusion that suits one's political predilections.

I am not arguing in favour of becoming apolitical, because the supposedly apolitical also have their unstated political prejudices. I am stating that (a) as far as possible we should make our political assumptions explicit (b) we should search out and have the courage to face those facts that go contrary to our predilections, and then root our conclusions in the facts, and (c) we should review any investigation sceptically which neatly confirms our original premises without offering any surprises.

All of us have certain culturally inherited prejudices which we may not be able entirely to overcome. Negative prejudices of this kind among higher status groups often take the form of considering lower status groups as irrational, unaware of their own interests, culturally backward or otherwise deficient and inferior. Europeans and Americans tend to have such prejudices against Africans and Asians: upper castes against lower castes; Hindus against Muslims; the rich against the poor. These prejudices may not always be stated; they could take the form of patronising condescension towards those perceived as backward. One may see oneself individually as being above prejudice, but if one belongs to the hegemonic community, which has a strong antipathy against the other community, one has to be particularly vigilant. It is not sufficient merely to accumulate the versions of more and more individuals when an entire community has begun to parrot a received version. In a situation where the two communities do not normally socialise, one's access to the other community in day-to-day life is in any case limited. No matter how liberal or radical one considers oneself, having a few friends from the other community does not materially alter the fact of one's essential distance from its felt life. Therefore, whenever violent conflict occurs, it is important to get the versions of ordinary members of the other community, as well as to have sufficient command over the available facts. Often, the real picture will be clouded by the contradictory versions of the two communities and one needs to probe at hard evidence to get an idea of how much credence to give to the various versions.

The Necessity of Hard Evidence

In order to have a better chance of obtaining these substantive facts, one needs to reach the site of conflict as quickly as possible, before the actual evidence has been removed. It is this evidence which often points to the possible falsity of the generally accepted interpretation of the events. Hearing multiple 'versions' is often not enough to develop valid conclusions, particularly when one has unequal access to the different groups, but the physical evidence of conflict may provide invaluable indications of what took place.

Take the example of the communal violence in Meerut in May-June 1987. A team of us form *Manushi* visited Meerut a few days after the violence, when curfew had been somewhat

304 Anthropological Journeys

relaxed. Since all of us were non-Muslims, we did not have
automatic access to Muslims and we had to seek it out. The few
contacts we had in the city were with Hindus.

Muslims are concentrated in certain areas of the city, and most
Hindus we met warned us against going there, telling dreadful
stories about the dangers that awaited Hindu women who dared
enter Muslim areas. We were solemnly told that we would never
return alive. The police and administration were also extremely
hostile to the idea of our entering Muslim areas. Their ostensible
reason was that they would be blamed if we came to harm there.
The real reason was that the law and order machinery had been
actively involved in a large-scale massacre of Muslims and thus
the police did not want reporters to meet the victims.

Had we gone only by the versions given by the people we
spoke to, we would have been confronted with two diametrically
opposed versions—one from Hindus and the other from
Muslims. Simply believing the majority would have meant
accepting the Hindu version since they were in a majority.
Otherwise, one would have ended up in confusion, not knowing
whom to believe.

Nearly all Hindus we met believed that most of the victims of
violence had been Hindus and that Hindus had lost more lives
as well as more property than Muslims had. Most Hindus also
believed that the government was prejudiced in favour of
Muslims, and that had it not been for the PAC's protective role,
Hindus would have suffered still more terrible losses. This
version was repeated by almost every Hindu, educated or
uneducated, rich or poor, man or woman, almost as if they had
memorised a tape-recorded message.

One had to be wary even of supposed eyewitness accounts.
The killers themselves often masqueraded as eyewitnesses, but
the inherent absurdities in the stories they told alerted us. Some
Hindu eyewitnesses told bizarre stories of how Muslims had
burnt their own homes in order to claim compensation, and how
Muslims burnt to death accidentally and their corpses
spontaneously leapt into distant wells, or that Muslims were the
aggressors even in areas where only Muslims had died.

We had to adopt different methods to arrive at an estimate of
the situation. First, we made a special effort to visit Muslim areas
in the face of hostility and obstruction from police and the Hindu

population. As soon as we did so, we came face to face with certain inescapable facts. For one thing, we saw a much larger number of Muslims with injuries and broken limbs than we did Hindus. Where in Hindu areas we had mainly heard rumour-based stories of Hindu deaths, but rarely met the families of any dead persons, in Muslim areas we met numerous families that had lost members who were killed by police or who 'disappeared' after arrest.

We also attempted a citywide survey of damage done during the violence. In the most seriously affected parts of the city, we did a house by house and shop by shop count to see how many establishments belonging to Muslims were damaged. These areas included the major markets of the city, where Hindu and Muslim shops were cheek by jowl. In each case, we also noted the nature and extent of the damage. The shops had not yet been cleaned up, and the wreckage was clearly visible. An overwhelming majority of the damaged shops, houses and vehicles belonged to Muslims. These ranged from small to medium-sized shops and stalls, factories, home-based weaving establishments, restaurants, rickshaws, scooters, buses, huts and three-storeyed houses. In comparison, the number of Hindus who had suffered losses was much smaller. In one area, a dozen large factories belonging to Hindus had been burnt, and in another, a petrol pump and a few nearby shops. The factories constituted a large visible loss which made a big impact in the local papers and on people's minds.

But thousands of Muslims, most of them poor and lower middle class, had lost their means of livelihood, and many were rendered homeless. These losses were downplayed in the local Hindi press, read by most Hindus, which was violently anti-Muslim in its tone. Muslims generally lived in separate colonies, and the wreckage in the interior of these colonies was not visible to Hindus who never entered them, especially at such times. Hindus dismissed the losses of Muslims with a contemptuous. 'What do those wretched rickshaw pullers have to lose anyway?' Even on the main roads, it was clear that Muslim establishments had been targeted for destruction. Neighbouring Hindu establishments were either untouched or slightly damaged, the latter generally due only to their proximity to the Muslim shops.

Most Muslim establishments were reduced to ashes and rubble, while in some areas whole colonies of Muslim homes were devastated as though by war, roofless and wrecked, while the adjoining Hindu colony was untouched. Yet most Hindus seemed not even to see such visible patterns.

We tried to get a community by community breakdown of deaths and arrests but the administration was extremely unwilling to disclose their figures. This reluctance was natural, given its complicity in the violence, and its consequent desire to let rumours favourable to the police version flourish. After much persuasion, we were allowed to look at some of the lists for a couple of cases. A simple count of Hindu and Muslim names confirmed the impression we had formed from surveys of Hindu and Muslim areas—that though far more Muslims than Hindus had died, far more Muslims than Hindus had been arrested as rioters.

If we had reached Meerut too late to see the evidence of the damage, and had been compelled to trust the versions given by the local people, the local media, the government and the press, we would have been led to believe that this was a riot between Hindus and Muslims in which Muslims had incited and led the violence. Examining the evidence with our own eyes showed us another reality.

From this experience, the realisation hit us forcefully that even so-called eyewitness accounts may not serve as an adequate basis for research in a hate-charged atmosphere wherein people's subjectivity is coloured by self-interest, or has been manipulated and distorted by politicians so systematically and over so long a period, that they have lost the ability to honestly register what they see and hear. Instead they may merely parrot the version that is transmitted to them by their incriminated leaders and by biased media, a version that conveniently falls within their immediate self-interest.

Even more caution in observing and listening is required when the communities involved are unevenly balanced in political power and economic resources. The dominant community's hegemony in the bureaucracy, police, government and mass media makes its version the authoritative and dominant one. When the researcher's own inherited bias coincides with the bias of the State machinery and of the majority of the population, it is often no longer safe to go by the 'people's version', namely the version put forward by the majority of the people.

How the majority version becomes the received version is evidenced also in the November 1984 massacre of Sikhs in Delhi still being referred to in documents and in the press as a 'riot' even though it is clear that it was an organised one-way attack on the Sikhs by armed gangs with the support of leading Congress (I) politicians and the assurance of noninterference by police.

Therefore, any description of a riot or massacre should include a realistic assessment of the relative strength and influence of the two communities. For instance, many Hindus are convinced Muslims are a pampered minority, but statistics and facts point to a situation of systematic discrimination against Muslims in most of northern India. If one does not have an accurate overall picture, one is unlikely to get facts, at a specific level, right.

What People Want

What then do I mean by emphasising the need to take people seriously, when I am at the same time arguing that people's version of their own lives as recounted to an activist is often insufficient to establish what is happening? Here I must distinguish between two kinds of information: while one needs to be sceptical, although not dismissive, about what people choose to reveal or conceal about themselves, their neighbours, relatives and friends, one needs to take people very seriously when they talk about what they want, what will improve their lives, and what they need in order to live with dignity, or even to survive.

We must be careful that the questions we ask regarding this last set of aspirations are relevant to the options available to a person, and not unrealistic or wholly imaginary. For instance, if a woman says she needs to have three or more children it is wrong to attribute this to her ignorance and to insist, without careful consideration, that it is in the 'national interest' as well as in her own long term interest to have no more than one or two children. In the case of such conflicts of interest, one must consider whether by 'nation' one is not actually indicating contrary interests which thwart the woman's own self-interest. When one seriously listens, it may become evident why she needs three, four or five children. If one reason turns out to be that she knows half of them are likely to die of malnutrition and related factors, one could try to help her fight against poverty and child disease, not as a bargaining point for a one-child family, but because that is what she needs and says she needs.

To take another example, when surveying the lives of maltreated wives, it is easy to assume that when a brutally maltreated woman says she wants to go back and live with the husband who beat her up and threw her out, it is solely because she suffers from lack of awareness and has low self esteem, and thus to believe that she should be persuaded, in her own interest, not to go back to him. It takes some time to realise that the woman's perception of her future, given her circumstances, could, in all likelihood, be the more realistic one, that in many instances she would end up leading a less dignified life in her parents' home, at the mercy of brothers and sisters-in-law, or as a single woman living on her own, than in her marital home where she might have at least some slightly enhanced socially acknowledged rights and status.

Some Suggestions

The following are some tentative rules of thumb evolved from the experiences described above, which may perhaps help us avoid making some of the same mistakes over and over again. I do not intend to imply that I have discovered a foolproof systematic new method of doing research, but merely to indicate some common and some more difficult areas where we need to be more vigilant.

When we begin to investigate a situation, we naturally have a set of expectations or notions about what the results might be. If the research ends up so completely confirming these notions that we could have written the report without having gathered any information, we should suspect that we are likely to have made some fundamental error. We should then review the entire process: the questions asked, the observations included, the respondents chosen, and the way the questions were formulated and the answers interpreted. It is possible that our preconceptions prevented us from asking searching enough questions, or led us unwittingly to give the respondents some signal that we preferred a particular type of response. We may also have excluded from the group of respondents certain relevant people who might have upset our preconceptions.

If at all possible, we should carefully discuss the various drafts of the report with the different groups of informants to see if it makes sense to them. Even if one believes that certain of the respondents may have biases that tend to distort their opinions, we should nevertheless listen to them carefully and take them seriously. They are likely to uncover complexities in the situation (including in our preconceptions) of which we were unaware.

We should avoid premature categorising of anticipated or actual respondents according to preconceived categories. For example, we cannot assume that most women will primarily or automatically describe their experience from the perspective of their 'status as women'. Other classifications may have far greater salience—for example, their religion, caste, landholding status, or relationship to other family members as a mother, mother-in-law, daughter or wife. One has patiently to untangle the cross-cutting allegiances and identities that even the most downtrodden member of a society maintains, in order to arrive at the information relevant to the category of most interest to one's investigation.

If the respondents do not respond in a way we expect them or would like them to respond, we should avoid assuming that the reason is that they are stupid, uneducated, ignorant or that they are at a low level of class (or any other kind of) consciousness, or that they are deliberately trying the mislead us. While these explanations are always possible, it is far more likely that it is the investigator who lacks mental flexibility. The unexpected and difficult answers are often the most fruitful clues to what is happening.

It is a mistake to think that we have a better comprehension of people's options and best interests than they do themselves. We should be particularly careful to talk about what it is they consider most important to improve their lives, and what is necessary for their survival. We are not likely to be able to offer them greater wisdom on what their real options are, given the particulars of their own situation.

We should not assume that because we have some things in common with our informants we automatically have greater insight into their lives. The investigator and the person interviewed may both be women, Dalits, teachers, mothers, but this commonality may not be the most salient factor influencing the investigation on a particular subject. The investigator's dissimilarities from the respondents are often even more significant than the similarities. Similarities with respondents may be helpful, but they cannot be a substitute for taking respondents' perceptions seriously even when they differ from our own.

We should also not assume that because we subscribe to an ideology that we believe is in the best interests of the people whose lives we are looking into, or because we genuinely believe we have their interests at heart, this will automatically give us greater insight into their situation, or that our perceptions are necessarily superior to their own regarding the possible solutions to their problems.

When the people we want to help and understand are dependent on others who may want to influence their replies, we have to develop better techniques to get the most forthright answers possible. One way to do this is to inform the respondents in explicit detail of the ways we will ensure confidentiality. We must then be stringent in abiding by our explicit or implicit promises.

Despite this, we also need to maintain proper scepticism about the answers received from those respondents who are in a relatively powerless position and could be injured by their answers becoming known to those on whom they are dependent. By the same token, it is equally essential that we cross-check the self-serving responses of the powerful, who have much to gain from their version of events.

One of the most difficult decisions for an investigator to make is what to do with information provided in distorted or even falsified ways, in a situation of hatred and stereotyping between groups. While discarding the falsified picture of events when trying to understand what in fact happened, it is nevertheless important to include the hateful prejudices and stereotypes prevalent as a crucial part of the prevailing situation. The existence of hate-inducing myths is an important factor in causing a so-called riot, for example. Therefore, knowledge of these myths, and examination of the hard evidence that serves to disprove them, is vital for those who try to find ways to improve the situation.

Notes

1. This paper first appeared in *Manushi*, 1990, No. 56.

Contributors

Maitrayee Chaudhuri teaches Sociology at the Jawaharlal Nehru University, Delhi.

Veena Das teaches Sociology at the Delhi School of Economics.

Saraswati Haider is a doctoral student at the Centre for the Study of Social Systems, School of Social Sciences, Jawaharlal Nehru University, Delhi.

Madhu Kishwar is founder editor of *Manushi* and currently, a Fellow at the Centre for the Study of Developing Societies, Delhi.

T.N. Madan is Honorary Professor in Sociology at the Institute of Economic Growth, Delhi, and Honorary Fellow of the Royal Anthropological Institute of Great Britian.

Kirin Narayan is Associate Professor of Anthropology and South Asian Studies at the University of Wisconsin at Madison.

Denzil Saldanha is Professor in the Sociology of Education at the Tata Institute of Social Sciences, Bombay.

Savyasaachi teaches Sociology at the Jamia Millia Islamia, Delhi.

Loes Schenk-Sandbergen is Associate Professor, Faculty of Social-Cultural Sciences, Anthropological-Sociological Centre, University of Amsterdam.

Amrit Srinivasan teaches sociology/social anthropology at the Department of Humanities and Social Sciences, IIT, Delhi.

Meenakshi Thapan teaches at the Faculty of Education, University of Delhi.

Index